ECONOMIC AND PHILOSOPHIC
MANUSCRIPTS OF 1844

Economic and Philosophic

Manuscripts of 1844

by KARL MARX

Edited With an Introduction
by Dirk J. Struik

Translated by Martin Milligan

INTERNATIONAL PUBLISHERS *New York*

SBN (cloth) 7178–0054–7; (paperback) 7178–0053–9

Library of Congress Catalog Card Number: 64-12877

Manufactured in the United States of America

PUBLISHER'S NOTE

Karl Marx's *Economic and Philosophic Manuscripts of 1844* was translated from the complete German text as first published in Marx-Engels, *Gesamtausgabe, Abt. I, Bd. 3* (*Collected Works*, Sec. I, Vol. 3), Berlin, 1932. The present text incorporates corrections of typographical errors and the author's obvious slips which were caught by the editors of subsequent editions in Marx-Engels, *Kleine ökonomische Studien*, Berlin, 1955; and the latest Russian edition prepared by the Institute of Marxism-Leninism, Moscow, 1956.

Included as an Appendix is Frederick Engels' "Outlines of a Critique of Political Economy," which was translated from the German text contained in *Gesamtausgabe, Abt. I, Bd. 2*, Berlin, 1930.

The translation is by Martin Milligan, who also supplied a note on Hegelian terminology and many of the explanatory notes. The present edition was prepared by Prof. Dirk J. Struik who compared Milligan's text (originally published by the Foreign Language Publishing House, Moscow, 1960) with the German editions of 1932 and 1955, and has made some changes in the translation. Besides contributing the Introduction, Prof. Struik has added to the note on Hegelian terminology and has supplied additional explanatory notes.

The original hand-written manuscripts consist of three parts, each with their own pagination, in Roman numerals. Each of the 27 pages of the first manuscript is broken up into three columns with two vertical lines; each column on each page has a heading written in beforehand—"Wages of Labor," "Profit of Capital," and "Rent of Land." Beginning with p. XVII only the column headed "Rent of Land" is filled in, and from p. XXII to the end of the first manuscript Marx wrote across the three columns, disregarding the headings. The text of these six pages (XXII-

XXVII) is given in the present book under the title, "Estranged Labor."

Only four pages of the second manuscript have been preserved, numbered XXXX-XLIII. The text starts in the middle of the sentence and has been entitled "Antithesis of Capital and Labor. Landed Property and Capital."

The third manuscript contains 43 large pages, divided into two columns. It begins with two appendices to lost pages XXXVI and XXXIX, presented here under two heads: "Private Property and Labor" and "Private Property and Communism." The further text is here given the title, "The Meaning of Human Requirements." Then, on pages XXIX-XL of the third manuscript we find the "Preface." This is followed, on pages XLI-XLIII, with a text which has been given the title, "The Power of Money in Bourgeois Society." Appended to this third manuscript is still another essay, independent of the others, which appears in the present volume under the head, "Critique of the Hegelian Dialectic and Philosophy as a Whole."

The parts of the manuscripts are published in the sequence in which Marx put them down, save the "Preface" which is given at the beginning, and the essay on Hegel which was placed at the end in accordance with the reference made by Marx in the "Preface." Except for the first three headings, which are Marx's own, titles for various parts of the *Manuscripts* have been supplied by the editors.

Passages crossed out by Marx in the original manuscripts are to be found in the Explanatory and Reference Notes at the back of the book. In the text proper all footnotes on the page are by Marx; the editor's notes are in the back.

CONTENTS

INTRODUCTION

1. PRELUDE, 1818-1843

The *Economic and Philosophic Manuscripts,* which are here presented in an English translation from the original German, date from March-August 1844, when Karl Marx was living in Paris. At that time turning 26 years of age, with a Ph.D. in philosophy from the University of Jena, he already had stormy days behind him as a contributor and later the editor of the *Rheinische Zeitung,* a radical-democratic daily published in Cologne. This newspaper, to which some of the most talented German liberals and radicals contributed, was harassed constantly by Prussian censorship, that finally killed it in March 1843.

Marx's work on the journal had brought the academic philosopher, reared in the school of Hegel, into direct contact with the burning political and economic questions of the day, to which the speculations of Hegel and even of his more radical followers— the so-called Young Hegelians—could give no satisfactory answers. In his search for self-clarification, Marx turned to the writings of the political economists, the socialists, and the communists. In a series of essays, of which only a few were published at the time, Marx gradually approached that new outlook on life which we now know as Marxism. The *Economic and Philosophic Manuscripts,* first published in German in 1932, form part of these essays, and are therefore of importance for an understanding of the genesis of Marxism. But as in the case of the early works of other men of genius, like Leibniz, Newton or Hegel, they are also of interest in themselves, worth study for their own sake. In their brilliant clarification of the relations between philosophy, economics, and socialism we can already recognize the greatness of the mature Marx.

When writing these essays Marx was still very much under the influence of the philosophy of Hegel with its universal sweep, masked by an involved structure and a highly technical language. It is necessary, therefore, to introduce the reader to some aspects of this philosophy and of other thinkers who influenced the younger Marx.[1]

Born May 5, 1818, in Trier (Treves), a provincial city of the Rhineland, then part of the kingdom of Prussia, he was the son of a well-known local lawyer, a man of liberal religious and political views. After graduation from the local Gymnasium (classical high school) and a year at the University of Bonn, he entered the University of Berlin in 1836 as a student of law. An arduous worker, he developed an interest in history and philosophy, on which he read as voraciously as on law.

At that time German philosophy, renewed by Kant in 1781 in his *Critique of Pure Reason* as a rebuttal of English empiricism and skepticism, was moving rapidly from one phase of speculative thought to another. During that stormy period, the influence was still fresh of the French Revolution, political heir of the Enlightenment, which had proclaimed the triumph of Reason. Philosophical thinking in France as in Germany reflected this optimistic belief, which expressed the political goals of the emergent middle classes. But where in France the middle classes had faced boldly the ancient powers of church and state and thus arrived at materialistic theories, conditions in Germany led to a different outlook since there the middle classes were too weak politically to fight the semi-feudal bureaucracy controlling church and state. In materialistic theories there is always to be found a militancy, and an anti-clerical militancy to boot. But German philosophers took another direction, less militant, more conciliatory to the existing powers. In this process they were able to dig deeply into the realm of pure thought, emerging with philosophies that hid their revolutionary potentials under an appearance of speculative contemplation. Since these thinkers proclaimed as the goal of reason the triumph of mind over matter, we speak of the speculative idealism of this great school of German philosophy.

French philosophy had defined the principal question of philosophy as the search for the relation between matter and mind. German speculative philosophy approached the same question by seeking for the relation of object to subject. Kant denied the subject essential knowledge of the object; Fichte struggling against Kant's agnosticism, let the subject ("Ego") determine the object ("Non-Ego") —but this subjective idealism also stressed the need for action: Fichte was a fighter for democracy. Schelling and Hegel returned to contemplation. Schelling, emphasizing nature, turned Fichte's subjectivism into an objective idealism, which Hegel completed by stripping philosophy of Fichte's and Schelling's one-sidedness. Hegel's system embraced all human knowledge in a systematic confrontation of subject and object on different levels, until object and subject were finally identified in the Absolute, the Absolute Mind in which nature "externalizes" itself in a process of repeated "mediation" and "alienation," first of consciousness, then of self-consciousness. Later we shall become better acquainted with the meaning of these terms.

This all-embracing system, which seemed to have shed all the weaknesses not only of Kant, Fichte, and Schelling, but of all previous philosophies (each expressing a particular phase in the development of the mind toward the Absolute), and which proclaimed the mastery of mind over matter, had a wide appeal in German academic circles. Marx could not escape its influence. In a letter of November 1837 to his father he described dramatically how he had wrestled with himself, even at the cost of his health, to attain clarity—and how he had finally surrendered to Hegel.

Hegel had taught at the University of Berlin from 1818 to his death in 1831. In his *Philosophy of Right* Hegel had proclaimed the state as the actualization of the ethical idea and also had found the state as then existing in the Germanic realm a reflection of the understanding of the principle of the unity of divine and human nature.[2] For these reasons Hegel's philosophy had received the encouragement (sometimes uneasy) of the Prussian authorities, who were willing to overlook many unorthodox and even subversive tendencies hidden in its method. But, especially in his later years, Hegel rarely agitated for future reforms, preferring speculation within the regions of the mind,[3] though he never was a dyed-in-the-wool reactionary, nor did he forget his youthful enthusiasm for the French Revolution. Yet, the Prussian police state of Frederick William III (1797-1840), as seen speculatively from the philosopher's lectern, appeared as the final embodiment of the concept of Right.

In 1821, when the *Philosophy of Right* appeared, the apparent stability of Europe after the Napoleonic wars seemed to justify the rather static outlook of the aging Hegel. The Holy Alliance was uniting Prussia, Austria, and Russia in an effort to maintain the status quo in Europe by opposing the demand for liberal reforms which the French Revolution had raised. These three countries were not yet deeply affected by the industrial revolution, which had been transforming England's social structure for decades, and had now also entered France. The industrial middle class, which already existed in the Rhineland and in a few other sections of Germany, was still politically weak. Although sympathizing with the reforms introduced by Napoleon, which had stimulated commerce and industry, this bourgeoisie was unwilling to put up a strong fight against the feudal, militaristic bureaucracy which dominated the Holy Alliance. Protests by students, reform agitation by middle class elements, the clamor for constitutional rights, for political representation, for freedom of the press, and for the unity of Germany (then broken up into many states) — all this was met with censorship, prison sentences, and other forms of intimidation. Some rebellious elements went abroad, to France or Switzerland, like the poet Heinrich Heine, who lived many years in Paris. There were many German artisans abroad, among them some who expressed politically advanced opinions *verboten* at home.

However, gradual industrialization continued to feed the reform movement, despite all suppression. The July Revolution of 1830 in France and the Reform Act of 1832 in England had their impact on Germany; the *Zollverein* (Customs Union) of 1833 was one of the signs that capitalism was also penetrating east of the Rhine. Steel, mining, and textiles flourished; in 1835 the first railroad appeared and within ten years the length of the German railroads was 1,000 miles. A working class developed under conditions of misery reminiscent of those in England and France. In 1844, there took place the revolt of the Silesian weavers.

These developments affected the pupils of Hegel, after his death in 1831. By 1837, when Marx joined their ranks, they were split into several groups. The "Old Hegelians," for a while basking in official favor, represented the political, religious, and philosophical status quo. The "Young Hegelians," among them the participants of the "Doctor's Club" which Marx had joined, expressed a certain amount of restlessness which could lead to opposition, if only in the realm of ideas. They began to compare Hegel's speculative state with the real Prussian bureaucratic state. Similarly, they began to contrast Hegel's speculative concept of the Christian religion as an advanced stage in man's philosophical development toward the Absolute with the actual Christian religion based on the gospel stories and tied to the state. And, finally, some of them began to ask whether Hegel's philosophical method necessarily had to lead to a conservative outlook on the world as a whole. The Young Hegelians came to different answers, but all sufficiently disagreeable to the Prussian authorities to render them unfit for academic positions, let alone promotions.

One of the first products of Young Hegelian emancipation was the *Leben Jesu* (*Life of Jesus*, 1835) by David Friedrich Strauss (1808-74). Hegel never had laid much stress on the gospel stories (which led his antagonists to say that at heart he was an atheist), but had based his argument on the philosophical significance of the dogmas. His pupil Strauss, however, analyzed the gospel stories and came to the conclusion that around the historic figure of Jesus the early Christians had spun a web of myths. This, he claimed, did not affect the deeper meaning of the Christian faith, but many of his readers were not convinced, and Strauss' book was seen as an attack on the Prussian religious status quo. Although Strauss was hardly a political fighter, his achievement gave many a Young Hegelian the courage to develop a critical attitude towards the established order.

In 1837 the Young Hegelians obtained their own periodical, the *Hallische Jahrbücher* (*Annals of Halle*). Leadership was taken by the publicist Arnold Ruge (1802-80) in Dresden, who as a student had served six years of imprisonment for his political activities. Most articles in the *Annals* were of a philosophical-theological nature, but some aimed at political reforms within the framework of the Prussian state. The ascent to the throne in 1840 of Frederick William IV fostered some liberal illusions, which were soon dispelled by sharper censorship. In 1841 Ruge's *Annals* were *verboten* in Prussia, and their successor, the *Deutsche Jahrbücher*, which Ruge continued to publish from Dresden in Saxony, shared the same fate in 1842. Ruge now decided to continue publication abroad, and in his *Anekdota*, published in Switzerland, appeared the first two published essays of Marx.[4]

Marx, in the meantime, had met in his Berlin "Doctor's Club" the theologian Bruno Bauer (1809-82), with whom he became a close friend. Starting as an Old Hegelian, who had criticized Strauss' book, Bauer had changed by 1840 to an academic radical, and during the next years wrote essays for Ruge's *Annals* and other periodicals. For Bauer, Strauss did not go far enough; his critique—a term which he used to such an extent that Marx would later make fun of Bauer's "critical critique"—denied the historicity of the gospels altogether. This cost him his position as an instructor (*Privatdozent*) at the University of Bonn, and also killed Marx's expectations of joining him there in an academic career.

Marx had received his Ph.D. in Jena in 1841 on a thesis dealing with the differences between the philosophies of Democritus and Epicurus, the leading materialists of Greek antiquity. The thesis was not published until 1913, but even now remains of importance for the understanding of Greek materialism.[5] Here Marx showed how Democritus, whose atoms moved in a straight line only, constructed a physical theory of strict determinism, whereas Epicurus, who allowed the atoms a slight deviation from the straight line, came to a much fuller world outlook that allowed freedom as well as determinism.[6] Thus Epicurus reached out for a full philosophy of life, wider and deeper than that of Democritus. In the objective world of Epicurus no room existed for superstition, and Marx considered him "the greatest Greek representative of the Enlightenment."

This praise of Epicurus, the materialist, already revealed the rebel in Marx. He left no doubt about his feelings: in the preface to his thesis, against the advice of Bauer, he glorified Prometheus, the rebel against the Gods and the friend of Man, as "the principal saint and martyr in the philosophical calendar." Marx's strong and imposing personality, his lust for life, and his already enormous erudition, impressed all he met. "He combines with the profoundest philosophical gravity the keenest wit: think of Rousseau, Voltaire, Holbach, Lessing, Heine, and Hegel united in one person—I say united, not thrown together—and you have Dr. Marx," wrote Moses Hess, the socialist, in 1841.[7]

For such a man, whose active temper would have led him in any case to rebel against a life of speculative contemplation, there was no room in a German university. Marx decided to become a newspaper correspondent. In 1842 he became first a contributor and later in the same year the editor of the *Rheinische Zeitung,* a daily founded in Cologne by prominent commercial interests. Its somewhat liberal and intellectual standards attracted Young Hegelians and other more or less radical elements. In his work for a leading newspaper Marx had to face the practical problems of the day, which he approached in the spirit of radical democracy. His articles attacked the still powerful feudal interests in the Rhineland, exposed parliamentary servility, defended the freedom of the press, and maintained the dignity of a liberal newspaper against the encroachments of an ever more obnoxious Prussian censorship.

It was in his activity as an editor that Marx first came in serious contact with socialism and communism. One of the contributors to the paper was Moses Hess (1812-75),[8] a fellow Rhinelander who had traveled in France and who was for a while the Paris correspondent of the *Rheinische Zeitung.* He had written two rather confused books in which religious mysticism mixed with a criticism of social and political conditions. The New Jerusalem, the kingdom of God, he claimed, could only be realized in a society without private property. Although these books made Hess the first German socialist writer, it is doubtful whether their mystical prophesies had much influence on Marx. We know that Hess, as a person, had some influence in those days on Frederick Engels. However, some later essays of a more mature Hess did have an effect on Marx's thinking.

A far more powerful influence on Marx during the period 1842-45 was the work of Ludwig Feuerbach (1804-72). Like Strauss, Feuerbach had studied under Hegel and had already made a name for himself as the author of several books, dealing mostly with the history of philosophy, and as a contributor to periodicals including those of Ruge. Then, in 1841, he shook the academic and theological world with his *Wesen des Christenthums (Essence of Christianity)*.[9] In this book he parted company with Strauss and Bauer, who despite all their criticism remained well within the limits of Hegel's idealist philosophy.

Feuerbach asserted that the search for truth, in particular for truth in religion, must lead beyond Hegel's abstract "Absolute" to man himself in his relation to nature. But when man is the starting point, then religion as well as theology is a product of man, is a reflection of man's state. Using in part Hegel's terminology, he explained how man by the "externalization" of his essential properties, of his properties not as an individual but as a species *(Gattungseigenschaften)*, creates God and makes Him the Creator of this world. By this externalization God, alien to man, is placed between man as a species and man as an individual entity. Religion is a form of alienation of man from himself, a self-alienation, which destroys his appropriate fulfillment as a "species being" *(Gattungswesen)* and lets it exist only as an illusion, in an imaginary world of God and heaven.

In simpler terms, it is not God who made man, but man who made God, constructing Him after his own image. Religion thus became nothing but a part of anthropology. Feuerbach conceived this anthropology quite abstractly, since he dealt with man in his abstract species being and not in his historical development. To return to man his true species being, the alienation expressed by religion must be destroyed. Only in this way can man's alienation from himself, that is, his egotistic, individualistic mode of living be replaced by a life which will allow man to live in accordance with his true destination, his true species being.

Expressed again in the language of abstract philosophy: the relation of subject and predicate had to be reversed.* Man from

---

* In a judgment a total conception is compared with a partial one, and we recognize that the latter constitutes an attribute of the former. One of these conceptions is the subject, the other the predicate. When we say that five is an odd number, five is the subject, odd number the predicate. God as a Man-maker is here opposed to Man as a God-maker.

being a predicate to the subject God had to become the subject himself and see God as its predicate. This step of inversion
taken by Feuerbach was therefore nothing less than a transition from mind to nature (with man as a product of nature)
as the primary element in the understanding of man's thinking.
It was a transition from the subject to the object, from
idealism to materialism, if only from a speculative, rational-
istic idealism, to an abstract, rationalist materialism, and so
far only in the field of theology. Since Feuerbach claimed that
Hegel's philosophy was nothing but a generalized form of theology, he did lay the cornerstone of a materialistic structure that
would subvert the whole of Hegel's idealism. However, the re-
building of the whole structure needed other men.

The definite break with the very nature of Hegel's philosophy
by a man who himself belonged to the sacred circle of Hegelians
was for many Germans an intellectual revelation. "One must
himself have experienced the liberating effect of this book to get
an idea of it. Enthusiasm was general; we all became at once
Feuerbachians," wrote Engels 45 years later in a reminiscent
mood.[10] Among those who studied Feuerbach thoroughly and
critically was Marx, although probably only after Feuerbach had
extended his criticism from religion to Hegel's philosophy in general in his *Vorläufige Thesen zur Reform der Philosophie (Preliminary Theses on the Reform of Philosophy*, 1842), which
appeared in 1843 in the same *Anekdota* of Ruge in which Marx
had his first (although anonymous) political essays. Feuerbach's
*Grundsätze der Philosophie der Zukunft (Principles of the Phi-
losophy of the Future*, 1843) followed in the same, equally
aphoristic vein.

2. SELF-CLARIFICATION, 1843-1844

The *Rheinische Zeitung*, gradually developing under Marx's
editorial leadership into a real opposition paper—something
unheard of in Prussia—could not survive constant harassment by
the Prussian censorship. Thus in March 1843, Marx again had to
look for a living. Neither an academic nor a journalistic career

seemed open in Germany. Closely allied to Ruge, whose radical-democratic convictions he shared at that time, Marx decided to become a free-lance writer, as so many other Young Hegelians had done. For some months he stayed at Kreuznach, in the Rhineland, where he married Jenny von Westphalen, that brave woman who was to share his difficult life.

He also collaborated with Ruge in the publication of a new set of *Annals,* now to be published in Paris in the hope that both German and French radicals would contribute. Ruge went to Paris, and in November 1843 Marx and his wife followed. The new *Annals* appeared early in 1844 and were entitled *Deutsch-Französische Jahrbücher.* Among the contributors to this brilliant and history-making periodical (of which only one double issue appeared)[1] in addition to Ruge and Marx, were Heinrich Heine and Frederick Engels. Attempts at obtaining French contributors had failed.

These months of 1843 and 1844 were for Marx a period of intense study and reflection. The crisis of 1837, in which he had wrestled with himself for self-clarification, was repeated under conditions of infinitely greater maturity (and, we may add, of personal happiness) . The philosophy of Hegel, as he saw it, needed revision badly, despite its universality, and he became convinced that Feuerbach's radical "inversion" of Hegel offered the key.

Feuerbach had developed a materialistic approach to the world, which tried to explain thought from being, mind from matter, and not the other way around, so that man's thought had to be explained from the world in which he lives. But, Marx found, Feuerbach conceived this world primarily as nature, in which an abstract species being lived in equally abstract natural surroundings. This was not enough. Man was a social being, and moreover not an abstract social being but living and above all *working* under specific social conditions historically determined. This role of labor had already been seen, if only abstractly and imperfectly expressed by Hegel, but was neglected by Feuerbach—one example out of many to show that his materialism, although in principle a step in advance of Hegel's idealism, was also poorer in content. By neglecting man's role as a social being, Feuerbach came thus to an abstract outlook on the world, materialistic in its foundation but leading in the social sphere to an abstract idealistic, even sentimental, theory which he called *humanism,* the theory of man as he truly should be according to the nature of his species being.

It was to this abstract humanism that Marx objected: for an understanding of true humanism it was necessary to study and understand society, history, politics, and that relatively new science, political economy. These thoughts led Marx, in particular, to the study of the French Revolution, the contemporary political situation in Western Europe, the writings of Adam Smith and other economists, and of the socialist and communist critics of society. He became conscious that modern industry had created a new class of men, the working class, with new ideals, a potentially revolutionary force for bringing about an entirely novel form of society.

Under such circumstances, research was not enough. Theory, he knew from his own newspaper experience and from Fichte and Hess and other militants as well, had to be enlivened by action; practice in its turn had to lead to a further understanding of theory. A basic revision of an all-embracing philosophy such as that of Hegel required a radical practice going to the very roots, the *radices,* of human existence.

Feuerbach, with his alienation theory, had come to the correct critique of religion, if only in principle. But religious alienation is only a special aspect of the full, all-embracing, social alienation resulting from our economic system. Even when extending his criticism to speculative philosophy as a whole, Feuerbach had missed this all-important point. Feuerbach's general philosophy of man as a species being had led him to an unhistorical anthropology. Marx, on the contrary, emphasized specific historical types of men, lords and serfs, bourgeois and proletarian. He thus saw his primary task in the analysis of the existing social order, proceeding from there to overhauling the whole of philosophy.

This activity resulted in a series of essays, of which at that time only a few were published. Now we can study all the relevant documents in print—thanks to the patient and painstaking scholarship of German and Soviet Marxists—and can trace Marx's stormy intellectual growth through his successive writings.

First came the criticism of Hegel's theory of the social order, contained in his *Philosophy of Right*. In a manuscript, written in 1843, but not published until 1927, we find a first attempt at such a criticism, singling out Hegel's theory of the state. Following Feuerbach's theory of "inversion," Marx declared that Hegel always "made the idea into subject and the true, real subject, as political attitude, into predicate. But the development always proceeds on the side of the predicate." In other words, a concrete entity like political attitude is derived by Hegel from an abstract "idea," while in reality abstract ideas follow from concrete conditions. In particular, claimed Marx, it is not the state in the abstract form of Hegel that determines civil society—Hegel called it *Bürgerliche Gesellschaft*—but society is the determining element in the state, and in human life as a whole. Man carries on his real life in civil society, and in the state only an illusory life. To solve this conflict between society and state—to allow man to live not an illusory life but a true life, corresponding to his species being—society has to be changed. Marx still sees this emancipation of society from the viewpoint of radical democracy, which would change society into a more collective, socially integrated form.

It was really not very clear; no wonder Marx never allowed this first attempt at a Hegel critique to be published. He saw clarity only when he began to understand the fundamental theses of the socialists and the role of the class struggle. And now he began to express his thoughts in a way approaching the classical form in which they have become familiar. First in time are his two articles *Zur Judenfrage (On the Jewish Question)*, written in late 1843. The perhaps unusual title is due to the fact that the articles were meant as an answer to Bruno Bauer, who had written on this subject, as had many others in Germany, where the Jews were threatened by the authorities with the loss of the rights of full citizenship which the French Revolution had brought.

Marx went far beyond the topic of his title, discussing the difference between limited political emancipation (not only of the

Jews) and human emancipation. Here we witness an advance far beyond Feuerbach: human emancipation is the liberation of man from the power of money, based on the existence of private property. Money transforms men into isolated individuals. Man can reach true human emancipation only by the abolition of the social order based on private property. Marx had become a communist.

Marx expounded this theory further in a radically revised Introduction to his *Contribution to the Critique of Hegel's Philosophy of Right*,[2] finished during his early weeks in Paris, where he witnessed the strong and militant working class movement. Published in the *Annals*, Marx announced his discovery that a new *class* had come into existence—the carrier of the social revolution, a class that can and must abolish private property—the working class, the proletariat. The theory which will lead this class to emancipation is the final result of German philosophy as it has developed from Hegelian doctrine, but in which the starting point has become *man*, living and acting in nature and in society:

"As philosophy finds its *material* weapon in the proletariat, so the proletariat finds its intellectual weapons in philosophy. . . .

"The head of this emancipation is philosophy, its heart the proletariat."

Speaking in terms of the quest for *freedom*, Hegel saw its realization in the philosophical mind which had reached the Absolute, Feuerbach in the conquest of alienation by abstract species-man, but Marx saw it in the achievement of a communist form of society as the result of the struggles of the working class in the money-dominated society of the present. Yet, the essays on the Jewish question and on Hegel's *Philosophy of Right* left many aspects of this struggle unexplored, of which Marx was well aware. A more concrete understanding of the forces of alienation was necessary and Marx found it in the study of political economy. Here he had to turn to England, the classical country of the new industrialism, which had produced Adam Smith, Ricardo, and other authoritative writers on this science of society. Although Marx at that time did not read English well, all pertinent literature was available in French. He later summarized the results of his studies in the following words:

> My investigation led to the conclusion that legal relations such as forms of state are to be grasped neither from themselves nor from the so-called general development of the human mind, but rather have their roots in the material conditions of life, the sum total of which Hegel, in accordance with the procedure of the Englishmen and Frenchmen of the eighteenth century, combined under the name of "civil society," but that the anatomy of civil society is to be sought in political economy.[3]

In this study neither Bauer nor Ruge nor even Feuerbach could be of much help. Bauer had become hopelessly outdated. Wrapped up in his academic "critique," he could only think in terms of abstract concepts, never in terms of human practice. From the height of his cardboard Hegelian tower he looked down upon the common people, in whose activity Marx was now learning to see the answer to some of the most fundamental problems of philosophy. Ruge, always a radical democrat, no longer could be a comrade on the new road that Marx was traveling. Feuerbach, living a retired life, let his materialism get stranded in a vague humanitarian sentimentalism—although he never showed hostility to socialism. However, where the old associates failed, Marx, at the right moment, found a new ally in Frederick Engels.

Engels (1821-1895), born in Barmen in the Rhineland, the son of an orthodox Protestant textile manufacturer, had spent the time of his military service in Berlin, where he had met the Young Hegelians.[4] Conquering his strong religious bias, he had studied Hegel's philosophy, though never following regular academic courses, at the same time writing literary and political articles for various periodicals. His Left Hegelianism had led him to the communist point of view even before Marx, partly under the influence of Hess. When he visited Manchester, England, in November 1842 as a representative of his father's firm, he was deeply impressed by the working-class movement, then reaching militant mass proportions under the banner of Chartism.* Con-

* The Chartists agitated for universal manhood suffrage, abolition of property qualifications for a seat in Parliament, vote by ballot, and other political reforms set forth in the People's Charter. They were very active between 1838 and 1849.

tinuing his literary activities, he kept his friends in Germany informed of conditions in England, and also reported in England about the continent. In his own way, still independent of Marx, he came to conclusions quite similar to those which Marx was reaching.

While "in Manchester," wrote Engels many years later, "I was forcibly brought to realize that economic facts, which so far have played no role or only a negligible one in the writing of history, are at least in the modern world a decisive historical force; that they form the *basis* for the origin of the present-day class antagonisms; that these class antagonisms, in the countries where they have become fully developed, thanks to large-scale industry, especially therefore in England, are in their turn the basis of the formation of political parties and of party struggles, and thus of all political history. Marx had not only arrived at the same view, but had already generalized it in the *Deutsch-Französische Jahrbücher* (1844), reaching the conclusion that it is not at all the state which conditions and regulates bourgeois society, but bourgeois society which conditions and regulates the state, and consequently that politics and the history of politics are to be explained from the economic conditions and their development, and not vice versa." [5]

Thus Engels studied the English political and economic scene, and read the writings of the political economists. His conclusions were published in the issue of the *Annals* in which Marx had his essays, and this article, "Outlines of a Critique of Political Economy," is included as an Appendix in the present volume. The essay, which probably was seen by Marx before publication since he did editorial work on the journal, was of the greatest aid to Marx in his work of self-clarification. Indeed, Engels took issue with the official political economists, including Malthus, pointing out how they considered the existing capitalist system with its competition and monopoly, its way of turning all values into cash and dehumanizing men, women, and children, as reasonable and necessary, as if it were in accordance with human nature. Here Engels developed the view that as the differences between the employers and workers become stronger, the small businessmen are increasingly thrown into the proletariat, and the class struggles

increase in size and importance, leading to a revolution which will
abolish the inhuman capitalist system and introduce a communist
form of society. Written in simple language without the obscurity
that cursed (and even now curses) the style of almost all German
philosophers, the essay appeals to the sense of justice and satisfies
the need for clarity. Despite certain theoretical weaknesses it is a
landmark in the genesis of scientific socialism. Marx understood
its importance immediately.

At the same time two articles appeared by Moses Hess which
may have had a direct affect on Marx's thinking. They were published in a Left-wing periodical with the curious name of *Einundzwanzig Bogen aus der Schweiz (Twenty-One Sheets from Switzerland)*.[6] Here Hess argued for a philosophy of action. Only through
action can man reach self-consciousness and become a true human
being, he held. But this is impossible in present civil society which
reduces the worker to the level of a slave. The reason is that society
is based on private property, which produces egotism and hunger
for profit. Man therefore can be free only in a communist society.
The alienation which Feuerbach had analyzed in the field of
religion, is in reality a reflection of the alienation of human
essence in civil society. Here the workers, by producing commodities, alienate themselves by means of their own product, and
become commodities themselves. Thus alienation is a typical trait
of civil society, which is in sharp contrast to true human society,
in which man by mastering nature can develop his faculties har-
moniously. In another paper, *Über das Geldwesen* ("On the Essence of Money") submitted to the *Annals* (but published only
in 1845 elsewhere), Hess complemented his analysis by sketching
the role of money, which had become an alien, inimical power, a
God worshipped by man and enslaving him. All men, exploiters as
well as exploited, had become the slaves of money. Only communism could save mankind.[7]

These articles of Engels, Hess, the economists, and the socialists
now led Marx to a thorough revision of his theory. In the early
months of 1844 he developed his ideas in several essays, which he
never published and of which only a part has been preserved.
These are the *Economic and Philosophic Manuscripts* that are
republished here, together with a supplementary analysis of

Hegel's work, this time of his fundamental *Phenomenology*. In these manuscripts Marx carried his analysis of civil society and of social change considerably further, probing the economic laws of capitalist society, the class struggle, and the devastating effect on man caused by the existence of private property. As in his previous essays, human emancipation remains Marx's basic concern, but now he consistently takes the point of view of the working class. The problems of alienation and of its final disappearance are no longer considered a political question, a question of the state, but are viewed in their social-economical form. Alienation and its conquest are now seen in terms of human labor and its emancipation, which can only be accomplished, as Marx sees it, in a communist form of society.

Before we take a closer look at the content of these manuscripts, we must add that Marx, after meeting Engels later in the same year of 1844, concluded that both had come to a similar outlook on life. They decided to complete their self-clarification in an elaborate criticism of the Young Hegelians. Thus followed *Die Heilige Familie (The Holy Family)*, which was published in 1845, and the more elaborate *Deutsche Ideologie (The German Ideology)*, written in 1845-46 but "left to the gnawing criticism of the mice" until it was rescued and first published in full in 1932.[8] It is in these writings that certain weaknesses of the *Economic and Philosophic Manuscripts* and the "Outlines of a Critique of Political Economy" were finally overcome, with the result that here we find an explicit formulation of that fundamental aspect of Marxism which we know as historical materialism, a mature result of the materialist approach to dialectics. The first published book with at least a partial exposition of the new outlook on the world was Marx's criticism of Proudhon: *La misère de la philosophie (The Poverty of Philosophy,* 1847). Then, in February 1848, appeared the *Communist Manifesto*.

3. FRENCH SOCIALISM

At the time of his departure for Paris, Marx was already acquainted to a certain extent with French socialist literature. Some was available in German translations since the early 1830's, especially part of Saint-Simon's work, but Marx, who knew French, hardly needed this. Hess had made him (and Engels) somewhat closer acquainted with French socialism at the time of the *Rheinische Zeitung.* In that period, in 1842, a book appeared that may have provided Marx, as it did many other Germans, with further information on the vast French socialist movement. It was *Der Sozialismus und der Communismus des heutigen Frankreichs (Socialism and Communism in Present-Day France),* written by Lorenz Stein, a young man who had made a study trip to France to collect material on the social forces active in that country (and incidentally to report to the German authorities).

The book, sympathetic to the peaceful efforts of the socialists, and full of misgivings concerning the revolutionary propaganda of the communists, was thorough and contained a mass of well organized information, as befitted a book written by a scholar who had learned from Hegel and Saint-Simon. He described the class struggle and was perfectly clear about the fact that "industrial society, the society of liberty and equality" has its poverty, "which is pauperism, industrial or mass poverty," in which "the worker, despite all legal liberty, is unfree, since he depends on the employer." Under such circumstances, Stein recognized, the struggle of the underlying class leads to utopias, to socialism and communism. After describing such ideas and systems as then existed in France, he warned the Germans: beware—this is also your own future!

Some statements made by Stein (who later became the highly respectable von Stein of Vienna University) remind us of Marx's analysis of the role of capitalism and the position of the working class. There is some controversy on Stein's influence on Marx; it is certain that neither Marx nor Engels thought much of his "compilation," [1] and they certainly did not need Stein to open their eyes to the facts of life. But among many Germans Stein did stimulate interest in the French Left; Hess discussed the book in his essays in *Einundzwanzig Bogen.* In his later polemic against Karl Grün's "true socialism," Marx pointed out in great detail Grün's dependence on Stein—which shows that Marx knew the book quite well.

Far more than Stein, or even Hess, Marx respected Wilhelm

Weitling (1808-71), a wandering journeyman-tailor, the *vater-landsloser Geselle* (the man without a fatherland). He was a militant leader of those rebellious German-speaking artisans and workers, of whom many had found employment in France or Switzerland. Among them, in 1836, the League of the Just was organized, with Weitling in the leadership. Weitling was in Paris in 1835, and from 1837 to 1841; then he went to Switzerland, where he was imprisoned in 1843. Discharged and expelled from the country, he came first to Hamburg and then to London. After 1849 he stayed in the United States, where he remained active in the German working class movement.

Weitling's best known book is his prophetic *Garantien der Harmonie und der Freiheit (Guarantees of Harmony and Freedom)*, published in 1842, an eloquent indictment of the institution of private property with its evils of money, war, and slavery, and its hoaxes of fatherland and official religion. Following some of Fourier's and Proudhon's ideas, he appealed directly to the masses of the exploited to reorganize society and bring about a communist system, ruled by philosophers and guaranteeing harmony and free development for all.

The book was popular and at that time gave some form of theoretical and practical foundation to the German socialist labor movement. Marx thought highly of it, praising Weitling's writings as "those of a genius, that theoretically often surpass those of Proudhon, even if they lack his ability of composition. Where could the bourgeoisie show such a work as Weitling's *Guarantees* in regard to its own emancipation?" He added: "It must be said that the German proletariat is the theoretician of the European proletariat, just as the English proletariat is its political economist and the French proletariat its politician." [2] This was, of course, before Marx had fully clarified his own ideas. But in Weitling with his militancy and his understanding of the role of the working class in the struggle for a communist society, Marx felt a congenial spirit.

Added to the influence of these writers was the impact on Marx of the French scene itself. Here, in Paris, he witnessed large and highly vocal reformist and revolutionary activities. The July Revolution of 1830 had brought the most influential sections of the bourgeoisie to power, the big industrialists and the bankers, who excluded from the government the working class, the small proprietors, and small businessmen. These groups were in opposition. All shades of radical democratic, socialist, and communist doctrines were advocated. For Marx and the other German radicals in Paris this contrast between their own country, without any opposition press, and a country with an almost unchecked freedom of expression must have seemed a step from utter darkness into the glory of the morning. No wonder that many radicals, like Ruge, did not go beyond the demand that a democracy of the French type be introduced into Germany.

The older socialists were followers of Henri de Saint-Simon and of Charles Fourier. Both were dead, Saint-Simon since 1825, Fourier since 1837. The Saint-Simonians were dispersed, their leaders active in banking and industry. The Fourierists were actively propagating their principle of association and dreaming of the building of phalansteries, which Albert Brisbane was already promoting in the United States. Both sects stayed away from political action. Among the different socialist groups could be found the Christian reformer De Lamennais and doctrinary writers like Pierre Leroux, each one in his way propagating some form of socialization of the means of production, to be attained by peaceful propaganda addressed mainly to the ruling classes and to the intellectuals. It was Pierre Leroux, it seems, who had introduced in 1832 the term "socialism"; [3] a few years earlier the Saint-Simonians had preached "to each according to his abilities, to each ability according to its products." [4]

A different type of language was used by Joseph Proudhon, whose *Qu'est ce que la Propriété (What is Property?)* had appeared in 1840 with the slogan, "Property is theft." Proudhon, a printer, who had a considerable following among the artisans and the working classes, preached a radical social reform essentially in behalf of the small proprietors, using a language partly borrowed from German philosophy. Like Marx, he believed that there was in Hegel's dialectic a lesson for those who struggled for the emancipation of the working class, but he lacked Marx's penetrating mind to interpret it successfully.

All these authors preached social reforms leading to a more equal distribution of wealth, but were without the historical perspective that would lead to more than mere utopias. Their principal and outstanding merit was their criticism of the existing capitalist system with its mass poverty amid growing and ostentatious wealth.

Far more radical in their opinions and actions were the communists, spokesmen of the more militant sections of the working class.[5] They propagated the social revolution, the abolition of private property, and the establishment of a communist society. The peaceful wing was represented by Etienne Cabet, who had studied Robert Owen in England and whose popular book *Voyage en Icarie* (1840) sketched a Christian communist form of society to be achieved by propaganda and education. He had a tremendous appeal among the artisans and the working class. Another communist school was represented by Théodore Dézamy, whose *Code de la Nature* (1842) was inspired by the teachings of the 18th century materialists.

The militants, organized in secret societies, lived in the tradition of the conspiracy of Babeuf, the communist executed in 1797 under the French Directory. The memory of this conspiracy of the "Equals" had been revived by Babeuf's old comrade Philippe Buonarotti, who in 1828 had published his book *La conspiration pour l'Egalité, dite de Babeuf (The Conspiracy for Equality, Named After Babeuf).*[6] Returning to France after the July Revolution, he assumed the role of a Nestor among the members of the secret societies until his death in 1837, when 1500 working men and women joined the funeral procession. Marx stressed his importance in *The Holy Family.*

The revolutionary movement, which began in 1789 in the *Cercle Social* and finally found its momentary defeat with Babeuf's conspiracy, had brought to light the *communist* idea, which Babeuf's friend, Buonarotti, introduced again into France after the revolution of 1830. This idea carried out consistently, is the *idea of a new world order.*[7]

In Babeuf's conspiratorial tradition, Auguste Blanque was restlessly active in preparing a proletarian dictatorship by means of armed revolt organized by secret societies. He led the Paris insur-

rection of 1839 and spent most of his life in prison. Many news-
papers and other journals, such as *Le Populaire* and *L'Avenir*,
propagated socialist and communist ideas, each in its own way.
There was a constant outpouring of pamphlets and books.

A large German colony also existed in Paris, estimated at a
hundred thousand persons, in many ranks of life, from the poet
Heine and the physician Hermann Ewerbeck to artisans of all
kinds—carpenters, shoemakers, tailors—many of whom eventually
returned to Germany. The more politically advanced among them
belonged to the League of the Just. Suppressed after the insurrec-
tion of 1839, it continued to exist in groups that met in different
cafés; their leaders were Ewerbeck and Herman Mäurer, the latter
living in the same house into which Marx and his wife had
moved. Marx never joined their organization with its confused
ideology of Blanquism, Icarianism, Christian socialism, Feuerbach humanism, and Weitling communism, but he enjoyed their
company, as well as that of their French comrades—to the amaze-
ment and disgust of Ruge. Here Marx tasted, as so many intellectuals have after him, the bracing atmosphere of proletarian
solidarity, the joy of life and the thirst for knowledge typical of
militant workers, undaunted by all possible handicaps. In the
Economic and Philosophic Manuscripts, as well as in *The Holy
Family*, Marx expressed his elation in no uncertain terms. Here,
he wrote, was an indication of the way in which, through the
struggle for proletarian emancipation, alienation could finally be
overcome.

Marx's reading, as usual, was thorough and was now directed
towards the deeper understanding, the checking and rechecking,
of the new philosophy of life which he had outlined in the *Annals*.
He studied the French Revolution and even played with the idea
of writing a history of the Convention of 1793. He read the his-
torians Thierry (who had been secretary to Saint-Simon), Mignet,
Thiers, and Guizot, who in their writings often stressed the decisive role of the class struggles in French history. He not only
studied the socialist and communist writers, but made personal
contact, spending many hours, for example, with Proudhon discussing German philosophy. His friendship with Heine was also

useful, since the poet had lived many years in Paris, following closely its political and intellectual movements; Marx in his turn inspired the poet with the brilliancy of his wit and understanding. Marx did not neglect his study of philosophy, and through Bacon, Descartes, Locke, and the French materialists came to a closer grip with that materialism which he had first learned to appreciate through Epicurus and Feuerbach. And last but not least, he turned to the political economists, studied Adam Smith, Ricardo, J. B. Say, and many others, including the mercantilists and the more recent physiocrats, in order to give his historical understanding of the role of the class struggle a solid economic foundation. Much of his economic reading of this period has left its traces in the *Manuscripts,* and also in the *Capital* of later years.

4. HEGEL

In the *Manuscripts* Marx is still the pupil of Hegel and Feuerbach, but already the emancipated pupil, who is finding his own way on the shoulders of the great men who preceded him. Above all he appreciated Hegel's method, which Hegel had called dialectics and with which he developed all concepts—whether from daily life, science, religion, law, morality or esthetics—in a chain of related reasoning until full understanding, and with it freedom, was reached in the Absolute.[1] New concepts were derived from previous concepts by analyzing their limitations and contradictions, "negating" every concept until a more embracing one was reached, and new light was thrown upon the older concept.

This method was different in principle from merely ordered classification, as in the Linnaean system of describing animals and plants. It also differed, as Hegel pointed out, from the mathematical method, in which the proof of a theorem, say that of Pythagoras, does not flow organically from the statement of the theorem: we need some tricks to prove it.[2] Hegel himself explained his dialectical method in the following terms:

There are three aspects in every thought which is logically real or true: the abstract or rational form, which says what something is; the dialectical negation, which says what something is not, the speculative—concrete comprehension: A is also that which it is not, A is non-A. These three aspects do not constitute three parts of logic, but are moments of everything that is logically real or true. They belong to every philosophical Concept. Every Concept is rational, is abstractly opposed to another, and is united in comprehension together with its opposites. This is the definition of dialectic.[3]

Wherever there is movement, wherever there is life, wherever anything is carried into effect in the actual world, there Dialectic is at work. It is also the soul of knowledge which is truly scientific. In the popular way of looking at things, the refusal to be bound by the abstract deliverances of understanding appears as fairness, which, according to the proverb Live and let live, demands that each should have its turn; we admit the one, but we admit the other also. But when we look more closely, we find that the limitations of the finite do not merely come from without; that its own nature is the cause of its abrogation, and that by its own act it passes into its counterpart. We say, for instance, that man is mortal, and seem to think that the ground of his death is in external circumstances only; so that if this way of looking were correct, man would have two special properties, vitality and—also—mortality. But the true view of the matter is that life, as life, involves the germ of death, and that the finite, being radically self-contradictory, involves its own self-suppression.[4]

Dialectics is therefore neither sophistry nor scepticism, nor is it a mere subjective seesaw of arguments pro and con.[5] Hegel often speaks of the unity of opposites, or even identity of opposites, as when he states that "the truth of Being and Nothing is the unity of the two, and this unity is Becoming." [6] This unity of opposites is often taken as a characteristic of dialectics. It was taken over by the materialist dialecticians and its profound common sense was stressed by Lenin:

The identity of opposites (more accurately, perhaps, their "unity," although the difference between the expressions "identity" and "unity" is not very essential here. In a certain sense both are correct) is the recognition (discovery) of the *mutually exclusive* and opposed tendencies in all the phenomena and processes of nature (including spirit and society). The condition of the knowledge of all processes of the world as in *"self-movement,"* in spontaneous development, conceived in its vital and living form, is the knowledge of the unity of their opposites. Development is "struggle" of opposites.[7]

Freed from its one-dimensional appearance and seen as a widening of concepts in many dimensions, and freed as well from the difficult technical language used by Hegel, dialectics makes common sense. With materialist, non-Hegelian dialectics, as developed by Marx, Engels, and Lenin, it is not difficult to see this in all domains of thought and also in the objective world. As was already pointed out, Hegel's dialectical exposition of the self-development of mind referred both to the inner growth of the philosophical mind and to the history of man. History thus was interpreted as the gradual evolution of the world-mind *(Weltgeist)* in which every phase (Antiquity, the Middle Ages, and Modern times, or the Chinese, the Greeks, and the Germanic races, or the philosophical systems) represented a definite stage in the self-fulfillment of the Absolute, also understood as the acquisition of freedom. This looks like the fulfillment of God's will in Christian doctrine and gives a clue to Feuerbach's assertion that Hegel's system was, in the last instance, theology. History ceased to be a collection of data on battles, princes, or governments, but a gradual unfolding process *with a sense.* This process was always conceived in terms of stages of the mind, behind which the social-economic relationships remain hidden, or better, appear in a mystified form—but they do appear at places, as Marx, Lenin, and others have pointed out.

We have also mentioned how religion entered into this scheme as a highly spiritualized advanced stage in philosophical progress. Likewise, the state is seen as the dialectical unity of the family and of civil society (not to be confused with bourgeois society), and as such is the final embodiment, in concept as well as in time, of morality and the ethical life. In his logic Hegel showed how the mind, having reached full understanding, is able to see the mutual relationship of concepts in terms of the categories (quantity, quality, measure, etc). These categories were not just explained and catalogued, as Aristotle and Kant had done, but were evolved from each other in a process of negation and a transcendence in a new negation that was also an affirmation. The relationship of quantity to quality, of which Engels has given illustrative examples, is perhaps the best known of such dialectical relationships.[8] Hegel also had a philosophy of nature, perhaps the weakest point in his speculative system.

This was an objective idealism, perhaps the most comprehensive in the history of philosophy. The individual was comprehended in the universal, the individual philosopher's mind in the world mind, all previous philosophy viewed as a phase of the new, dialectical philosophy—Kant's "thing in itself," Leibniz' "monad," Spinoza's "substance," Fichte's "Ego" and "Non-Ego," all conquered in Hegel's Absolute, or so he thought. Is it then a wonder that this philosophy had enormous attraction for a generation that, in the full view of great continental events, wanted to storm Olympus, but not being able to get anywhere in the political-economic world had to be satisfied by storming an Olympus of the mind?

What strikes us in Hegel is his optimism. Proclaiming the possibility of acquiring full and adequate understanding of the world (that is, the world of the mind), he taught the triumph of speculative reason:

> Man ought to honor himself and deem himself worthy of the highest. He cannot think too much of the greatness and power of the spirit. The essence of the universe, closed though it is for itself, has no barrier to defend itself against the courage to know it. It must disclose its treasures; its depth is there for us to behold, to know, to enjoy.[9]

Philosophy thus is not a specialist's professional field, but involves the whole of man. We see Hegel carrying out his program in the *Phenomenology* of 1806, the work that Marx analyzes in his *Economic and Philosophic Manuscripts.* Here Hegel describes the development of the mind, its appearances (phenomena), from the most elementary acts of individual consciousness to absolute knowledge and freedom. Like Bunyan leading us on his Christian's pilgrimage to Eternity, Hegel leads us on a philosopher's voyage of discovery to the Absolute:

> I have set forth the movement of consciousness, from the first crude opposition between itself and the object, up to absolute knowledge. This process goes through all the forms of the *relation of thought to the object,* and reaches the concept of a *theory of knowledge (Wissenschaft)* as its result.[10]

Hegel begins with subjective certainty of the individual in the most elementary actions of daily life, where he faces an exterior, an alien, world.[11] This process is described in the first five chapters, which Marx entitles "Consciousness" and Hegel later summarized under the title "Subjective Mind."[12] I, the subject, see a house (the object). This is sense-certainty, both subject and object appear as individuals, as "pure immediacy" *(reine Unmittelbarkeit)*. But the house and I may be "negated," the house may be replaced by another object within my vision, I may be replaced by someone else. This leads to the concepts of "here" and "now," which are universals. Hegel says that the universal is the "truth" of sense-certainty. This process of reaching universals is "negation" *(Verneinung)* and "mediation" *(Vermittlung)*.

At this moment sense-certainty turns into perception *(Wahrnehmung,* literally, the taking of truth). This deals with "things," permanent under changes of here and now. Things have certain properties or "determinatenesses." The thing is posited *(gesetzt)* explicitly *(für sich,* for itself) as absolute negation of all other entities, it is both unity and multiplicity, it is a unity of opposites. The unity in the diversity of the properties is the "thinghood" *(Dingheit)*.

In this way the abstract analysis proceeds, we leave the realm of perception and move into that of appearance *(Erscheinung)*. Understanding *(Verstand)* is past, we reach for reason *(Vernunft)*. In this higher world of knowledge the ways of consciousness have opened into those of self-consciousness, where we enter into the inner realm of truth. In the sphere of self-consciousness I see not only myself, but us *(Wir)*.

Here Hegel suddenly moves into the social atmosphere. It is typical of the *Phenomenology* that it not only describes the personal experiences of the mind, but also the experiences of man in history; also typical is the obscurity of the language, which almost never moves away from the abstract, and in which explicit references hardly ever occur,[13] often making it difficult to see what specific event or episode is on the author's mind. But, here in the opening sections of the part on Self-Consciousness, we have no doubt where we stand. Hegel points out that I and the other are not alike, self-consciousness is in conflict with self-opposition, and this leads to the split between Lord and Servant *(Herr und Knecht)*, one of the most remarkable sections of the *Phenomenology*.

The relationship between Lord and Servant, to which Marx refers in his *Manuscripts*, is expressed in highly abstract terms. The Lord is conscious being for itself, which is mediated with itself through another consciousness; he, as master, is thus related to the servant through mediation by the independent existence of the servant, for that is precisely what keeps this servant in thrall. But an interesting thing happens. This relationship of Lord and Servant (or Lord and Bondsman, as Baillie translates it) is established through *labor*—by which the consciousness of the servant comes to itself. In the product of his labor he finds himself, and while it appeared to be alien to him, it destroys this extraneous alien negative and sets itself up as a negative in the element of permanence—in other words, it becomes his own. Thus the servant attains the consciousness that he exists in his own right and on his own account, implicitly and explicitly *(an und für sich)*. "Thus precisely in labor where there seemed to be merely some outsider's mind and ideas involved, the servant becomes aware, through this rediscovery of himself by himself, of having and being a 'mind of his own.' " [14] The servant has spiritually overcome the master.

Thus Hegel sketches the dialectics of servitude, by which through the labor process not only the master, but also the oppressed finds his own mind—though only, at this stage, on the level of understanding, not yet of reason. But the idea of freedom can enter even here: the self is established as ultimately a free self.[15]

Hegel now proceeds to search for the "freedom of self-consciousness," and finds it in history. He discusses as stages in this process the stoicism and scepticism of the Roman empire and the "unhappy consciousness" of religious life in the Middle Ages. We need not follow him further when he passes through the stages of reason, where mind faces nature, and through the stages of objective mind, where it faces law, ethics, culture, language, morality, and religion. At last he reaches the final stage of Absolute knowledge, where the mind has freed itself and all previous modes of consciousness appear in their own place. "This process of releasing itself from the form of itself is the highest freedom and security of its knowledge of itself." Hegel's goal of freedom is reached, it is a philosophical freedom, a state of mind.

We have seen that in the dialectical process the object faces the subject on different levels of consciousness. This process, whereby the object is posited outside of the subject, and then is taken back in a newer form, is called objectivization *(Vergegenständlichung)*, externalization *(Entäusserung)*, disunity *(Entweiung)*, and estrangement or alienation *(Verfremdung)*. The concept of alienation expresses the greatest amount of tension, as in the case of the unhappy consciousness, and later, in the domain of objective spirit, Hegel even speaks of *self-alienation*. It is this term which Marx (via Feuerbach) took over, though in a new, a materialistic sense, and which in our time has received so much attention that the Marxist concept of alienation has become the topic of an ever-growing series of essays and books.

The term alienation itself is old and appears originally with a religious connotation, as in "alienation from God." [16] Fichte seems to have used it first in a philosophical sense, considering the positing of an object an alienation of the subject. Hegel took it over and used it in a far more comprehensive sense as an essential element in the dialectical process. We have seen how it is labor that externalizes "the pure self-existence" of the servant's consciousness, but how in the labor process itself this extraneous alien element is transcended while the servant enters into his own mind. When Hegel, in his section on nature, introduces spiritual and material mechanism (we speak of mechanical materialism) he characterizes it by the fact that the concepts with which it deals remain external to the mind and to one another.

Again, in the section of the *Phenomenology* which is called "Spirit in Self-Estrangement" we meet the concept in the realm of culture and civilization. Here Hegel points out that the life of the spirit as found in social self-consciousness is split into the universal spirit, the social spirit, and the individual spirit. The individual seeks to remove the contrast, which places his true life outside of himself, and a strong tension develops which the spirit wants to remove by struggle. This struggle can take intellectual, economic, religious or ethical forms, and is typical of what we call culture or civilization. Hegel follows it through several sections of European history, where it culminates in the Enlightenment and the French Revolution.[17] He stresses the importance of this process in the words: "Self-consciousness is only something definite, it only has real existence, insofar as it alienates itself from itself. By doing so, it puts itself in the position of something universal, and this universality is its validity, and its actuality *(Wirklichkeit)*."

Both nature and history are thus externalizations, the alienated essences of the mind in search of the Absolute. Matter and mind are a unity, matter being the alienated self of mind. Alienation is a relation of opposites, a disunity in what is finally a unity. In its development the mind endeavors to conquer this alienation. Eventually, in absolute knowledge, "self-consciousness attains the form of universality, and what remains is its true notion, the notion that has attained its realization—the notion in its truth, i.e., in unity with its externalization."

It is only natural that critical minds like Feuerbach and Marx, while wondering at this speculative jargon should at the same time realize that Hegel had something very important to say, and therefore asked themselves: what lies behind it? And it was Marx who eventually saw the light: the jargon mystified the process by which man obtains true knowledge of the objective world of nature and of man; alienation is a social process, active in history, and history is determined by property relations and the class struggle.

Feuerbach, as we have seen, took a first and important step, but confined himself mainly to theology, in which he saw the key to Hegel's philosophy. Theology he saw as a form of anthropology, but of an abstract anthropology.[18] He then tried to apply his newly acquired understanding to Hegel's philosophy in general, but also only in abstract terms:

The secret of theology is anthropology, but the secret of speculative philosophy is theology—the speculative theology which is distinguished from ordinary theology in that it places the divine being, removed by ordinary theology in the Beyond, due to fear and stupidity, into the Herebelow, that is, it makes it present and definite, real. Theology is belief in spooks, ordinary theology has its spooks in sensuous imagination, speculative theology in unsensuous abstraction. We have only to invert speculative theology in order to have the unmystified, pure, white truth. And since everything on earth is found again in the heaven of theology, therefore we find everything in nature back in the heaven of Hegel's logic: equality, quantity, measure, being, chemistry, mechanism and organism. In theology we have everything twice, once abstract, the other time concrete, and so we have everything twice in Hegelian philosophy: once as object of logic and then again as object of the philosophy of nature and mind.

To abstract means to place the essence of nature outside of nature, the essence of man outside of man, the essence of thought outside of the art of thinking. Hegel's philosophy has *alienated man from himself*, since his total system is based on these acts of abstraction. True, it identifies again what it separates, but only in a manner which itself is again separable, mediate. Hegel's philosophy lacks in immediate unity, immediate certainty, immediate truth.[19]

This is how Marx found the critique of German philosophy, when on the strength of his understanding of the social process he set himself the task of completing Feuerbach's process of "inversion." In the light in which he began to see the world of mind and man, the whole concept of the relation of men to nature and to society took a new form, in which also the principle of alienation changed its meaning entirely. In this process he emancipated himself completely from Feuerbach. However, despite his basic criticism of the great dialectician, Marx always looked upon Hegel with the greatest respect as a thinker who, if often only intuitively, had grasped some of the fundamentals of human thought and conduct.

5. The Manuscripts

Early in 1845 (after the *Manuscripts* were written) Marx summarized his opinion of Feuerbach: starting from the fact of religious self-alienation, the duplication of the world into an imaginary religious and a real one, Feuerbach had dissolved the religious world into its secular foundation. But, said Marx, Feuerbach overlooks the fact that having completed his work, the principal thing still remains to be done. The secular foundation itself must first be understood in its contradiction, and by removing it, be revolutionized in practice. Not satisfied with abstract thinking, Marx continued, Feuerbach appeals to sensuous contemplation, but does not conceive sensuousness as a practical human-sensuous activity. His standpoint, that of old materialism, is civil society. The standpoint of the new materialism is human society or socialized humanity.[1]

In the *Economic and Philosophic Manuscripts of 1844* we can see how Marx came to reach this position. He is full of scorn for the idle, speculative "critical" idealism of Bauer. Feuerbach is still his hero because of his true materialism based on the relationship of man to nature. This, Marx wrote, is criticizing Hegel from a positive, constructive side. Hegel never was able to get out of theology, even if in his abstract way he tried to overcome it. This same abstract point of view prevented Hegel from conceiving human history as the history of living, concrete, suffering men, for him it is always a speculative process. Marx already hints here that Feuerbach, by seeing man too much as a species being, and specifically as a species being in nature and not in a social setting, does not radically conquer Hegel, but Marx's full understanding came only somewhat later, in the *Theses on Feuerbach* and *The German Ideology*.[2] Thus, starting with the materialist outlook into which Feuerbach has led him, in the *Manuscripts* Marx opens his critique of the *Phenomenology*.[3]

He discovers two fundamental errors. The first is that when Hegel conceives wealth, state power, etc., as essences alienated from human essence, he accomplishes this only in thought. His whole alienation theory, both its appearance out of externalization and its transcendence, is only the production theory of abstract thought. Hence, secondly, since mind is for Hegel the true essence of man, he conceives religion, wealth, etc., only as spiritual entities. Hegel therefore has not written the real history of man, but only an abstract, speculative impression of it. Hegel, conceiving man as mind and mind as self-consciousness, sees all alienation of man as alienation of self-consciousness. Instead of natural objects he posits an abstract "thinghood." Objectivation of man becomes pure negativity; Hegel never gets out of his world of ideas. But a being which has no object outside of itself is an *un-being (Unwesen)*; the history of such un-beings becomes quite unreal.

Despite his spooky performance, Hegel's analysis is thorough and a great achievement. All elements of a correct analysis are in it, but too often hidden, unclear, obscure, mystified.

Now Marx points out one of these achievements. Hegel conceives the self-creation of man as a process, the "objectivization" as "externalization," and its transcendence as a result of his own *labor*. Hegel here sees man in his proper reality, he understands the essence of the labor process. In labor, man as a species being creates all his species powers, in other words, mankind has created all human faculties by labor. But this is a process which is possible only in the form of alienation (estrangement). In pointing this out, Hegel takes a great step ahead with respect to all other philosophers.

At the same time Hegel shows his one-sidedness. He takes the point of view of political economy, by which Marx means, in the first place, the doctrines of Adam Smith, in stressing the fundamental role of labor. But he sees only its positive side, labor as the act of self-creation of man as a species being. This act of self-creation is interpreted as alienation. But, as Marx saw it, Hegel, living in a world of abstractions, only recognizes abstract labor, which is labor of the mind, the labor of thinking and knowing. This is the reason that Hegel's alienation is eventually transcended only in the mental process.

The key to the *Phenomenology*, to the history of man, is therefore the labor process, the process of concrete, living man in creating his existence in daily practice, where he breathes and eats and loves and suffers. The forms of alienation and their transcendence must have their roots in human practice. This is what Hegel fails to see.

This latter point of view is now built up in considerable detail, and from several angles. It is Marx's materialist answer to Hegel's mystifying idealism, and we will not repeat it here. Much of the argument is itself clothed in the terminology that Hegel and Feuerbach use, and is hard to understand by anyone but a specialist. But the gist is clear. Against Hegel's point of view that "man is regarded as a non-objective, spiritual being," Marx asserts that man is directly a natural being with natural powers of life. The objects of his perception exist outside of him, yet he needs them. To be sure, the Hegelian dialectic has its positive moments, if we consider objectivization and externalization, negation, and alienation and its transcendence as processes in the objective world, as true negations of negations. Atheism as negation and transcendence of God, communism as transcendence of private property, are no mere flights in the realm of thought, but are actual, real conditions for the realization of man's powers, for true humanism.

In his criticism of the *Phenomenology* Marx thus has rescued labor, and with it the externalization and alienation processes, from the cloudy realms of speculation, and placed them in the everyday, the real world in which we live. Now their true nature has to be explained. Marx finds it in political economy. After having rescued labor from Hegel's philosophical, ontological category, Marx turns to a science—and a rather modern science— for a closer study. This is analogous to what Galileo and Newton had done to some of the scholastic categories such as substance. The abstract concept becomes historically concrete.

Accordingly, the first chapters of the *Manuscripts* are devoted to an analysis of the most important English and French economists of the day—Adam Smith, Ricardo, James Hill, McCulloch, J. B. Say, Destutt de Tracy, Boisguillebert, and the now almost for-gotten Wilhelm Schulz. Their principal merit is that they agree in conceiving labor as the source of all wealth, contrary to the mercantilists who had conceived precious metals and to the more recent physiocrats who had conceived land as the source of wealth—where labor entered as a factor in agriculture. Only by modern economists, writes Marx, has labor been recognized in its full generality and its full abstraction as the source of wealth, no longer tied to a specific element such as land.

With Adam Smith, for example, all wealth is industrial wealth, industry is labor in its fully developed form, as the factory system is the fully developed form of private property.

From this point of view mercantilists and physiocrats, who place the source of wealth outside of man, appear as fetish worshippers, as Catholics. Engels has therefore called Adam Smith the Luther of economics. Just as Luther opposed Catholic paganism by returning religiosity to man's inner self, so has Adam Smith destroyed the type of wealth outside of man and has incorporated wealth in man himself.

However, by making religion the affair of man's inner self Luther did not abolish religion. Nor did Adam Smith abolish private property by making it an inner affair of man in the form of labor. But since Smith places man in the setting of private property, recognition of the role of labor leads to dehumanization of man, because he has become the essence of private property. Political economy thus leads to the capture of man by private property, depicting the horrors of private property as if they were natural, necessary phenomena, at the same time professing concern for the human essence, man's freedom, and his independence. But in this way bourgeois political economy has been compelled to shed its hypocrisy and in the course of development—from Adam Smith to Say, Ricardo, and Mill—has had to reveal its utter cynicism. Thus political economy has brought into the open, more and more clearly, man's alienation from nature and from his fellow man.

Here Marx breaks with classical political economy and takes fully the point of view of the working class. Instead of justifying the present form of civil or bourgeois society he attacks it, showing its inhuman character by analyzing the three basic forms of income in the capitalist system, the wages of labor, the profits of capital, and ground rent.

The exposition is so clear that only a few words are necessary to explain the character of this analysis, or, better said, this indictment. Labor is the source of all wealth, but the laborer gets only the smaller part of it, barely enough to continue working. The product of his labor goes to the capitalists. This leads to a bitter struggle between capital and labor, in which the advantages are all on the side of the capitalist. In this class struggle, the aim of the capitalists is to keep wages to a minimum. Labor has become a commodity on the market, where all human relations are reduced to money relations.

Marx shows how the worker is degraded, the capitalist enriched. In his analysis of profit he notes a trend towards concentration of capital in fewer hands, and how profit is increased by monopoly. Eventually, the contradictions of the system lead to its annulment through competition. This holds both for industry and for agriculture, where capitalist exploitation destroys the romantic myth still attached to the soil. Thus the way is opened to eventual association of producers, and the soil will become the home of truly free men.

When we study Marx's exposition in detail, we find the beginning of his mature analysis of capitalist society—in his treatment of the machine, division of labor, dehumanization of labor, concentration of capital, and the class struggle. Later Marx will correct and complete his theory, especially by developing the labor theory of value, the distinction between use value and exchange value, and the theory of surplus value. In the many notes Marx made while studying the economists (and which have been published) [4] we see him struggling with the law of value, but, like Engels at that time, he had not yet come to a conclusion. They both played with the idea that value is determined by competition and expressed by price.[5] The distinction between labor and labor power also is still missing.

What conclusions can be drawn from this analysis with respect to the theory of alienation? Marx points out that bourgeois political economy proceeds from the fact that private property exists, but takes its existence for granted. The only motives recognized are greed and competition. But the situation can be understood only if we start from the fundamental fact that the object produced by labor confronts it as something alien, as an object, a power, independent of the producer. It does not belong to him; it turns against him. The Hegelian concepts of objectification and externalization followed by alienation get blood and life. They become the concrete objectivization of labor in its product, and its subsequent loss in alienation. Just as in religion, as Feuerbach has observed, the more man places into God, the less he retains himself, so the greater the laborer's product, the less he retains himself, the less he is himself.

The alienation is twofold. First, it is to be found in the relation of the worker to his product, as an alien object which has power over him, and which is at the same time his relation to the outside world as a whole. Second, alienation is expressed in the relation of labor to the act of production itself: the worker's activity does not belong to him; indeed, it is turned against him. Estranged labor turns man against man, takes away from him the natural, spontaneous activity to which he is entitled as a member of the human race (as a species being) and degrades him to working for mere existence, like a horse.

If in estranged labor the product of the laborer is alien to the worker, to whom does it belong? The answer is clear: it belongs to the master of labor, the capitalist. Private property is thus the product of alienated labor. At one place Marx qualifies this by saying that while private property originates as the consequence of alienated labor, later there is a reciprocal relationship. But the whole tenor leads to Marx's conclusion of the priority of private property. We witness here historical materialism in the making.

Hence, annulment of alienation means annulment of private property. This means communism, to which the labor movement leads. But there are different kinds of communism, including the crude type which wants to destroy all private property that cannot be possessed by all and also wants to destroy talent and the natural relationship of man and woman (for example, some of the followers of Babeuf). Still negative, it is ruled by envy, and cannot overcome alienation. Then there is a political communism that wants to destroy the state, but it would retain enough vestiges of private property to leave strong remnants of alienation (for example, Proudhon).

Marx's concept of communism is far more comprehensive, being the positive annulment of private property and with this of human self-alienation. Man then becomes truly human; he will be able to develop all his creative faculties, and the acquired material and cultural wealth of mankind in its entirety truly will be appropriated by the whole of mankind. Man will be a social, a human being, in harmony with nature and with man himself, the contradictions between his existence and his essence, between necessity and freedom, between individual and species having come to an end. This is the true solution of Feuerbach's quest for humanism and naturalism. It is found in communism.

Thus the analysis ends. The problem of alienation that Hegel divined to reside in man's relation to the labor process, and Feuerbach saw in man's relation to the deity, finds its solution in the abolition of private property. Communism emerges as the final answer to one of the most fundamental problems raised by classical German philosophy.

By way of summary, these are the main characteristic traits of alienation according to Marx, or, as he states it more precisely, of the "alienation of the worker in his object," an all important fact which political economy (and we may add, philosophy) so far had hidden:

(1) *Alienation of labor from its product* (which is the alienation of the laborer from the object of his production), *alienation from the object:*

(a) Labor is independent of, alien to its product, which is in other hands; labor remains a thing outside the laborer, it is only his exterior state: "appropriation is alienation," "realization of labor is its derealization" (even so far as starvation).

(b) The life that labor has given the obect of its labor confronts it as a hostile force.

(c) Labor becomes the slave of its object, since only through it can the laborer continue to exist, not only as a worker, but as a human being.

(2) *Alienation of labor from the act of production, self-alienation:*

(a) Since labor is exterior to the laborer, labor is forced labor, a means to satisfy needs, not a need itself: "What is animal in man becomes human, what is human becomes animal."

(3) *Alienation of man from nature, hence from his species, mankind:*

(a) Since mankind's deepest need is to produce, to create, and alienation makes productive life only a means to satisfy needs, individual man is alienated from mankind: "man makes his essence only a means of his existence."

(b) Since alienated labor takes species-life away from man, it takes his advantage over the animal away from him. A worker may as well be a horse the way society treats him: he gets just enough to keep going.

(c) The life of mankind is alienated as a whole; man is not what he should be as a human being, but finds himself treated as a means, a tool.

(d) Hence, man is alienated from his fellow man, since he treats him also as a means, a tool.

Hence alienation appears in three forms: (1) alienation from the object of one's labor, (2) self-alienation, and (3) alienation of man from man, of man from mankind.

6. THE REACTION TO MARX'S MANUSCRIPTS

In the last thirty years, but especially in the period after the second world war, great interest has developed in the formative period of Marxist thought. What were the factors, intellectual as well as social, that led Karl Marx to his daring new philosophy? In 1842, when Marx, a 24-year-old Doctor of Philosophy, became the editor of a radical-democratic paper in the Rhineland, there was no Marxism, only some revolt among the pipe-smoking metaphysicians in Germany who debated the social and religious implications of Hegel's philosophy in taverns and in ephemeral little periodicals, against a background of encroaching capitalism and resulting political dissent.

The first explicit formulation of historical materialism in terms of a materialist dialectics dates from 1845. What happened in these years in which an academic metaphysics clothed in an obscure technical language was transformed into a theory that would shake the world, and with a message understandable to the fisherman and the peasant, the industrial worker and the student, a message not only for contemplation, but also for action?

One of the reasons for this interest is technical, since a large number of Marx's early writings remained unpublished until 1927 when the *Gesamtausgabe* [1] began to appear. Several of these writings have revealed ideas of Marx which he rarely took up again in later days, ideas concerning man's thoughts and sufferings and final triumph in the full human dignity of the individual, ideas developed in elaborate critical studies of the philosophies of Hegel and Feuerbach. It so happened that early writings of Hegel also have been brought to light, which have contributed to a new interest in Hegel, and even in some of the almost forgotten Young Hegelians. In addition, a new prominence has been reached by one of the latest trends in philosophical thinking, existentialism, which like Marxism has some roots in Hegelianism, or better said in a criticism of Hegelianism.

All this has led the interest in Marxism, of friend and enemy alike, somewhat away from economics and history—the central points for study and controversy in previous days—to the philosophical roots of Marxism. The position of the anti-Marxists can be summarized in the words of a recent author: "The expansive force of the communist ideology can be met actively only by returning to its origins." [2] However, the general interest in these questions is rooted in deeper ground, in the crisis of the capitalist system, which has brought philosophy again into the focus of attention. This can be observed most clearly in the natural sciences.

Indeed, capitalism, in its imperialistic stage, is caught in its own contradictions, and its total elimination is the goal of an ever-growing part of mankind. Already it has lost large sections of the world, where socialism on the whole has been remarkably successful. Marxism, in particular, has captured the mind and is directing the actions of millions of people. Marxism has come to fruition, it cannot be ignored; on the contrary, as is realized more and more, it is not merely an economic or historical theory, but a universal outlook on the world, more universal than Hegelianism, since it appeals not only to the head, but also to the hand and the heart of mankind. The study of Marx's early writings, therefore, can contribute to a better understanding of the mature Marxist theory and practice and to a better grasp of some of the essentials of dialectical materialism, as of thought in general.

Such an understanding can be attained only by a critical approach to the early writings. Much of these are still embryonic, sketchy—the first stage in the development of Marxist thoughts. The language is often taken straight from Hegel and Feuerbach and shows traces of idealism and of abstract materialism. The later Marx never wanted the unpublished manuscripts published, or the published essays reprinted. Not that he was ashamed of them.[3] But when Wilhelm Liebknecht, in 1871, wanted to reprint some early essays of Marx and Engels, both men objected, because they saw no useful purpose in doing so. "But you must reprint rather long sections from *Capital*," added Marx.[4] *The importance, the validity, of the early writings can be judged only from the point of view of fully developed Marxism.*

Whether one may agree with this conclusion or not, the interest is there and does not wane. An enormous number of essays and books, often exhibiting considerable erudition, have appeared on the subject of young Marx.[5] Many non-Marxists participate in this discussion, often with full or grudging admiration and a desire for understanding that many a friend of the Marxist outlook may well emulate. Philosophers and psychologists, economists and theologians, Protestants and Catholics, are filling the shelves of our libraries with their commentaries, the majority of them written in French or German. Each one has his own axe to grind, so that there is a veritable spectrum of opinions.

Many questions are being raised. What can now be said about the relation of Marxist and Hegelian philosophy? What is the difference between the Marx of the formative years and the mature Marx of *Capital* and the International Workingmen's Association? Can we understand the economic theory of *Capital* better by the study of the early economic writings? Why did not Marx, in his later days, elaborate on the alienation theory of his formative years? Many other points have been touched upon, such as the relationship of Marx to Engels or to his later pupils, Kautsky, Plekhanov, and Lenin. Other questions that deserve attention deal with the central thesis of Marx relating alienation to private property (Marx, in 1844, did not yet speak of the abolition of the private ownership of the means of production, although his attention usually was focussed there). And what do Marx's hints at human relationships "beyond" communism mean?

For these reasons the *Manuscripts* have become a treasure trove for the students of the early Marx, and the chief interest is that section of the *Manuscripts* that deals with alienation, although useful work could also be done in comparing the economic doctrines of the same writings with those of *Capital*.[6] The reason is clear. Alienation has become a standard term in our dictionary. Capitalism, in more than a hundred years of development since Marx stressed the role of alienation as a social phenomenon, has affected the relation of man to his work and of man to man to such an extent that alienation has become a matter of grave concern to thousands of worried students of society.

Indeed, viewing alienation as Marx has described it, we are shocked to see how aptly it fits our present-day civilization. Here, as in so many other fields, Marx has anticipated the ideas of others by several decades. As a matter of fact, alienation has become more pronounced, more inclusive, more devastating, more monstrous than ever before. How can labor's product turn man against himself more starkly than in nuclear weapons? How can any moral code be rejected so utterly as in the propaganda to make these weapons acceptable? "Man alone," "the lonely crowd," are but two of the expressions coined to show how alienation has affected our daily life. Enormous is the list of books and papers dealing with the phenomenon in the present time, with or without reference to Marx, with or without specifying particular aspects, such as loneliness, frustration, hostility, insanity, crime, or dehumanization.[7]

Moreover, phenomena of alienation also occur, albeit often in modified form, in the new socialist societies. Although socialism offers perspective for man's harmonious development and for true humanism that capitalism cannot offer, the process leading to the eventual abolition of alienation is long and secular, as with all concrete historic processes having its ups and downs, advances and retrogressions. As a result, the meaning of young Marx's writings is also being ardently discussed in the socialist world. Marxists debate with non-Marxists, existentialists with Catholics—the debate crosses many fronts and frontiers.[8]

However, the debate on alienation in connection with Marx serves still another, quite different purpose. Can the "idealistic" young Marx be played off against the supposedly cynical, disillusioned, older Marx, or Marx, the lover of lifelong freedom, against the "authoritarians" of the modern working-class movement? If so, it then may be deemed possible to undermine the foundations of Marxism, or at least to discredit the present workers' parties which base themselves on Marxism. *One way is to suppress the connection between Marx's ideas on alienation and on the class struggle.*

An early German edition of the *Manuscripts*—or at any rate, part of them—by Landshut and Mayer (1932) gives an example of this interpretation.[9] Not the mature Marx, but the young Marx is the true philosopher: the *Manuscripts* form "the nodal point of Marx's whole development of thought, in which the principles of his economic analysis originate immediately from the idea of the true actuality of man. They show Marx on the most finished height of his position, the only document which in itself spans the whole dimension of Marx's spirit." This whole dimension is identified with what Marx calls "real humanism." Then the political motivation of this curious distortion is given away: "Everything which usually is connected with the concept of communism and by which it understands itself today, Marx has clearly rejected in anticipation."

No wonder that the authors proclaim that according to their novel interpretation of Marxism the famous sentence of *The Communist Manifesto* which declares that all history so far has been a history of class struggles, might also have been written: "All history so far is the history of self-alienation of man." [10] In this way the authors, instead of leading us from Hegel to Marx, have brought us back safely from Marx to Hegel.

A similar attempt to take the class struggle out of Marxism and

in its place substitute "alienation" can be studied in a book by
H. Popitz called *Der entfremdete Mensch (Alienated Man)*, where
a chapter heading reads: "The Alienated Man (The Philosophical
Foundation of Dialectical Materialism) ." [11]

In Europe, with large and powerful Marxist parties, such writings seek to show that the policies of these parties are not based
on the theory of "true" Marxism, and thus to add to the confusion.
In the United States where knowledge of Marxism as yet is
limited and access to it is bedeviled by obscurantist libels published by legislative committees and agents of the secret police,
attempts have been made by better informed authors to upgrade
Marx to a more respectable position. Here again the notion of
alienation plays a role. Since alienation is being discussed so
widely, the man who so clearly understood the issue should be
known. This is the theme of *Marx's Concept of Man* by the psy-
choanalyst Erich Fromm,[12] whose description of alienation in
Marx deserves commendation. Moreover, he recognizes the unity
of thought that connects the young and the mature Marx:

> Socialism, for Marx, is a society which permits the actualization of
> man's essence, by overcoming his alienation. It is nothing less than
> creating the conditions for the truly free, rational, active and inde-
> pendent man; it is the fulfillment of the prophetic aim: the destruction
> of the idols. . . . For Marx, the aim of socialism was freedom . . .
> based on man's standing on his own feet, using his own powers and
> relating himself to the world productively.

This is well expressed, even though Marx used the term "communism" rather than "socialism." But the historic sense is missing.
It is typical of both the Landshut-Mayer and the Fromm editions
of the *Manuscripts* that they only reproduce the "alienation"
parts, and omit the economic sections, which stress the class struggle. And the class struggle is a very concrete, historical process
with ups and downs, as are revolution and socialist reconstruction.
In Fromm's eyes, Marxism is thus the heir of prophetic Messian-
ism, opposed to the church as well as to liberalism, and to all
"authoritarianism," whether that of Lenin, Stalin or Khrushchev.
It is an absolute, non-historic Marxism that emerges from
Fromm's explanation of alienation. Despite his appreciation of

Marx the thinker and Marx the man, his Marx is but a glorified Hess or Weitling.

A more ambitious attempt to present Marxism as a philosophy is the book by Professor R. C. Tucker, *Philosophy and Myth in Karl Marx*.[13] Much in this book can be recommended as supplementary to the very concise sketch which we had to give of Marx's relation to Feuerbach and classical German philosophy. Like Fromm, Tucker sees the unity between the work of the young and of the older Marx. But with Fromm, Tucker seems unaware of how much human practice and concrete historical understanding lie behind even Marx's earliest philosophical and economic writings. Marxism ends up for Tucker in a myth: "Marx's myth of the warfare of labour and capital." "What Marx produced in *Capital* was not a work of ethics but a book of revelation;" Marx is declared not a social scientist, but "a philosopher become mythmaker." The path of Tucker's Marx thus leads, like Fromm's Marx, back to the utopians of the more eschatological kind, in this case via Georges Sorel and those syndicalists who were the real protagonists of the theory of the myth.

Many more examples of confusing interpretation can be given. An interesting one is the claim that Marx's theory was just another metaphysics:

> The phenomenology of the Mind has simply been changed into that of labor, the dialectics of human alienation into that of capital, the metaphysics of absolute Knowledge into that of absolute communism. History maintains all along the same meaning, the Marxian "intention" is as large, as ambitious, as the Hegelian intention.

This passage is from *Marxisme et humanisme* by Bigo,[14] who misses the point that Marx, though in his earlier work still using some terminology of speculative metaphysics, constructs a theory based on the facts of real life, as lived by man in a historical setting, in which science is called upon to serve in the reconstruction of society. It makes little sense to speak of a "metaphysics of absolute communism." Communism emerges as a result of the historical process, carried out by the mass action of the underlying classes of society. The carriers of the revolution are no metaphysicians, they are the common men, who, as Lincoln once said, must have been loved by God because he made so many of them. The road from Bigo's "metaphysics" to Tucker's "myth" is not very long.

Another theme which deserves special attention is the role played by alienation in the debate between the Marxists and the existentialists.[15] Both outlooks on life stem from opposition to the abstract character of Hegel's philosophy, in which real, living, loving suffering man appears only in a mythified form, since Hegel leaves the actual individual and his subjective life unaffected. Both stress the dignity of man, or at any rate, his right to such dignity, his uniqueness, his importance. From there Marx proceeded to a philosophy based on man as a social being whose task it is to overcome alienation in the class struggle and in the subsequent building of a new form of society in which his freedom will be realized. In contrast, Søren Kierkegaard (1813-55), often considered the founder of existentialism, tried to find his way in life through the struggle of the individual man with his God. In a profound state of inner tension, always haunted by the consciousness of sin, man can overcome his alienation—if ever he can overcome it—in an intensely personalized religion. The Marxist can see in this only an attempt to replace one kind of alienation with another—an attitude which in Kierkegaard reflected the economically undeveloped state of the Danish society of his day.

Both Marxist and existentialist probably will agree on the fundamental fact that man's existence is in conflict with his essence, even though there is an abstract, unhistorical, Feuerbachian flavor to this term "essence." But where the Marxist outlook is essentially optimistic, since he sees the working classes of the world coming to a collective reconstruction of society, existentialism is pessimistic, seeing man alone in a hostile world, and if he loses his God, facing *le Néant*, Nothingness. Freedom is for Marx a historic concept, to be realized for the individual man in a society in harmony with nature and the whole of mankind, while existentialists seek freedom in the isolation of the struggling individual—without much of a past or a future.

However, laying emphasis on the intense personal side of man, existentialism has often touched upon a very important element in man's struggle against alienation, an element which Marxists too often have neglected in a one-sided concentration on the economic and political struggle. Marx's outlook on life was deeply ethical, and his life-long struggle was inspired by his passion for freedom, but in his writings after 1847 he intentionally concentrated on political and economic subjects, and the world has been the richer for that. He had little opportunity to elaborate on the subject of the *Manuscripts* in a more mature form. This, however, is no reason why Marxism should neglect the personal, ethical side of individual man. Marx was a humanist, moreover, a socialist humanist; and Marxism is socialist humanism, if nothing else. This aspect of Marxism is recognized more and more, especially in the socialist countries, the discussion around the *Manuscripts* being a contributing factor.

Finally, the point has been raised why Marx never again took up the subject of alienation after having written the *Manuscripts* and locked them up in his desk. Did he lose interest in the personal value of man? Did he lose sight of the individual in the masses?

Nothing in the nature of Marxism or in the personal life of Marx warrants this opinion—as Fromm and others have pointed out—even if the published works of the later Marx and Engels deal almost exclusively with economics, history, and the class struggle. This was the task they had set themselves; the world, let us repeat, is the richer for this. Actually, not for a moment did they think of overlooking the existence of alienation; on the contrary, it remained a subject of the deepest concern to them. It reappears in the fetishism of the commodity which is one of the fundamental concepts of *Capital*. Even if the term "alienation" tends to disappear, together with many other Hegelian words which had outlived their usefulness for Marx and Engels, such as exteriorization and objectivation, it is still used very effectively as late as the third volume of *Capital*.[16] Nonetheless, it is gratifying that resumption of discussion around the subject of alienation has opened a new period in the evaluation of Marxist philosophy in general and of Marxist ethics in particular.

In conclusion, I wish to thank Robert Cohen, Fritz Pappenheim and Howard Selsam, as well as James S. Allen of International Publishers, for helpful suggestions in preparing this introduction. *Belmont, Mass., May 5, 1963.* DIRK J. STRUIK

TRANSLATOR'S AND EDITOR'S NOTE ON TERMINOLOGY

The translator of Hegel's language meets many difficulties. He meets them also in the translation of the present text, since Marx uses the language of Hegel in many of his expositions.

The first difficulty lies, of course, in the subject matter of Hegel's philosophy itself. He often found no adequate words in German to express the fullness of his ideas, so that he either used existing words, but charged with a special meaning, or created his own terms. It is difficult to render such expressions into readable English. How, for instance, shall we render *aufheben, entäussern, Wesen, Begriff, Geist, Verstand, an sich, bei sich, für sich,* etc., in such a way that the flavor is preserved?

The difficulty is increased by the peculiar use Hegel makes of the roots of the German language, so that his terms have a meaning different from common use. Take, for instance, a simple word like *wirklich,* of which the English equivalent is "real." But we must always expect that in Hegel *wirklich* may well mean *was wirkt,* hence, "what works," "effective," "actual." Similarly, *Begriff,* "concept" in translation, is in Hegel's sense connected with the verb *greifen,* to grasp, so that *Begriff* is a concept that has a full grasp on its content. The term *sinnlich,* translated by "sensuous," is what belongs to the *Sinne,* "senses," and is not to be rendered by "sensual."

The translator offers the following notes on certain of these German terms, partly to explain the way in which they have been translated, and partly as an aid to understanding the texts.

Aufheben (past tense: *hob auf,* p.p. *aufgehoben;* noun: *Aufhebung*).

Aufheben (literally "to raise up") has two opposed meanings in popular speech. (1) It can mean "to abolish," "to cancel," "to annul," "to do away with," etc. (2) It can mean "to preserve." Hegel, valuing the word just because of this double, negative and positive, meaning,[1] uses it to describe the positive-negative action by which a higher logical category or form of nature or spirit, in superseding a lower, both "annuls" it and "incorporates its truth." Unfortunately, there is no single English word with the same double meaning, except "sublate," a technical term adopted for the purpose by some translators of Hegel; but as this is likely to be unintelligible to the general reader, it has not been used in the present volume. Instead, "supersede" has generally been used to render *aufheben,* where is seemed that the word was being used in this double, positive-negative sense, and occasionally it has been rendered as "transcend." Where, on the other hand, it seemed that *aufheben* was being used simply or predominantly in its common-place negative sense, the negative words listed above—"abolish," "annul," etc.—have been employed.

Entäussern (p.p. *entäussert;* noun: *Entäusserung*).

The ordinary dictionary meanings of *entäussern* are "to part with," "to renounce," "to cast off," "to sell," "to alienate" (a right, or one's property). The last of these best expresses the sense in which Marx usually uses this term. For "alienate" is the only English word which combines, in much the same way as does *entäussern,* the ideas of "losing" something which nevertheless remains in existence over-against one, of something passing from one's own into another's hands, as a result of one's own act, with the idea of "selling" something: that is to say, both "alienate" and *entäussern* have, at least as one possible meaning, the idea of a sale, a transference of ownership, which is simultaneously a re-nunciation. At the same time, the word *entäussern* has, more strongly than "alienate," the sense of "making external to oneself," and at times, when this has seemed to be the aspect of its meaning uppermost in the author's mind, the word "externalize" has been used to render it in English. *Veräussern,* whose occurrence is noted at one point in the text, means "to sell" and "to alienate" in the same way as *entäussern,* but without the overtone of "renuncia-tion" or of the counter-position of the thing alienated to the one who has alienated.

Entfremden (p.p. *entfremdet*; noun: *Entfremdung*).

The ordinary dictionary meanings for *entfremden* are "to estrange," "to alienate," but in the present volume "estrange" has always been used. The reason is not only that "alienate" was needed for *entäussern* (see above), but also that *enfremden* is only equivalent to "alienate" in *one* sense of the English word—in the sense in which we speak of two people being "alienated," or of someone's affections being "alienated." *Entfremden* has not the legal-commercial undertones of "alienate," and would not be used, for instance, to describe a transfer of property. Hence, despite the fact that translators of Marx have often rendered *entfremdet* as "alienated," "estranged" seems better, especially as Marx does also use *entäussert,* which *is* the equivalent of "alienated" in its legal-commercial sense.

Wesen

There is no English word with the same range of meaning as *Wesen.*

Wesen can mean, for one thing, "essence," and some translators of Marx have treated it as if it could mean nothing else. But even when it does mean "essence," "essence" should be understood, not in the sense of something super-mundane or rarefied, but almost in the opposite sense of the "solid core" of something—its essential, as against its inessential, characteristics—its "substance" as against its accidental features—the "essential nature" or even the "very being" of something.

But secondly, *Wesen* is also the quite commonplace German word for a "being," in such phrases as "a human being" (*ein menschliches Wesen*); or the "Supreme Being" (*das höchste Wesen*).

Thirdly, *Wesen*, as Hegel points out, "in ordinary life frequently means only a collection or aggregate: *Zeitungswesen* (the press), *Postwesen* (the post office), *Steuerwesen* (the revenue). All that these terms mean is that the things in question are not to be taken singly, in their immediacy, but as a complex, and then, perhaps, in addition, in their various bearings." Hegel adds that:

"This usage of the term is not very different in its implications from our own." [2]

This last usage of the term is also not very different from Marx's, when, for instance, he seeks to make positive use of the concept of *das menschliche Wessen*. "The human essence," he says, "is no abstraction inherent in each single individual. In its reality it is the ensemble of the social relations." [3]

In the texts translated in the present volume, Marx frequently plays on the various meanings of *Wesen*, using it at times in two or even more of its senses in the one sentence. The English translator can only render the different senses by different English words, and explain their common equivalent in a note, as has been done in this volume.

ECONOMIC AND PHILOSOPHIC
MANUSCRIPTS OF 1844

PREFACE

I have already announced in the *Deutsch-Französische Jahrbücher* the critique of jurisprudence and political science in the form of a critique of the *Hegelian* Philosophy of Right. While preparing it for publication, the intermingling of criticism directed only against speculation with criticism of the various subjects themselves proved utterly unsuitable, hampering the development of the argument and rendering comprehension difficult. Moreover, the wealth and diversity of the subjects to be treated could have been compressed into *one* work only in a purely aphoristic style; whilst an aphoristic presentation of this kind, for its part, would have given the *impression* of arbitrary systematism. I shall therefore publish the critique of law, ethics, politics, etc., in a series of distinct, independent pamphlets, and afterwards try in a special work to present them again as a connected whole showing the interrelationship of the separate parts, together with a critique of the speculative elaboration of that material. For this reason it will be found that the interconnection between political economy and the state, law, ethics, civil life, etc., is touched upon in the present work only to the extent to which political economy itself *ex professo* [expressly] touches upon these subjects.

It is hardly necessary to assure the reader conversant with political economy that my results have been attained by means of a wholly empirical analysis based on a conscientious critical study of political economy.[1]

It goes without saying that besides the French and English Socialists I have also used German socialist works. The only *original* German works of substance in this science, however—other than Weitling's writings—are the essays by Hess published in *Einundzwanzig Bogen*,[2] and Engels' *Umrisse zu einer Kritik der Nationalökonomie* in the *Deutsch-Französische Jahrbücher*, where I have also indicated in a very general way the basic elements of this work.[3]

It is only with *Feuerbach* that positive, humanistic and natural-
istic criticism begins. The less noise they make, the more certain,
profound, widespread, and enduring is the effect of *Feuerbach's*
writings, the only writings since Hegel's *Phänomenologie* and
Logik to contain a real theoretical revolution.

In contrast to the *critical theologians*[4] of our day, I have
deemed the concluding chapter of the present work—the settling
of accounts with *Hegelian dialectic* and Hegelian philosophy as a
whole—to be absolutely necessary, a task not yet performed. This
lack of thoroughness is not accidental, since even the *critical* theologian remains a *theologian*. Hence, either he has to start from
certain presuppositions of philosophy accepted as authoritative;
or, if in the process of criticism and as a result of other people's
discoveries, doubts about these philosophical presuppositions have
arisen in him, he abandons them without vindication and in a
cowardly fashion, *abstracts* from them, thus showing his servile
dependence on these presuppositions and his resentment at this
dependence merely in a negative, unconscious and sophistical
manner.[5]

On close inspection *theological criticism*—genuinely progres-
sive though it was at the inception of the movement[6]—is seen
in the final analysis to be nothing but the culmination and consequence of the old *philosophical*, and especially the *Hegelian*,
transcendentalism, twisted into a *theological caricature*. This
interesting example of historical justice, which now assigns to
theology, ever philosophy's spot of infection, the further role
of portraying in itself the negative dissolution of philosophy, i.e.,
the process of its decay—this historical nemesis I shall demonstrate
on another occasion.[7]

WAGES OF LABOR

Wages are determined through the antagonistic struggle between capitalist and worker. Victory goes necessarily to the capitalist. The capitalist can live longer without the worker than can the worker without the capitalist. Combination among the capitalists is customary and effective; workers' combination is prohibited and painful in its consequences for them.[1] Besides, the landowner and the capitalist can augment their revenues with the fruits of industry; the worker has neither ground rent nor interest on capital to supplement his industrial income. Hence the intensity of the competition among the workers. Thus only for the workers is the separation of capital, landed property, and labor an inevitable, essential and detrimental separation. Capital and landed property need not remain fixed in this abstraction, as must the labor of the workers.

The separation of capital, ground rent, and labor is thus fatal for the worker.

The lowest and the only necessary wage rate is that providing for the subsistence of the worker for the duration of his work and as much more as is necessary for him to support a family and for the race of laborers not to die out. The ordinary wage, according to Smith, is the lowest compatible with common humanity, that is, with cattle-like existence.[2]

The demand for men necessarily governs the production of men, as of every other commodity. Should supply greatly exceed demand, a section of the workers sinks into beggary or starvation. The worker's existence is thus brought under the same condition as the existence of every other commodity. The worker has become a commodity, and it is a bit of luck for him if he can find a buyer. And the demand on which the life of the worker depends, depends on the whim of the rich and the capitalists. Should the quantity in supply exceed the demand, then one of the constituent

65

parts of the price—profit, ground rent or wages—is paid below its *rate* [3]; a part of these factors is therefore withdrawn from this application, and thus the market price gravitates towards the natural price as the center point. But (1) where there is considerable division of labor it is most difficult for the worker to direct his labor into other channels; (2) because of his subordinate relation to the capitalist, he is the first to suffer.

Thus in the gravitation of market price to natural price it is the worker who loses most of all and necessarily. And it is just the capacity of the capitalist to direct his capital into another channel which either renders the worker, who is restricted to some particular branch of labor destitute, or forces him to submit to every demand of this capitalist.

The accidental and sudden fluctuations in market price hit ground rent less than they do that part of the price which is resolved into profit and wages; but they hit profit less than they do wages. In most cases, for every wage that rises, one remains *stationary* and one *falls*.

The worker need not necessarily gain when the capitalist does, but he necessarily loses when the latter loses. Thus, the worker does not gain if the capitalist keeps the market price above the natural price by virtue of some manufacturing or trading secret, or by virtue of monopoly or the favorable situation of his property.

Furthermore, *the prices of labor are much more constant than the prices of provisions.* Often they stand in inverse proportion. In a dear year wages fall on account of the decrease in demand, but rise on account of the increase in the prices of provisions—and thus balance. In any case, a number of workers are left without bread. In cheap years wages rise on account of the rise in demand, but decrease on account of the fall in the prices of provisions—and thus balance. [4]

Another respect in which the worker is at a disadvantage: *The labor prices of the various kinds of workers show much wider differences than the profits in the various branches in which capital is applied.* In labor all the natural, spiritual, and social variety of individual activity is manifested and is variously rewarded, whilst

dead capital always shows the same face and is indifferent to
real individual activity.

In general it has to be observed that in those cases where worker
and capitalist equally suffer, the worker suffers in his very existence, the capitalist in the profit on his dead mammon.

The worker has to struggle not only for his physical means of
subsistence; he has to struggle to get work, i.e., the possibility, the
means, to perform his activity. Let us take the three chief conditions in which society can find itself and consider the situation of
the worker in them: [5]

(1) If the wealth of society declines the worker suffers most of
all, and for the following reason: although the working class cannot gain so much as can the class of property owners in a prosperous state of society, *no one suffers so cruelly from its decline as the
working class.*[6]

(2) Let us take now a society in which wealth is increasing.
This condition is the only one favorable to the worker. Here competition between the capitalists sets in. The demand for workers
exceeds their supply. But:

In the first place, the raising of wages gives rise to *overwork*
among the workers. The more they wish to earn, the more must
they sacrifice their time and carry out slave labor, completely losing all their freedom in the service of greed. Thereby they shorten
their lives. This shortening of their life span is a favorable circumstance for the working class as a whole, for as a result of it an ever-
fresh supply of labor becomes necessary. This class has always to
sacrifice a part of itself in order not to be wholly destroyed.

Furthermore: When does a society find itself in a condition of
advancing wealth? When the capitals and the revenues of a
country are growing. But this is only possible:

(*a*) As the result of the accumulation of much labor, capital
being accumulated labor; as the result, therefore, of the fact that
more and more of his products are being taken away from the
worker, that to an increasing extent his own labor confronts him
as another man's property and that the means of his existence and
his activity are increasingly concentrated in the hands of the
capitalist.

(*b*) The accumulation of capital increases the division of labor, and the division of labor increases the number of the workers. Conversely, the number of workers increases the division of labor, just as the division of labor increases the accumulation of capital. With this division of labor on the one hand and the accumulation of capital on the other, the worker becomes ever more exclusively dependent on labor, and on a particular, very one-sided, machine-like labor at that. Just as he is thus depressed spiritually and physically to the condition of a machine and from being a man becomes an abstract activity and a belly, so he also becomes ever more dependent on every fluctuation in market price, on the application of capital, and on the whim of the rich. Equally, the increase in the class of people wholly dependent on work intensifies competition among the workers, thus lowering their price. In the factory system this situation of the worker reaches its climax.

(*c*) In an increasingly prosperous society only the richest of the rich can continue to live on money interest. Everyone else has to carry on a business with his capital, or venture it in trade. As a result, the competition between the different capitalists becomes more intense. The concentration of capital increases, the big capitalists ruin the small, and a section of the erstwhile capitalists sinks into the working class, which as a result of this supply again suffers to some extent a depression of wages and passes into a still greater dependence on the few big capitalists. The number of capitalists having been diminished, their competition with respect to the workers scarcely exists any longer; and the number of workers having been increased, their competition among themselves has become all the more intense, unnatural, and violent. Consequently, a section of the working class falls into beggary or starvation just as necessarily as a section of the middle capitalists falls into the working class.

Hence even in the condition of society most favorable to the worker, the inevitable result for the worker is overwork and premature death, decline to a mere machine, a bond servant of capital, which piles up dangerously over and against him, decline to more competition, and to starvation or beggary for a section of the workers.

The raising of wages excites in the worker the capitalist's mania to get rich, which he, however, can only satisfy by the sacrifice of his mind and body. The raising of wages presupposes and entails the accumulation of capital, and thus sets the product of labor against the worker as something ever more alien to him. Similarly, the division of labor renders him ever more one-sided and dependent, bringing with it the competition not only of men but also of machines. Since the worker has sunk to the level of a machine, he can be confronted by the machine as a competitor. Finally, as the amassing of capital increases the amount of industry and therefore the number of workers, it causes the same amount of industry to manufacture a *greater amount of product,* which leads to over-production and thus either ends by throwing a large section of workers out of work or by reducing their wages to the most miserable minimum. Such are the consequences of a state of society most favorable to the worker—namely, of a state of *growing, advancing wealth.*

Eventually, however, this state of growth must sooner or later reach its peak. What is the worker's position now?

(3) "In a country which has attained that full complement of riches . . . both the wages of labour and the profits of stock would probably be very low. . . . The competition for employment would necessarily be so great as to reduce the wages of labour to what was barely sufficient to keep up the number of labourers, and, the country being already fully peopled, that number could never be augmented."[7]

The surplus would have to die.

Thus in a declining state of society—increasing misery of the worker; in an advancing state—misery with complications; and in a fully developed state of society—static misery.

Since, however, according to Smith, a society is not happy, of which the greater part suffers[8]—yet even the wealthiest state of society leads to this suffering of the majority—and since the *economic system* [9] (and in general a society based on private interest) leads to this wealthiest condition, it follows that the goal of the economic system is the *unhappiness* of this system.

Concerning the relationship between worker and capitalist we should add that the capitalist is more than compensated for the raising of wages by the reduction in the amount of labor time, and that the raising of wages and the raising of interest on capital operate on the price of commodities like simple and compound interest respectively.

Let us put ourselves now wholly at the standpoint of the political economist, and follow him in comparing the theoretical and practical claims of the workers.

He tells us that originally and in theory the *whole produce* of labor [10] belongs to the worker. But at the same time he tells us that in actual fact what the worker gets is the smallest and utterly indispensable part of the product—as much, only, as is necessary for his existence, not as a man, but as a worker, and for the propagation, not of humanity but of the slave class of workers.

The political economist tells us that everything is bought with labor and that capital is nothing but accumulated labor; but at the same time he tells us that the worker, far from being able to buy everything, must sell himself and his human identity.

Whilst the rent of the lazy landowner usually amounts to a third of the product of the soil, and the profit of the busy capitalist to as much as twice the interest on money, the "something more" which the worker himself earns at the best of times amounts to so little that of four children of his, two must starve and die. Whilst according to the political economists it is solely through labor that man enhances the value of the products of nature, whilst labor is man's active possession, according to this same political economy the landowner and the capitalist, who *qua* landowner and capitalist are merely privileged and idle gods, are everywhere superior to the worker and lay down the law to him.

Whilst according to the political economists labor is the sole constant price of things, there is nothing more uncertain than the price of labor, nothing exposed to greater fluctuations.

Whilst the division of labor raises the productive power of labor and increases the wealth and refinement of society, it impoverishes the worker and reduces him to a machine. Whilst labor brings about the accumulation of capital and with this the increasing prosperity of society, it renders the worker ever more dependent on the capitalist, leads him into competition of a new intensity, and drives him into the headlong rush of over-production, with its subsequent corresponding slump.

Whilst the interest of the worker, according to the political economists, never stands opposed to the interest of society, society always and necessarily stands opposed to the interest of the worker.

According to the political economists, the interest of the worker is never opposed to that of society: (1) because the raising of wages is more than compensated by the reduction in the amount of labor time, together with the other consequences set forth above; and (2) because in relation to society the whole gross product is the net product, and only in relation to the private individual has the "net product" any significance.

But that labor itself, not merely in present conditions but in so far as its purpose in general is the mere increase of wealth—that labor itself, I say, is harmful and pernicious—follows from the political economist's line of argument, without his being aware of it.

In theory, ground rent and profit on capital are *deductions* suffered by wages. In actual fact, however, wages are a deduction which land and capital allow to go to the worker, a concession from the product of labor to the workers, to labor.

When society is in a state of decline, the worker suffers most severely. The specific severity of his burden he owes to his position as a worker, but the burden as such to the position of society.

But when society is in a state of progress, the ruin and impoverishment of the worker is the product of his labor and of the wealth produced by him. The misery results, therefore, from the *essence* of present-day labor itself.

Society in a state of maximum wealth—an ideal, but one which is more or less attained, and which at least is the aim of political economy as of civil society—means for the workers *static misery*.

It goes without saying that the *proletarian,* i.e., the man who, being without capital and rent, lives purely by labor, and by a one-sided, abstract labor, is considered by political economy only as a *worker*. Political economy can therefore advance the proposition that the proletarian, the same as any horse, must get as much as will enable him to work. It does not consider him when he is not working, as a human being; but leaves such consideration to criminal law, to doctors, to religion, to the statistical tables, to politics and to the poorhouse overseer.

Let us now rise above the level of political economy and try to answer two questions on the basis of the above exposition, which has been presented almost in the words of the political economists:

(1) What in the evolution of mankind is the meaning of this reduction of the greater part of mankind to abstract labor?

(2) What are the mistakes committed by the piecemeal reformers, who either want to *raise* wages and in this way to improve the situation of the working class, or regard *equality* of wages (as Proudhon does) the goal of social revolution? [11]

In political economy *labor* occurs only in the form of *wage-earning activity*.

"It can be asserted that those occupations which presuppose specific talents or longer training have become on the whole more lucrative; whilst the proportionate reward for mechanically monotonous activity in which one person can be trained as easily and quickly as another has fallen with growing competition, and was inevitably bound to fall. And it is just *this* sort of work which in the present state of the organization of labor is still by far the commonest. If therefore a worker in the first category now earns seven times as much as he did, say, fifty years ago, whilst the earnings of another in the second category have remained unchanged, then of course both are earning *on the average* four times as much. But if the first category comprises only a thousand workers in a particular country, and the second a million, then 999,000 are no better off than fifty years ago—and they are *worse off* if at the same time the prices of the necessaries of life have risen. With such superficial *calculations of averages* people try to deceive themselves about the most numerous class of the population. Moreover, the size of the *wage* is only one factor in the estimation of the *worker's income*, because it is essential for the measurement of the latter to take into account the assurance of its *permanence*—of which there is obviously no possibility in the anarchy of so-called free competition, with its ever-recurring fluctuations and periods of stagnation. Finally, the *hours of work* customary formerly and now have to be considered. And for the English cotton-workers these have been raised, as a result of the entrepreneurs' mania for profit, to between twelve and sixteen hours a day during the past twenty-five years or so—that is to say, precisely during the period of the introduction of labor-saving machines; and this rise in one country and in one branch of industry inevitably asserted itself elsewhere to a greater or lesser degree for the right of the unlimited exploitation of the poor by the rich is still universally recognized." (Wilhelm Schulz, *Movement of Production*, p. 65.) [12]

"But even if it were as true as it is false that the average income of *every* class of society has increased, the income-differences and *relative* income-distances may nevertheless have become greater and the contrasts between wealth and poverty accordingly stand out more sharply. For just *because* total production rises—and in the same measure as it rises—needs, desires and claims also multiply and thus *relative* poverty can increase whilst absolute poverty diminishes. The Samoyed living on fish oil and rancid fish is not poor for in his secluded society all have the same needs. But in a state *that is forging ahead*, which in the course of a decade, say, increased by a third its total production in proportion to the population, the worker who is getting as much at the end of ten years as at the beginning has not remained as well off, but has become poorer by a third." (*Ibid.*, pp. 65-66.)

But political economy knows the worker only as a working animal—as a beast reduced to the strictest bodily needs.

"To develop in greater spiritual freedom, a people must break their bondage to their bodily needs—they must cease to be the slaves of the body. They must, therefore, above all, have *time* at their disposal for spiritual creative activity and spiritual enjoyment. The developments in the labor-organism gain this time. Indeed with new motive forces and improved machinery, a single worker in the cotton factories now not infrequently performs the work formerly requiring a hundred, or even 250 to 350 workers. Similar results can be observed in all branches of production, because external natural forces are being compelled to participate to an even-greater degree in human labor. If the satisfaction of a given amount of material needs formerly required a certain expenditure of time and human effort which has later been reduced by half, then without any loss of material comfort the scope for spiritual activity and enjoyment has been simultaneously extended by as much. . . . But again the way in which the booty, that we win from old Kronos[13] himself in his most private domain, is shared out is still decided by the dice-throw of blind, unjust Chance. In France it has been calculated that at the present stage in the development of production an average working period of five hours a day by every person capable of work could suffice for the satisfaction of all the material interests of society. . . . Notwithstanding the time saved by the perfecting of machinery, the duration of the slave labor performed by a large population in the factories has only increased." (*Ibid.*, pp. 67, 68.)

"The transition from compound manual labor rests on a breakdown of the latter into its simple operations. At first, however, only *some* of the uniformly-recurring operations will devolve on machines, while some devolve on men. From the nature of things, and from confirmatory experience, it is clear that unendingly monotonous activity of this kind is as harmful to the mind as to the body; thus this *combination* of machinery with mere division of labor among a greater number of hands must inevitably show all the disadvantages of the latter. These disadvantages appear, among other things, in the greater mortality of factory workers. . . . Consideration has not been given . . . to this big distinction as to how far men work *through* machines or how far *as* machines." (*Ibid.*, p. 69.)

"In the future life of the peoples, however, the inanimate forces of nature working in machines will be our slaves and serfs." (*Ibid.*, p. 74.)

"The English spinning mills employ 196,818 females and only 158,818 men. For every 100 male workers in the cotton factories of Lancashire there are 103 female workers, and in Scotland as many as 209. In the English flax mills of Leeds, for every 100 male workers there were found to be 147 female workers. In Druden and on the East Coast of Scotland as many as 280. In the English silk mills . . . many female workers; male workers predominate in the wool mills where the work requires greater physical strength. In 1833, no fewer than 38,927 females were employed alongside 18,593 men in the North American cotton mills. As a result of the changes in the labor organism, a wider sphere of gainful employment has thus fallen to the share of the female sex. . . . Women now occupying an economically more independent position . . . the two sexes are drawn closer together in their social conditions." (*Ibid.*, pp. 71, 72.)

"Working in the English steam and water-driven spinning mills in 1835 were: 20,558 children between the ages of eight and twelve; 35,867 between the ages of twelve and thirteen; and, lastly, 108,208 children between the ages of thirteen and eighteen. . . . Admittedly, further advances in mechanization, by more and more removing all monotonous work from human hands, are operating in the direction of a gradual elimination of this social evil. But standing in the way of these more rapid advances is the very circumstance that the capitalists can, in the easiest and cheapest fashion, appropriate the energies of the lower classes down to the children, to be employed and *instead* of mechanical aids." (*Ibid.*, pp. 70-71.)

"Lord Brougham's call to the workers—'Become capitalists.' . . . The evil that millions are only able to earn a bare pittance for themselves by strenuous labor which is shattering the body and crippling them morally and intellectually; that they are even obliged to consider the misfortune of finding *such* work a piece of good fortune." (*Ibid.*, p. 60.)

"In order to live, then, the non-owners are obliged to place themselves, directly or indirectly, *at the service* of the owners—to put themselves, that is to say, into a position of dependence upon them." (Pecqueur, *Théorie nouvelle d'économie soc., etc.*, p. 409.) [14]

"Servants—pay; workers—wages; employees—salary or emoluments." (*Ibid.*, pp. 409, 410.)

"To hire out one's labor"; "To lend one's labor at interest"; "To work in another's place."

"To hire out the materials of labor"; "To lend the materials of labor at interest." "To make others work in one's place." (*Ibid.*, p. 411.)

"Such an economic order condemns men to occupations so mean, to a degradation so devastating and bitter, that by comparison savagery seems like a kingly condition." (*Ibid.*, pp. 417, 418.) "Prostitution of the non-owing class in all its forms." (*Ibid.*, p. 421 *f.*) "Ragmen."

Charles Loudon, in the book *Solution du problème de la population, etc.*, Paris, 1842,[15] declares the number of prostitutes in England to be between sixty and seventy thousand. The number of women of doubtful virtue is said to be equally large (p. 228).

"The average life of these unfortunate creatures on the streets, after they have embarked on their career of vice, is about six or seven years. To maintain the number of sixty to seventy thousand prostitutes, there must be in the three kingdoms at least eight to nine thousand women who commit themselves to this degrading profession each year, or about twenty-four new victims each day—in average of *one* per hour; and it follows that if the same proportion holds good over the whole surface of the globe, there must constantly be in existence one and a half million unfortunate women of this kind." (*Ibid.*, p. 229.)

"The population of the poverty-stricken grows with their poverty, and at the extreme limit of destitution human beings are crowded together in the greatest numbers contending with each other for the right to suffer. . . . In 1821 the population of Ireland was 6,801,827. In 1831 it had risen to 7,764,010—an increase of 14 per cent in ten years. In Leinster, the wealthiest province, the population increased by only 8 per cent; whilst in Connaught, the most poverty-stricken province, the increase reached 21 per cent. (*Extract from the Enquiries Published in England on Ireland*, Vienna, 1840.)" (Buret, *De la misère, etc.*, t. 1, pp. 36, 37.) [16]

Political economy considers labor in the abstract as a thing; "labor is a commodity." If the price is high, then the commodity is in great demand; if the price is low, then the commodity is in great supply.

"the price of labor as a commodity must fall lower and lower." This is made inevitable partly by the competition between capitalist and worker, and partly by the competition amongst the workers. "The working population, the seller of labor, is necessarily reduced to accepting the most meager part of the product. . . . Is the theory of labor as a commodity anything other than a theory of disguised bondage?" (*Ibid.*, p. 43.) "Why then has nothing but an exchange value been seen in labor?" (*Ibid.*, p. 44.) The large workshops prefer to buy the labor of women and children, because this costs less than that of men. (*Ibid.*) "The worker is not at all in the position of a *free seller vis-à-vis* the one who employs him. . . . The capitalist is always free to use labor, and the worker is always forced to sell it. The value of labor is completely destroyed if it is not sold every instant. Labor can neither be accumulated nor even be saved, unlike true commodities. Labor is life, and if life is not each day exchanged for food, it suffers and soon perishes. To claim that human life is a commodity, one must, therefore, admit slavery." (*Ibid.*, pp. 49, 50.) If, then, labor is a commodity, it is a commodity with the most unfortunate attributes. But even by the principles of political economy it is no commodity, for it is not the *free result of a free transaction.* The present economic regime simultaneously lowers the price and the remuneration of labor; it perfects the worker and degrades the man. (*Ibid.*, pp. 52-53.) "Industry has become a war, and commerce a gamble." (*Ibid.*, p. 62.)

The cotton-working machines (in England) alone represent 84,000,000 manual workers. (*Ibid.*, p. 193.)

Up to the present, industry has been in a state of war—a war of conquest: "It has squandered the lives of the men who made up its army with the same indifference as the great conquerors. Its aim was the possession of wealth, not the happiness of men." (Buret, *loc. cit.,* p. 20.) "These interests (that is, economic interests), freely left to themselves . . . must necessarily come into conflict; they have no other arbiter but war, and the decisions of war assign defeat and death to some, in order to give victory to the others. . . . It is in the conflict of opposed forces that science seeks order and equilibrium: *perpetual war,* according to it, is the sole means of obtaining peace; that war is called competition." (*Ibid.*, p. 23.)

"The industrial war, to be conducted with success, demands large armies which it can amass on one spot and profusely decimate. And it is neither from devotion nor from duty that the soldiers of this army bear the exertions imposed on them, but only to escape the hard necessity of hunger. They feel neither attachment nor gratitude towards their bosses, nor are these bound to their subordinates by any feeling of benevolence. They do not know them as men, but only as instruments of production which have to yield as much as possible with as little cost as possible. These populations of workers, ever more crowded together, have not even the assurance of always being employed. Industry, which has called them together, only lets them live while it needs them, and as soon as it can get rid of them it abandons them without the slightest scruple; and the workers are compelled to offer their persons and their powers for whatever price they can get. The longer, more painful and more disgusting the work they are given, the less they are paid. There are those who, with sixteen hours' work a day and unremitting exertion, scarcely buy the right not to die." (*Ibid.*, pp. 68-69.)

"We are convinced . . . as are the commissioners charged with the enquiry into the condition of the hand-loom weavers, that the large industrial towns would in a short time lose their population of workers if they were not all the time receiving from the neighboring rural areas constant recruitments of healthy men, a constant flow of fresh blood." (*Ibid.*, p. 362.)

PROFIT OF CAPITAL

1. CAPITAL

(1) What is the basis of *capital*, that is, of private property in the products of other men's labor?

"For if capital itself does not merely amount to theft or fraud, it requires still the cooperation of legislation to sanctify inheritance." (Say, t. I, p. 136, footnote.) [1]

How does one become a proprietor of productive stock? How does one become owner of the products created by means of this stock?

By virtue of *positive law.* (Say, t. II, p. 4.)

What does one acquire with capital, with the inheritance of a large fortune, for instance?

"The person who either acquires, or succeeds to a great fortune, does not necessarily acquire or succeed to any political power. . . . The power which that possession immediately and directly conveys to him, is the *power of purchasing;* a certain command over all the labour, or over all the produce of labour, which is then in the market." (*The Wealth of Nations,* by Adam Smith, Vol. 1, pp. 26-27.)

Capital is thus the *governing power* over labor and its products. The capitalist possesses this power, not on account of his personal or human qualities, but inasmuch as he is an *owner* of capital. His power is the *purchasing* power of his capital, which nothing can withstand.

Later we shall see first how the capitalist, by means of capital, exercises his governing power over labor, then, however, we shall see the governing power of capital over the capitalist himself.

What is capital?

"A certain quantity of *labour stocked* and stored up to be employed." (*Ibid.,* Vol. I, p. 295.)

Capital is *stored-up labor.*

(2) *Fonds,* or stock, is any accumulation of products of the soil

or of manufacture. Stock is called *capital* only when it yields to its owner a revenue or profit *(Ibid.*, Vol. I, p. 243.)

2. THE PROFIT OF CAPITAL

The *profit or gain of capital* is altogether different from the *wages of labour.* This difference is manifested in two ways: in the first place, the profits of capital are regulated altogether by the value of the capital employed, although the labour of inspection and direction associated with different capitals may be the same. Moreover in large works the whole of this labour is committed to some principal clerk, whose salary bears no regular proportion to the capital of which he oversees the management. And although the labour of the proprietor is here reduced almost to nothing, he still demands profits in proportion to his capital. *(Ibid.*, Vol. I, p. 43.) [2]

Why does the capitalist demand this proportion between profit and capital?

He would have no *interest* in employing the workers, unless he expected from the sale of their work something more than to replace the stock advanced by him as wages and he would have no *interest* to employ a great stock rather than a small one, unless his profits were to bear some proportion to the extent of his stock. *(Ibid.*, p. 42.)

The capitalist thus makes a profit, first, on the wages, and secondly on the raw materials advanced by him.

What proportion, then, does profit bear to capital?

If it is already difficult to determine the usual average level of wages at a particular place and at a particular time, it is even more difficult to determine the profit on capitals. A change in the price of the commodities in which the capitalist deals, the good or bad fortune of his rivals and customers, a thousand other accidents to which commodities are exposed both in transit and in the warehouses—all produce a daily, almost hourly variation in profit. *(Ibid.*, pp. 78-79.)

But though it is impossible to determine with precision what are the profits on capitals, some notion may be formed of them from the *interest of money.* Wherever a great deal can be made by the use of money, a great deal will be given for the use of it; wherever little can be made by it, little will be given. *(Ibid.*, p. 79.)

The proportion which the usual market-rate of interest ought to bear to the rate of clear profit, necessarily varies as profit rises or falls. Double interest is in Great Britain reckoned what the merchants call

un profit honnête, modéré, raisonnable,[3] terms which mean no more
than a *common and usual profit.* (*Ibid.,* p. 87.)

What is the *lowest* rate of profit? And what the *highest*?

The *lowest rate* of ordinary profit on capital must always be *something more* than what is sufficient to compensate the occasional losses
to which every employment of stock is exposed. It is this surplus only
which is neat or clear profit. The same holds for the lowest rate of
interest. (*Ibid.,* p. 86.)

The *highest rate* to which ordinary profits can rise is that which in
the price of the greater part of commodities *eats up the whole of the
rent of the land,* and reduces the wages of labour contained in the
commodity supplied to the *lowest rate,* the bare subsistence of the
labourer during his work. The worker must always be fed in some way
or other while he is required to work; ground-rent can disappear entirely. For example: the servants of the East India Company in Bengal.
(*Ibid.,* pp. 86-87.)

Besides all the advantages of limited competition which the
capitalist may *exploit* in this case, he can keep the market price
above the natural price by quite decorous means.

For one thing, by keeping *secrets in trade* if the market is at a great
distance from those who supply it, that is, by concealing a price change,
its rise above the natural level. This concealment has the effect that
other capitalists do not follow him in investing their capital in this
branch of industry or trade.

Then again by keeping *secrets in manufacture,* which enable the
capitalist to reduce the costs of production and supply his commodity
at the same or even at lower prices than his competitors while obtaining a higher profit. (Deceiving by keeping secrets is not immoral?
Dealings on the stock exchange.) *Furthermore,* where production is
restricted to a particular locality (as in the case of a rare wine), and
where the *effective demand* can never be satisfied. *Finally,* through
monopolies exercised by individuals or companies. Monopoly-price is
the highest possible. (*Ibid.,* pp. 53-54.)

Other fortuitous causes which can raise the profit on capital: the
acquisition of new territories, or of new branches of trade, often increases the profit on capital even in a wealthy country, because they
withdraw some capital from the old branches of trade, reduce competition, and cause the market to be supplied with fewer commodities,
the prices of which then rise: those who deal in these commodities can
then afford to borrow at a higher rate of interest. (*Ibid.,* p. 83.)

The more a commodity comes to be manufactured—the more it becomes an object of manufacture—the greater becomes that part of the price which resolves itself into wages and profit in proportion to that which resolves itself into rent. In the progress of the manufacture of a commodity, not only the number of profits increases, but every subsequent profit is greater than the foregoing; because the capital from which it is derived must always be greater. The capital which employs the weavers, for example, must always be greater than that which employs the spinners; because it not only replaces that capital with its profits, but pays, besides, the wages of weavers; and the profits must always bear some proportion to the capital. (*Ibid.*, p. 45.)

Thus the advance made by human labor in converting the product of nature into the manufactured product of nature increases, not the wages of labor, but in part the number of profitable capital investments, and in part the size of every subsequent capital in comparison with the foregoing.

With regard to the advantage which the capitalist derives from the division of labor, more later.

He profits doubly—first, by the division of labor; and secondly, in general, by the advance which human labor makes on the natural product. The greater the human share in a commodity, the greater the profit of dead capital.

In one and the same society the average rate of capital profits is much more nearly on the same level than the wages of the different sorts of labour. (*Ibid.*, p. 100.) In the different employments of capital, the ordinary rate of profit varies with the certainty or uncertainty of the returns. "The ordinary profit of stock, though it rises with the risk, does not always seem to rise in proportion to it." (*Ibid.*, pp. 99-100.)

It goes without saying that profits also rise if the means of circulation become less expensive or easier available (e.g., paper money).

3. The Rule of Capital over Labor
and the Motives of the Capitalist

The consideration of his own private profit is the sole motive which determines the owner of any capital to employ it either in agriculture, in manufactures, or in some particular branch of the wholesale or retail trade. The different quantities of *productive labour* which it may put into motion, and the different values which it may add to the annual produce of the land and labour of his country, according as it is employed in one or other of those different ways, never enter into his thoughts. (*Ibid.*, p. 335.)

The most useful employment of capital for the capitalist is that which, risks being equal, yields him the greatest profit. This employment is not always the most useful for society; the most useful employment is that which draws benefit from the productive powers of nature. (Say, t. II, pp. 130-31.)

The plans and speculations of the employers of capitals regulate and direct all the most important operations of labour, and *profit* is the end proposed by all those plans and projects. But the rate of profit does not, like rent and wages, rise with the prosperity and fall with the declension of the society. On the contrary, it is naturally low in rich and high in poor countries, and it is always highest in the countries which are going fastest to ruin. The interest of this class, therefore, has not the same connection with the general interest of the society as that of the other two.[4] The particular interest of the dealers in any particular branch of trade or manufactures is always in some respects different from, and frequently even in sharp opposition to, that of the public. To widen the market and to narrow the sellers' competition is always the interest of the dealer. This is a class of people whose interest is never exactly the same as that of society, a class of people who have generally an interest to deceive and to oppress the public. (Smith, Vol. I, pp. 231-32.)

4. THE ACCUMULATION OF CAPITALS AND THE COMPETITION AMONGST THE CAPITALISTS

The *increase of stock*, which raises wages, tends to lower the capitalists' profit, because of the *competition* amongst the capitalists. (*Ibid.*, p. 78.)

"If, for example, the capital which is necessary for the grocery trade of a particular town is divided between two different grocers, their competition will tend to make that each of them sells cheaper than if it were in the hands of one only; and if it were divided among twenty, their competition would be just so much the greater, and the chance of their combining together, in order to raise the price, just so much less." (*Ibid.*, p. 322.)

Since we already know that monopoly prices are as high as possible, since the interest of the capitalists, even from the point of view commonly held by political economists, stands in hostile opposition to society, and since a rise of profit operates like compound interest on the price of the commodity (*Ibid.*, pp. 87-88) ,[5] it follows that the sole defense against the capitalists is *competition*, which according to the evidence of political economy acts beneficently by both raising wages and lowering the prices of commodities to the advantage of the consuming public.

But competition is only possible if capital multiplies, and is held in many hands. The formation of many capital investments is only possible as a result of multilateral accumulation, since capital comes into being only by accumulation; and multilateral accumulation necessarily turns into unilateral accumulation. Competition among capitalists increases the accumulation of capital.

Accumulation, where private property prevails, is the *concentration* of capital in the hands of a few, it is in general an inevitable consequence if capital is left to follow its natural course, and it is precisely through competition that the way is cleared for this natural destination of capital.

We have been told that the profit on capital is in proportion to the size of the capital. A large capital therefore accumulates more quickly than a small capital in proportion to its size, even if we disregard for the time being deliberate competition.

Accordingly, the accumulation of large capital proceeds much more rapidly than that of smaller capital, quite irrespective of competition. But let us follow this process further.

With the increase of capital the profits on capital diminishes, because of competition. The first to suffer, therefore, is the small capitalist.

The increase of capital and a large number of capital investments presupposes, further, a condition of advancing wealth in the country.

"In a country which has acquired its full complement of riches, the ordinary rate of clear profit is so small, that usual rate of interest which could be afforded out of it is so low as to render it impossible for any but the very wealthiest people to live upon the interest of their money. All people of middling fortunes must be obliged to superintend themselves the employment of their own stocks." (*Ibid.*, p. 86.)

This is the situation most dear to the heart of political economy.

"The proportion between capital and revenue, therefore, seems everywhere to regulate the proportion between industry and idleness; wherever capital predominates, industry prevails; wherever revenue, idleness." (*Ibid.*, p. 301.)

What about the employment of capital, then, in this condition of increased competition?

"As stock increases, the quantity of stock to be lent at interest grows gradually greater and greater. As the quantity of stock to be lent at interest increases, the interest . . . diminishes. . . ." (i) because the market-price of things commonly diminishes as their quantity increases. . . . and (ii) because with the *increase of capitals in any country*, "*it becomes gradually more and more difficult* to find within the country a profitable method of employing any new capital. There arises in consequence a competition between different capitals, the owner of one endeavouring to get possession of that employment which is occupied by another. But upon most occasions he can hope to jostle that other out of this employment by no other means but by dealing upon more reasonable terms. He must not only sell what he deals in somewhat cheaper, but in order to get it to sell, he must sometimes, too, buy it dearer. The demand for productive labour, by the increase of the funds which are destined for maintaining it, grows every day greater and greater. Labourers easily find employment, but the owners of capitals find it difficult to get labourers to employ. Their competition raises the wages of labour and sinks the profits of stock." (*Ibid.*, p. 316.)

Thus the small capitalist has the choice: (1) either to consume his capital, since he can no longer live on the interest—and thus cease to be a capitalist; or (2) to set up a business himself, sell his commodity cheaper, buy dearer than the wealthier capitalist, and pay increased wages—thus ruining himself, the market price being already very low as a result of the intense competition presupposed. If, however, the big capitalist wants to squeeze out the smaller capitalist, he has all the advantages over him which the capitalist has as a capitalist over the worker. The larger size of his capital compensates him for the smaller profits, and he can even bear temporary losses until the smaller capitalist is ruined and he finds himself freed from this competition. In this way, he accumulates the small capitalist's profits.

Furthermore, the big capitalist always buys cheaper than the small one, because he buys bigger quantities. He can therefore well afford to sell cheaper.

But if a fall in the rate of interest turns the midde capitalists from rentiers into business men, the increase in business capital and the resulting smaller profit produce conversely a fall in the rate of interest.

"When the profits which can be made by the use of a capital are . . . diminished, . . . the price which can be paid for the use of it, . . . must necessarily be diminished with them." (*Ibid.*, p. 316.)

"As riches, improvement, and population have increased, interest has declined," and consequently the profit of capitals, "after these are diminished, stock may not only continue to increase, but to increase much faster than before. . . . A great stock though with small profits, generally increases faster than a small stock with great profits. Money, says the proverb, makes money." (*Ibid.*, p. 83.)

When, therefore, this large capital is opposed by small capitalists with small profits, as it is under the presupposed condition of intense competition, it crushes them completely. The necessary result of this competition is a general deterioration of commodities, adulteration, fake production and universal poisoning, evident in large towns.

An important circumstance in the competition of large and small capital is, furthermore, the relationship between *fixed capital* and *circulating capital*.[6]

"*Circulating capital* is a capital which is employed in manufacturing or purchasing goods, and selling them again. The capital employed in this manner yields no revenue or profit to its employer while it either remains in his possession or continues in the same shape. It is continually going from him in one particular shape in order to return to him in another, and it is only by means of such circulation, or such successive exchanges and transformations that it yields any profit. *Fixed capital* consists of capital invested in the improvement of land, the purchase of useful machines, instruments of trade, and such-like things." (*Ibid.*, pp. 243-44. [In quoting, Marx has abbreviated this passage.])

"Every saving in the expense of supporting the fixed capital is an improvement of the net revenue of the society. The whole capital of the undertaker of every work is necessarily divided between his fixed and his circulating capital. While his whole capital remains the same, the smaller the one part, the greater must necessarily be the other. It is the circulating capital which furnishes the materials and wages of labour, and puts industry into motion. Every saving, therefore, in the expense of maintaining the fixed capital, which does not diminish the productive powers of labour, must increase the fund which puts industry into motion." (*Ibid.*, p. 257.)

It is clear from the outset that the relationship of fixed capital and circulating capital is much more favorable to the big capitalist than to the smaller capitalist. The extra fixed capital required by a very big banker as against a very small one is insignificant. Their fixed capital amounts to nothing more than the office. The equipment of the bigger landowner does not increase in proportion to the size of his estate. Similarly, the credit which a big capitalist enjoys compared with a smaller one means for him all the greater saving in fixed capital—that is, in the amount of ready money he must always have at hand. Finally, it is obvious that where industrial labor has reached a high level, and where therefore almost all manual labor has become factory labor, the entire capital of a small capitalist does not suffice to provide him even with the necessary fixed capital.*

It is generally true that the accumulation of large capital is also accompanied by a proportional concentration and simplification of fixed capital, as compared to the smaller capitalists. The big capitalist introduces for himself some kind of organization of the instruments of labor.

"Similarly, in the sphere of industry every manufactory and mill is already a more comprehensive combination of a larger material fortune with numerous and varied intellectual capacities and technical skills serving the *common* purpose of production. . . . Where legislation preserves landed property in large units, the surplus of a growing population flocks into trades, and it is therefore as in Great Britain in the field of industry, principally, that proletarians aggregate in great numbers. Where, however, the law permits the continuous division of the land, the number of small, debt-encumbered proprietors increases, as in France; and the continuing process of fragmentation throws them into the class of the needy and the discontented. When eventually this

* Marx has made here the following note in French: "As is well known, large-scale cultivation usually provides employment only for a small number of hands."

fragmentation and indebtedness reaches a higher degree still, big landed property once more swallows up small property, just as large-scale industry destroys small industry. And as larger estates are formed again, large numbers of propertyless workers not required for the cultivation of the soil are again driven into industry." (Schulz, *Bewegung der Produktion*, pp. 58, 59.)

"Commodities of the same kind change in character as a result of changes in the method of production, and especially as a result of the use of machinery. Only by the exclusion of human power has it become possible to spin from a pound of cotton worth 3 shillings and 8 pence 350 hanks of a total length of 167 English miles (i.e., 36 German miles), and of a commercial value of 25 guineas." (*Ibid.*, p. 62.)

"On the average the prices of cotton cloth have decreased in England during the past 45 years by eleven-twelfths, and according to Marshall's calculations the same amount of manufactured goods for which 16 shillings was still paid in 1814 is now supplied at 1 shilling and 10 pence. The greater cheapness of industrial products expands both consumption at home and the market abroad, and because of this the number of workers in cotton has not only not fallen in Great Britain after the introduction of machines but has risen from forty thousand to one and a half million. As to the earnings of industrial entrepreneurs and workers: the growing competition between the factory owners has resulted in their profits necessarily falling relative to the amount of products supplied by them. In the years 1820-33 the Manchester manufacturer's gross profit on a piece of calico fell from four shillings 1⅓ pence to one shilling 9 pence. But to make up for this loss, the volume of manufacture has been correspondingly increased. The consequence of this is . . . that separate branches of industry experience over-production to some extent; that frequent bankruptcies occur causing property to fluctuate and vacillate unstably *within* the class of capitalists and masters of labor, thus throwing into the proletariat some of those who have been ruined economically; and that, frequently and suddenly, close-downs or cuts in employment become necessary, the painful effects of which are always bitterly felt by the class of wage laborers." (*Ibid.*, p. 63.)

"To hire out one's labor is to begin one's enslavement. To hire out the materials of labor is to establish one's freedom. . . . Labor is man; but the materials of labor, on the other hand, contain nothing human." (Pecqueur, *Théorie sociale*, etc., pp. 411-12.)

"The element of *matter*, which is quite incapable of creating wealth without the other element, *labor*, acquires the magical virtue of being fertile for them [who own this matter] as if by their own action they had placed there this indispensable element." (*Ibid.*)

"Supposing that the daily labor of a worker brings him on the average 400 francs a year and that this sum suffices for every adult to live some sort of crude life, then any proprietor receiving 2,000 francs in interest or rent, from a farm, a house, etc., compels indirectly five men to work for him; an income of 100,000 francs represents the labor of 250 men, and that of 1,000,000 francs the labor of 2,500 individuals (hence 300 million [Louis Philippe] therefore the labor of 750,000 workers)." (*Ibid.*, pp. 412-13.)

"The human law has given owners the right to use and to abuse—that is to say, the right to do what they will with the materials of labor. . . . They are in no way obliged by law to provide work for the propertyless when required and at all times, or to pay them always an adequate wage, etc." (*Ibid.*, p. 413.) "Complete freedom concerning the nature, the quantity, the quality and the opportunity of production; concerning the use and the disposal of wealth; and full command over the materials of all labor. Everyone is free to exchange what belongs to him as he thinks fit, without considering anything other than his own interest as an individual." (*Ibid.*, p. 413.)

"Competition is merely the expression of the freedom to exchange, which itself is the immediate and logical consequence of the individual's right to use and abuse all the instruments of production. The right to use and abuse, freedom of exchange, and arbitrary competition—these three economic moments, which form one unit, entail the following consequences; each produces what he wishes, as he wishes, when he wishes, where he wishes, produces well or produces badly, produces too much or not enough, too soon or too late, at too high a price or too low a price; none knows whether he will sell, how he will sell, when he will sell, where he will sell, to whom he will sell. And it is the same with regard to purchases. The producer is ignorant of needs and resources, of demand and supply. He sells when he wishes, when he can, where he wishes, to whom he wishes, at the price he wishes. And he buys in the same way. In all this he is ever the plaything of chance, the slave of the law of the strongest, of the least harassed, of the richest. . . . Whilst at one place there is scarcity, at another there is glut and waste. Whilst one producer sells a lot or at a very high price, and at an enormous profit, the other sells nothing or sells at a loss. . . . The supply does not know the demand, and the demand does not know the supply. You produce, trusting to a taste, a fashion, which prevails amongst the consuming public. But by the time you are ready to deliver the commodity, the whim has already passed and has settled on some other kind of product. . . . The inevitable consequences: bankruptcies occurring permanently and universally; miscalculations, sudden ruin and unexpected fortunes, commercial crises, unemployment, periodic gluts or shortages; instability and depreciation of wages and profits, the loss or enormous waste of wealth, time and effort in the arena of fierce competition." (*Ibid.*, pp. 414-16.)

Ricardo in his book (Rent of Land): Nations are merely production-shops; man is a machine for consuming and producing; human life is a kind of capital; economic laws blindly rule the world. For Ricardo men are nothing, the product everything. In the 26th chapter of the French translation it says: "To an individual with a capital of £20,000 whose profits were £2,000 per annum, it would be a matter quite indifferent whether his capital would employ a hundred or a thousand men. . . . Is not the real interest of the nation similar? Provided its net real income, its rent and profits be the same, it is of no importance whether the nation consists of ten or of twelve millions of inhabitants." "In fact, says M. Sismondi (t. II, p. 331), nothing remains to be desired but that the King, living quite alone on the island, should by continuously turning a crank cause automatons to do all the work of England."[7]

"The master who buys the worker's labor at such a low price that it scarcely suffices for the worker's most pressing needs is responsible neither for the inadequacy of the wage nor for the excessive duration of the labor: he himself has to submit to the law which he imposes. . . . Poverty is not so much caused by men as by the power of things." (Buret, *loc. cit.* p. 82.)

"The inhabitants of many different parts of Great Britain have not capital sufficient to improve and cultivate all their lands. The wool of the southern counties of Scotland is, a great part of it, after a long land carriage through very bad roads, manufactured in Yorkshire, for want of capital to manufacture it at home. There are many little manufacturing towns in Great Britain, of which the inhabitants have not capital sufficient to transport the produce of their own industry to those distant markets where there is demand and consumption for it. If there are any merchants among them, they are properly only the agents of wealthier merchants who reside in some of the greater commercial cities." (Smith, *loc. cit.*, Vol. 1, pp. 326-27.)

"The annual produce of the land and labour of any nation can be increased in its value by no other means but by increasing either the *number of its productive labourers* or *the productive powers of those labourers* who had before been employed. . . . In either case an additional capital is almost always required." (*Ibid.*, pp. 306-07.)

"As the *accumulation* of stock must, in the nature of things, be previous to the division of labour, so labour can be more and more subdivided in proportion only as stock is previously more and more accumulated. The quantity of materials which the same number of people can work up, increases in a great proportion as labour comes to be more and more subdivided; and as the operations of each work-

man are gradually reduced to a greater degree of simplicity, a variety
of new machines come to be invented for facilitating and abridging
those operations. As the division of labour advances, therefore, in order
to give constant employment to an equal number of workmen, an
equal stock of provisions, and a greater stock of materials and tools
than what would have been necessary in a ruder state of things, must
be accumulated beforehand. But the number of workmen in every
branch of business generally increases with the division of labour in
that branch, or rather it is the increase of their number which enables
them to class and subdivide themselves in this manner." (*Ibid.*, pp.
241-42.)

"As the accumulation of stock is previously necessary for carrying
on this great improvement in the productive powers of labour, so that
accumulation naturally leads to this improvement. The person who
employs his stock in maintaining labour, necessarily wishes to employ
it in such a manner as to produce as great a quantity of work as
possible. He endeavours, therefore, both to make among his workmen
the most proper distribution of employment, and to furnish them with
the best machines which he can either invent or afford to purchase.
His abilities in both these respects are generally in proportion to the
extent of his stock, or to the number of people whom it can employ.
The quantity of industry, therefore, not only increases in every
country with the *increase of the stock* which employs it, but, in consequence of that increase, the same quantity of industry produces a much
greater quantity of work." (*Ibid.*, p. 242.) Hence *over-production*.

"More comprehensive combinations of productive forces . . . in industry and trade by uniting more numerous and more diverse, human
and natural powers in larger-scale enterprises. Already here and there,
closer association of the chief branches of production. Thus, big
manufacturers will try to acquire also large estates in order to become
independent of others for at least a part of the raw materials required
for their industry; or they will go into trade in conjunction with their
industrial enterprises, not only to sell their own manufactures, but
also to purchase other kinds of products and to sell these to their
workers. In England, where a single factory owner sometimes employs
ten to twelve thousand workers . . . it is already not uncommon to
find such combinations of various branches of production controlled
by *one* brain, such smaller states or provinces within the state. Thus,
the mine owners in the *Birmingham* area have recently taken over the
whole process of iron production, which was previously distributed
among various entrepreneurs and owners. (See '*Der bergmännische
Distrikt bei Birmingham*,' *Deutsche Viertel-jahrsschrift*, No. 3, 1838.)
Finally in the large joint-stock enterprises which have become so numerous, we see far-reaching combinations of the financial resources of

many participants with the scientific and technical knowledge and skills of others to whom the carrying out of the work is handed over. The capitalists are thereby enabled to apply their savings in more diverse ways and perhaps even to employ them simultaneously in agriculture, industry and commerce. As a consequence their interest becomes more comprehensive, and the contradictions between agricultural, industrial, and commercial interests are reduced and disappear. But this increased possibility of applying capital profitably in the most diverse ways cannot but intensify the antagonism between the propertied and the non-propertied classes." (Schulz, *loc. cit.*, pp. 40-41.)

The enormous profit which the landlords of houses make out of poverty. House rent stands in inverse proportion to industrial poverty.[8]

So does the interest obtained from the vices of the ruined proletarians. (Prostitution, drunkenness; the pawn broker.) The accumulation of capital increases and the competition between capitalists decreases, when capital and landed property are united in the same hand, also when capital is enabled by its size to combine different branches of production.

Indifference towards men. Smith's twenty lottery-tickets.[9]

Say's net and gross revenue.

RENT OF LAND

Landlords' right has its origin in robbery. (Say, t. I, p. 136, footnote.) The landlords, like all other men, love to reap where they never sowed, and demand a rent even for the natural produce of the earth. (Smith, *loc. cit.*, I, p. 44.)

"The rent of land, it may be thought, is frequently no more than a reasonable profit or interest for the stock laid out by the landlord upon its improvement. This, no doubt, may be partly the case upon some occasions; . . . The landlord demands (1) a rent even for un-improved land, and the supposed interest or profit upon the expense of improvement is generally an addition to this original rent. (2) Those improvements, besides, are not always made by the stock of the landlord, but sometimes by that of the tenant. When the lease comes to be renewed, however, the landlord commonly demands the same augmentation of rent as if they had been all made by his own. (3) He sometimes demands rent for what is altogether incapable of human improvement." (*Ibid.*, p. 131.)

Smith cites as an instance of the last case kelp, a species of seaweed which, when burnt, yields an alkaline salt, useful for making glass, soap, etc. It grows in several parts of Great Britain, particularly in Scotland, upon such rocks only as lie within the high water mark, which are twice every day covered with the sea, and of which the produce, therefore, was never augmented by human industry. The landlord, however, whose estate is bounded by a kelp shore of this kind, demands a rent for it as much as for his corn fields. The sea in the neighborhood of the Islands of Shetland is more than commonly abundant in fish, which makes a great part of the subsistence of their inhabitants. But in order to profit by the produce of the water they must have a habitation upon the neighboring land. The rent of the landlord is in proportion, not to what the farmer can make by the land, but to what he can make both by the land and by the water. (*Ibid.*, p. 131.)

"This rent may be considered as the produce of those *powers of nature*, the use of which the landlord lends to the farmer. It is greater or smaller according to the supposed extent of those powers, or in other words, according to the supposed natural or improved fertility of the land. It is the work of nature which remains after deducting or compensating everything which can be regarded as the work of man." (*Ibid.*, pp. 324-25.)

"*The rent of land*, therefore, considered as the price paid for the use of the land, is naturally a *monopoly price*. It is not at all proportioned to what the landlord may have laid out upon the improvement of the land, or to what he can afford to take; but to what the farmer can afford to give." (*Ibid.*, p. 131.)

Of the three original classes, that of the landlords is the one "whose revenue costs them neither labour nor care, but comes to them, as it were, of its own accord, and independent of any plan or project of their own." (*Ibid.*, p. 230.)

We have already learnt that the size of the rent depends on the degree of *fertility* of the land.

Another factor in its determination is *situation*.

"The rent of land not only varies with its *fertility*, whatever be its produce, but with its *situation*, whatever be its fertility." (*Ibid.*, p. 133.)

"The produce of land, mines and fisheries, when their natural fertility is equal, is in proportion to the extent and proper application of the capitals employed about them. When the capitals are equal and equally well applied, it is in proportion to their natural fertility." (*Ibid.*, p. 249.)

These propositions of Smith are important, because, given equal costs of production and capital of equal size, they reduce the rent of land to the greater or lesser fertility of the soil. Thereby showing clearly the perversion of concepts in political economy, which turns the fertility of the land into an attribute of the landlord.

Now, however, let us consider the rent of land as it is formed in real life.

The rent of land is established as a result of the *struggle between tenant and landlord*. We find that the hostile antagonism of interests, the struggle, the war is recognized throughout political economy as the basis of social organization.

Let us see now what the relations are between landlord and tenant.

"In adjusting the terms of the lease, the landlord endeavours to leave him no greater share of the produce than what is sufficient to keep up the stock from which he furnishes the seed, pays the labour, and purchases and maintains the cattle and other instruments of husbandry, together with the ordinary profits of farming stock in the neighbourhood. This is evidently the smallest share with which the tenant can content himself without being a loser, and the landlord seldom means to leave him any more. Whatever part of the produce, or, what is the same thing, whatever part of its price is over and above this share, he naturally endeavours to reserve to himself as the rent of his land, which is evidently the highest the tenant can afford to pay in the actual circumstances of the land. . . . This portion, however, may still be considered as the natural rent of land, or the rent for which it is naturally meant that land should for the most part be let." (*Ibid.*, pp. 130-31.)

"The landlords," says Say, "operate a certain kind of monopoly against the tenants. The demand for their commodity, site and soil, can go on expanding indefinitely; but there is only a given, limited amount of their commodity. . . . The bargain struck between landlord and tenant is always advantageous to the former in the greatest possible degree. . . . Besides the advantage he derives from the nature of the case, he derives a further advantage from his position, his larger fortune and greater credit and standing. But the first by itself suffices to enable him and him *alone* to profit from the favorable circumstances of the land. The opening of a canal, or a road; the increase of population and of the prosperity of a district, always raise the rent. . . . Indeed, the tenant himself may improve the ground at his own expense; but he only derives the profit from this capital for the duration of his lease, with the expiry of which it remains with the proprietor of the land; henceforth it is the latter who reaps the interest thereon, without having made the outlay, for there is now a proportionate increase in the rent." (Say, t. II, pp. 142-43.)

"Rent, considered as the price paid for the use of land, is naturally the highest which the tenant can afford to pay in the actual circumstances of the land." (Smith, *loc. cit.*, p. 130.)

"The rent of an estate above ground commonly amounts to what is supposed to be a third of the gross produce; and it is generally a rent certain and independent of the occasional variations in the crop." (*Ibid.*, p. 153.) This rent "is seldom less than a fourth . . . of the whole produce." (*Ibid.*, p. 325.)

Ground rent cannot be paid on all commodities. For instance, in many districts no rent is paid for stones.

"Such parts only of the produce of land can commonly be brought to market of which the ordinary price is sufficient to replace the stock which must be employed in bringing them thither, together with its ordinary profits. If the ordinary price is more that this, the surplus part of it will naturally go to the rent of the land. If it is not more, though the commodity may be brought to market, it can afford no rent to the landlord. Whether the price is or is not more depends upon the demand." (*Ibid.*, p. 132.)

"Rent, it is to be observed, therefore, enters into the composition of the *price of commodities* in a *different way* from wages and profit. *High or low wages and profit* are the *causes* of high or low prices; high or low rent is the *effect* of it." (*Ibid.*, p. 132.)

Food belongs to the *products* which always yield a *ground rent*.

"As men, like all other animals, naturally multiply in proportion to the means of their subsistence, food is always, more or less, in demand. It can always purchase or command a greater or smaller quantity of labour, and somebody can always be found who is willing to do something in order to obtain it. The quantity of labour, indeed, which it can purchase is not always *equal* to what it could maintain, if managed in the most economical manner, on account of the high wages which are sometimes given to labour. But it can always purchase such a quantity of labour as it can maintain, according to the rate at which the sort of labour is commonly maintained in the neighbourhood. But land, in almost any possible situation, produces a greater quantity of food than what is sufficient to maintain all the labour necessary for bringing it to market in the most liberal way in which that labour is ever maintained. The surplus, too, is always more than sufficient to replace the stock which employed that labour, together with its profits. Something, therefore, always remains for a rent to the landlord." (*Ibid.*, pp. 132-33.)

"Food is in this manner not only the original source of rent, but every other part of the produce of land which afterwards affords rent derives that part of its value from the improvement of the powers of labour in producing food by means of the improvement and cultivation of land." (*Ibid.*, p. 150.)

"Human food seems to be the only produce of land which always and necessarily affords some rent to the landlord." (*Ibid.*, p. 147.)

"Countries are populous not in proportion to the number of people whom their produce can clothe and lodge, but in proportion to that of those whom it can feed." (*Ibid.*, p. 149.)

"After food, clothing and lodging are the two great wants of mankind." They usually yield a rent, but not inevitably. (*Ibid.*, p. 147.)

Let us now see how the landlord exploits everything from which society benefits.

(1) The rent of land increases with population. (*Ibid.*, p. 146.)

(2) We have already learnt from Say how the rent of land

increases with railways, etc., with the improvement, safety, and multiplication of the means of communication.

(3) "Every improvement in the circumstances of the society tends either *directly* or *indirectly* to raise the real rent of land, to increase the real wealth of the landlord, his power of purchasing the labour, or the produce of the labour of other people. The extension of improvement and cultivation tends to raise it directly. The landlord's share of the produce necessarily increases with the increase of the produce. The rise in the real price of those parts of the rude produce of land, . . . the rise in the price of cattle, for example, tends too to raise the rent of land directly, and in a still greater proportion. The real value of the landlord's share, his real command of the labour of other people, not only rises with the real value of the produce, but the proportion of his share to the whole produce rises with it. That produce, after the rise in its real price, requires no more labour to collect it than before. A smaller proportion of it will, therefore, be sufficient to replace, with the ordinary profit, the stock which employs that labour. A greater proportion of it must, consequently, belong to the landlord." (Smith, I, pp. 228-29.)

The greater demand for raw produce, and therefore the rise in value, may in part result from the increase of population and from the increase of their needs. But every new invention, every new application in manufacture of a previously unused or little-used raw material, augments the rent of the land. Thus, for example, there was a tremendous rise in the rent of coal mines with the advent of the railways, steamships, etc.

Besides this advantage which the landlord derives from manufacture, discoveries, and labor, there is yet another, as we shall presently see.

(4) "All those improvements in the productive powers of labour, which tend directly to reduce the real price of manufactures, tend indirectly to raise the real rent of land. The landlord exchanges that part of his rude produce, which is over and above his own consumption, or what comes to the same thing, the price of that part of it, for manufactured produce. Whatever reduces the real price of the latter, raises that of the former. An equal quantity of the former becomes thereby equivalent to a greater quantity of the latter; and the landlord is enabled to purchase a greater quantity of the conveniencies, ornaments, or luxuries, which he has occasion for." (*Ibid.*, p. 229.)

But it is silly to conclude, as Smith does, that since the landlord exploits every benefit which comes to society, the interest of the landlord is always identical with that of society. (*Ibid.*, p. 230.) In the economic system, under the rule of private property, the interest which an individual has in society is in precisely inverse proportion to the interest society has in him—just as the interest of the money-lender in the spendthrift is by no means identical with the interest of the spendthrift.

We shall mention only in passing the landlord's obsession with monopoly directed against the landed property of foreign countries, from which the corn laws, for instance, originate. Likewise, we shall here pass over medieval serfdom, the slavery in the colonies, and the miserable condition of the country folk, the day laborers, in Great Britain. Let us confine ourselves to the propositions of political economy itself.

(1) The landlord being interested in the welfare of society means, according to the principles of political economy, that he is interested in the growth of its population, production of the arts, in the expansion of its needs—in short, in the increase of wealth; and this increase of wealth is, as we have already seen, identical with the increase of poverty and slavery. The relation between increasing house rent and increasing poverty is an example of the landlord's interest in society, for the ground rent, the interest obtained from the land on which the house stands, goes up with the rent of the house.

(2) According to the political economists themselves, the landlord's interest is inimically opposed to the interest of the tenant farmer—and thus already to a significant section of society.

(3) As the landlord can demand all the more rent from the tenant farmer the less wages the farmer pays, and as the farmer forces down wages all the lower the more rent the landlord demands, it follows that the interest of the landlord is just as hostile to that of the farm workers as is that of the manufacturers to their workers. It forces down wages to the minimum in just the same way.

(4) Since a real reduction in the price of manufactured products raises the rent of land, the landowner has a direct interest in

lowering the wages of industrial workers, in competition amongst the capitalists, in over-production, in all the misery associated with industrial production.

(5) While, thus, the landlord's interest, far from being identical with the interest of society, stands inimically opposed to the interest of tenant farmers, farm laborers, factory workers and capitalists, on the other hand, the interest of one landlord is not even identical with that of another, on account of the competition which we will now consider.

In general the relationship of large and small landed property is like that of big and small capital. But in addition, there are special circumstances which lead inevitably to the accumulation of large landed property and to the absorption of small property by it.

(1) Nowhere does the relative number of workers and implements decrease more with increases in the size of the stock than in landed property. Likewise, the possibility of all-round exploitation, of economizing production costs, and of effective division of labor, increases nowhere more with the size of the stock than in landed property. However small a field may be, it requires for its working a certain irreducible minimum of implements (plough, saw, etc.), whilst the size of a piece of landed property can be reduced far below this minimum.

(2) Big landed property accumulates to itself the interest on the capital which the tenant farmer has employed to improve the land. Small landed property has to employ its own capital, and therefore does not get this profit at all.

(3) While every social improvement benefits the big estate, it harms small property, because it increases its need for ready cash.

(4) Two important laws concerning this competition remain to be considered:

(a) The rent of the cultivated land, of which the produce is human food, regulates the rent of the greater part of other cultivated land. (Smith, I, p. 144.)

Ultimately, only the big estate can produce such food as cattle, etc. Therefore it regulates the rent of other land and can force it down to a minimum.

The small landed proprietor working on his own account stands then to the big landowner in the same relation as an artisan possessing his *own* tool to the factory owner. Small property in land has become a mere instrument of labor. Rent of land entirely disappears for the small proprietor; there remains to him at the most the interest on his capital, and his wages. For ground rent can be driven down by competition till it is nothing more than the interest on capital not invested by the proprietor.

(b) In addition, we have already learnt that with equal fertility and equally efficient exploitation of lands, mines and fisheries, the produce is proportionate to the size of the capital. Hence the victory of the big landowner. Similarly, where equal capitals are employed the product is proportionate to the fertility. Hence, where capitals are equal, victory goes to the proprietor of the more fertile soil.

(*a*) "A mine of any kind may be said to be either fertile or barren, according as the quantity of mineral which can be brought from it by a certain quantity of labour is greater or less than what can be brought by an equal quantity from the greater part of other mines of the same kind." (*Ibid.*, p. 151.)

"The most fertile coal-mine, too, regulates the price of coals at all other mines in its neighbourhood. Both the proprietor and the undertaker of the work find, the one that he can get a greater rent, the other that he can get a greater profit, by somewhat underselling all their neighbours. Their neighbours are soon obliged to sell at the same price, though they cannot so well afford it, and though it always diminishes, and sometimes takes away altogether both their rent and their profit. Some works are abandoned altogether; others can afford no rent, and can be wrought only by the proprietor." (*Ibid.*, pp. 152-53.) "After the discovery of the mines of Peru, the silver mines of Europe were, the greater part of them, abandoned. . . . This was the case, too, with the mines of Cuba and St. Domingo, and even with the ancient mines of Peru, after the discovery of those of Potosi." (*Ibid.*, p. 154.)

What Smith here says of mines applies more or less to landed property generally:

(*b*) "The ordinary market-price of land, it is to be observed, depends everywhere upon the ordinary market rate of interest. . . . If the rent of land should fall short of the interest of money by a greater difference, nobody would buy land, which would soon reduce its ordinary price. On the contrary, if the advantages should much more than compensate the difference, everybody would buy land, which again would soon raise its ordinary price." (*Ibid.*, p. 320.)

From this relation of ground rent to interest on money it follows that rent must fall more and more, so that eventually only the wealthiest people can live on rent. Hence the ever greater competition between landowners who do not lease their land to tenants. Ruin of some of these—further accumulation of large landed property.

This competition has the further consequence that a large part of landed property falls into the hands of the capitalists and that capitalists thus become simultaneously landowners, just as the smaller landowners are on the whole already nothing more than capitalists. Similarly, a section of large landowners becomes at the same time industrialists.

The final consequence is thus the abolition of the distinction between capitalist and landowner, so that there remain altogether only two classes of the population—the working class and the class of capitalists. This huckstering with landed property, the transformation of landed property into a commodity, constitutes the final overthrow of the old and the final establishment of the money aristocracy.

(1) We will not join in the sentimental tears wept over this by romanticism. Romanticism always confuses the shamefulness of *huckstering the land* with the perfectly rational consequence, inevitable and desirable within the realm of private property, of the *huckstering of private property* in land. In the first place, feudal landed property is already by its very nature huckstered land— the earth which is estranged from man and hence, confronts him in the shape of a few great lords.

The domination of the land as an alien power over men is already inherent in feudal landed property. The serf is the adjunct of the land. Likewise, the lord of an entailed estate, the first-born son, belongs to the land. It inherits him. Indeed, the dominion of private property begins with property in land—that is its basis. But in feudal landed property the lord at least *appears* as the king of the estate. Similarly, there still exists the semblance of a more intimate connection between the proprietor and the land than that of mere *material* wealth. The estate is individualized with its lord: it has his rank, is baronial or ducal with him, has his privileges, his jurisdiction, his political position, etc. It appears as the inorganic body of its lord. Hence the proverb *nulle terre sans maître* [there is no land without its master], which expresses the fusion of nobility and landed property. Similarly, the rule of landed property does not appear directly as the rule of mere capital. For those belonging to it, the estate is more like their fatherland. It is a constricted sort of nationality.

In the same way, feudal landed property gives its name to its lord, as does a kingdom to its king. His family history, the history of his house, etc.—all this individualizes the estate for him and makes it literally his house, personifies it. Similarly those working on the estate have not the position of *day laborers;* but they are in part themselves his property, as are serfs; and in part they are bound to him by ties of respect, allegiance, and duty. His relation to them is therefore directly political, and has likewise a human, *intimate* side. Customs, character, etc., vary from one estate to another and seem to be one with the land to which they belong; later, on the other hand, a man is bound to his land, not by his character or his individuality, but only by his purse strings. Finally, the feudal lord does not try to extract the utmost advantage from his land. Rather, he consumes what is there and calmly leaves the worry of producing to the serfs and the tenants. Such is *nobility's* relationship to landed property, which casts a romantic glory on its lords.

It is necessary that this appearance be abolished—that landed property, the root of private property, be dragged completely into the movement of private property and that it become a commodity; that the rule of the proprietor appear as the undisguised rule of private property, of capital, freed of all political tincture; that the relationship between proprietor and worker be reduced to the economic relationship of exploiter and exploited; that all personal relationship between the proprietor and his property cease, property becoming merely *objective,* material wealth; that the marriage of convenience should take the place of the marriage of honor with the land; and that the land should likewise sink to the status of a commercial value, like man. It is essential that that which is the root of landed property—filthy self-interest—make its appearance, too, in its cynical form. It is essential that the immovable monopoly turn into the mobile and restless monopoly, into competition; and that the idle enjoyment of the products of other peoples' blood and toil turn into a bustling commerce in the same commodity. Lastly, it is essential that in this competition landed property, in the form of capital, manifest its dominion over both the working class and the proprietors themselves who are either being ruined or raised by the laws governing the movement of capital. The medieval proverb *nulle terre sans seigneur* [there is no land without its lord] is thereby replaced by that other proverb, *l'argent n'a pas de maître* [money knows no master], wherein is expressed the complete domination of dead matter over mankind.

(2) Concerning the argument of division or non-division of landed property, the following is to be observed.

The division of landed property negates the *large-scale monopoly* of property in land—abolishes it; but only by *generalizing* this monopoly. It does not abolish the source of monopoly, private property. It attacks the existing form, but not the essence, of monopoly. The consequence is that it falls victim to the laws of private property. For the division of landed property corresponds to the movement of competition in the sphere of industry. In addition to the economic disadvantages of such a dividing-up of the instruments of labor, and of separated labor (to be clearly distinguished from the division of labor: in separated labor the work is not shared out amongst many, but each carries on the same work by himself, it is a multiplication of the same work) this division of land, like competition in industry, necessarily turns again into accumulation.

Therefore, where the division of landed property takes place, there remains nothing for it but to return to monopoly in a still more malignant form, or to negate, to abolish the division of landed property itself. To do that, however, is not to return to feudal ownership, but to abolish private property in the soil alto-

gether. The first abolition of monopoly is always its generalization, the broadening of its existence. The abolition of monopoly,
once it has come to exist in its utmost breadth and inclusiveness,
is its total annihilation. Association, applied to land, shares the
economic advantage of large-scale landed property, and first brings
to realization the original tendency inherent in land division,
namely, equality. In the same way association also reestablishes,
now on a rational basis, no longer mediated by serfdom, overlord-
ship and the silly mysticism of property, the intimate ties of man
with the earth, since the earth ceases to be an object of huckstering,
and through free labor and free enjoyment becomes once more a
true personal property of man. A great advantage of the division
of landed property is that its mass, which can no longer resign
itself to servitude, perishes through property in a different way
than in industry.[1]

As for large landed property, its defenders have always, sophis-
tically, identified the economic advantages offered by large-scale
agriculture with large-scale landed property, as if it were not precisely as a result of the abolition of property, that this advantage,
for one thing, would receive its greatest possible extension, and,
for another, only then would be of social benefit. In the same way,
they have attacked the huckstering spirit of small landed property,
as if large landed property did not contain huckstering latent
within it, even in its feudal form—not to speak of the modern
English form, which combines the landlord's feudalism with the
tenant farmer's huckstering and industry.

Just as large landed property can return the reproach of monopoly leveled against it by partitioned land, since partitioned land
is also based on the monopoly of private property, so can partitioned landed property likewise return to large landed property
the reproach of partition, since partition also prevails there,
though in a rigid and crystallized form. Indeed, private property
rests altogether on partitioning. Morever, just as division of the
land leads back to large landed property as a form of capital
wealth, so must feudal landed property necessarily lead to partitioning or at least fall into the hands of the capitalists, turn and
twist as it may.

For large landed property, as in England, drives the overwhelm-

ing majority of the population into the arms of industry and reduces its own workers to utter wretchedness. Thus, it engenders
and enlarges the power of its enemy, capital, industry, by throwing
poor people and an entire activity of the country on to the
other side. It makes the majority of the people of the country
industrial and thus opponents of large landed property. Where
industry has attained to great power, as in England at the present
time, it progessively forces from large landed property its monopolies against foreign countries and throws them into competition with landed property abroad. For under the sway of industry
landed property could keep its feudal grandeur secure only by
means of monopolies against foreign countries, thereby protecting
itself against the general laws of trade, which are incompatible
with its feudal character. Once thrown into competition, landed
property obeys the laws of competition, like every other commodity subjected to competition. It begins thus to fluctuate, to
decrease and to increase, to fly from one hand to another; and no
law can keep it any longer in a few predestined hands. The immediate consequence is the splitting up of the land amongst many
hands, and in any case subjection to the power of industrial
capitals.

Finally, large landed property which has been forcibly preserved in this way and which has begotten by its side a tremendous industry leads even more quickly to crisis than the partitioning of land, by whose side the power of industry remains
constantly of second rank.

Large landed property, as we see in England, has already cast off
its feudal character and adopted an industrial character in so far
as it is aiming to make as much money as possible. To the
owner it yields the utmost possible rent, to the tenant farmer the
utmost possible profit on his capital. The workers on the land,
in consequence, have already been reduced to the minimum, and
the class of tenant farmers already represent within landed property the power of industry and capital. As a result of foreign competition, rent of land in most cases can form no longer an independent income. A large number of landowners have to displace
farmers, some of whom in this way sink into the proletariat. On

the other hand, many farmers will take over landed property; for the big proprietors who with their comfortable incomes have mostly given themselves over to extravagance are for the most part not competent to conduct large-scale agriculture, and in some cases possess neither the capital nor the ability for the exploitation of the land. Hence a section of this class, too, is completely ruined. Eventually wages, which have already been reduced to a minimum, must be reduced yet further, to meet the new competition. This then necessarily leads to revolution.

Landed property had to develop in each of these two ways so as to experience in both its necessary downfall, just as industry both in the form of monopoly and in that of competition had to ruin itself so as to learn to believe in man.

ESTRANGED LABOR[1]

We have proceeded from the premises of political economy. We have accepted its language and its laws. We presupposed private property, the separation of labor, capital and land, and of wages, profit of capital and rent of land—likewise division of labor, competition, the concept of exchange-value, etc. On the basis of political economy itself, in its own words, we have shown that the worker sinks to the level of a commodity and becomes indeed the most wretched of commodities; that the wretchedness of the worker is in inverse proportion to the power and magnitude of his production; that the necessary result of competition is the accumulation of capital in a few hands, and thus the restoration of monopoly in a more terrible form; and that finally the distinction between capitalist and land rentier, like that between the tiller of the soil and the factory worker, disappears and that the whole of society must fall apart into the two classes—the property *owners* and the propertyless *workers*.

Political economy starts with the fact of private property, but it does not explain it to us. It expresses in general, abstract formulas the *material* process through which private property actually passes, and these formulas it then takes for *laws*. It does not *comprehend* these laws, i.e., it does not demonstrate how they arise from the very nature of private property. Political economy does not disclose the source of the division between labor and capital, and between capital and land. When, for example, it defines the relationship of wages to profit, it takes the interest of the capitalists to be the ultimate cause, i.e., it takes for granted what it is supposed to explain. Similarly, competition comes in everywhere. It is explained from external circumstances. As to how far these external and apparently accidental circumstances are but the expression of a necessary course of development, political economy teaches us nothing. We have seen how exchange itself appears

106

to it as an accidental fact. The only wheels which political economy sets in motion are *greed* and the war *amongst the greedy—competition.*

Precisely because political economy does not grasp the way the movement is connected, it was possible to oppose, for instance, the doctrine of competition to the doctrine of monopoly, the doctrine of the freedom of the crafts to the doctrine of the guild, the doctrine of the division of landed property to the doctrine of the big estate—for competition, freedom of the crafts and the division of landed property were explained and comprehended only as accidental, premeditated and violent consequences of monopoly, of the guild system, and of feudal property, not as their necessary, inevitable and natural consequences.

Now, therefore, we have to grasp the essential connection between private property, greed, and the separation of labor, capital and landed property; between exchange and competition, value and the devaluation of men, monopoly and competition, etc.— the connection between this whole estrangement and the *money* system.

Do not let us go back to a fictitious primordial condition as the political economist does, when he tries to explain. Such a primordial condition explains nothing; it merely pushes the question away into a gray nebulous distance. It assumes in the form of a fact, of an event, what the economist is supposed to deduce— namely, the necessary relationship between two things—between, for example, division of labor and exchange. Theology in the same way explains the origin of evil by the fall of man; that is, it assumes as a fact, in historical form, what has to be explained.

We proceed from an economic fact *of the present.*

The worker becomes all the poorer the more wealth he produces, the more his production increases in power and size. The worker becomes an ever cheaper commodity the more commodities he creates. With the *increasing value* of the world of things proceeds in direct proportion the *devaluation* of the world of men. Labor produces not only commodities: it produces itself and the worker as a *commodity*—and this in the same general proportion in which it produces commodities.

This fact expresses merely that the object which labor produces —labor's product—confronts it as *something alien,* as a *power independent* of the producer. The product of labor is labor which has been embodied in an object, which has become material: it is the *objectification* [2] of labor. Labor's realization is its objectification. In the sphere of political economy this realization of labor appears as *loss of realization* [3] for the workers; objectification as *loss of the object* and *bondage to it;* appropriation as *estrangement,* as *alienation.* [4]

So much does labor's realization appear as loss of realization that the worker loses realization to the point of starving to death. So much does objectification appear as loss of the object that the worker is robbed of the objects most necessary not only for his life but for his work. Indeed, labor itself becomes an object which he can obtain only with the greatest effort and with the most irregular interruptions. So much does the appropriation of the object appear as estrangement that the more objects the worker produces the less he can possess and the more he falls under the sway of his product, capital.

All these consequences result from the fact that the worker is related to the *product of his labor* as to an *alien* object. For on this premise it is clear that the more the worker spends himself, the more powerful becomes the alien world of objects which he creates over and against himself, the poorer he himself—his inner world—becomes, the less belongs to him as his own. It is the same in religion. The more man puts into God, the less he retains in himself. The worker puts his life into the object; but now his life no longer belongs to him but to the object. Hence, the greater this activity, the greater is the worker's lack of objects. Whatever the product of his labor is, he is not. Therefore the greater this product, the less is he himself. The *alienation* of the worker in his product means not only that his labor becomes an object, an *external* existence, but that it exists *outside him,* independently, as something alien to him, and that it becomes a power on its own confronting him. It means that the life which he has conferred on the object confronts him as something hostile and alien.

Let us now look more closely at the *objectification,* at the production of the worker; and in it at the *estrangement,* the *loss* of the object, of his product.

The worker can create nothing without *nature,* without the *sensuous external world.*[5] It is the material on which his labor is realized, in which it is active, from which and by means of which it produces.

But just as nature provides labor with the *means of life* in the sense that labor cannot *live* without objects on which to operate, on the other hand, it also provides the *means of life* in the more restricted sense, i.e., the means for the physical subsistence of the *worker* himself.

Thus the more the worker by his labor *appropriates* the external world, hence sensuous nature, the more he deprives himself of *means of life* in a double manner: first, in that the sensuous external world more and more ceases to be an object belonging to his labor—to be his labor's *means of life;* and secondly, in that it more and more ceases to be *means of life* in the immediate sense, means for the physical subsistence of the worker.

In both respects, therefore, the worker becomes a slave of his object, first, in that he receives an *object of labor,* i.e., in that he receives *work;* and secondly, in that he receives *means of subsistence.* Therefore, it enables him to exist, first, as a *worker;* and, second as a *physical subject.* The height of this bondage is that it is only as a *worker* that he continues to maintain himself as a *physical subject,* and that it is only as a *physical subject* that he is a *worker.*

(The laws of political economy express the estrangement of the worker in his object thus: the more the worker produces, the less he has to consume; the more values he creates, the more valueless, the more unworthy he becomes; the better formed his product, the more deformed becomes the worker; the more civilized his object, the more barbarous becomes the worker; the more powerful labor becomes, the more powerless becomes the worker; the more ingenious labor becomes, the less ingenious becomes the worker and the more he becomes nature's bondsman.)

Political economy conceals the estrangement inherent in the nature of labor by not considering the direct relationship between the worker (labor) *and production.* It is true that labor produces for the rich wonderful things—but for the worker it produces privation. It produces palaces—but for the worker, hovels. It produces beauty—but for the worker, deformity. It replaces labor by machines, but it throws a section of the workers back to a barbarous type of labor, and it turns the other workers into machines. It produces intelligence—but for the worker stupidity, cretinism.

The direct relationship of labor to its products is the relationship of the worker to the objects of his production. The relationship of the man of means to the objects of production and to production itself is only a *consequence* of this first relationship—and confirms it. We shall consider this other aspect later.

When we ask, then, what is the essential relationship of labor we are asking about the relationship of the *worker* to production.

Till now we have been considering the estrangement, the alienation of the worker only in one of its aspects, i.e., the worker's *relationship to the products of his labor.* But the estrangement is manifested not only in the result but in the *act of production,* within the *producing activity,* itself. How could the worker come to face the product of his activity as a stranger, were it not that in the very act of production he was estranging himself from himself? The product is after all but the summary of the activity, of production. If then the product of labor is alienation, production itself must be active alienation, the alienation of activity, the activity of alienation. In the estrangement of the object of labor is merely summarized the estrangement, the alienation, in the activity of labor itself.

What, then, constitutes the alienation of labor?

First, the fact that labor is *external* to the worker, i.e., it does not belong to his essential being; that in his work, therefore, he does not affirm himself but denies himself, does not feel content but unhappy, does not develop freely his physical and mental energy but mortifies his body and ruins his mind. The worker therefore only feels himself outside his work, and in his work feels outside himself. He is at home when he is not working, and when he is working he is not at home. His labor is therefore not voluntary, but coerced; it is *forced labor*. It is therefore not the satisfaction of a need; it is merely a *means* to satisfy needs external to it. Its alien character emerges clearly in the fact that as soon as no physical or other compulsion exists, labor is shunned like the plague. External labor, labor in which man alienates himself, is a labor of self-sacrifice, of mortification. Lastly, the external character of labor for the worker appears in the fact that it is not his own, but someone else's, that it does not belong to him, that in it he belongs, not to himself, but to another. Just as in religion the spontaneous activity of the human imagination, of the human brain and the human heart, operates independently of the individual—that is, operates on him as an alien, divine or diabolical activity—so is the worker's activity not his spontaneous activity. It belongs to another; it is the loss of his self.

As a result, therefore, man (the worker) only feels himself freely active in his animal functions—eating, drinking, procreating, or at most in his dwelling and in dressing-up, etc.; and in his human functions he no longer feels himself to be anything but an animal. What is animal becomes human and what is human becomes animal.

Certainly eating, drinking, procreating, etc., are also genuinely human functions. But abstractly taken, separated from the sphere of all other human activity and turned into sole and ultimate ends, they are animal functions.

We have considered the act of estranging practical human activity, labor, in two of its aspects. (1) The relation of the worker to the *product of labor* as an alien object exercising power over him. This relation is at the same time the relation to the sensuous external world, to the objects of nature, as an alien world inimically opposed to him. (2) The relation of labor to the *act of production* within the *labor* process. This relation is the relation of the worker to his own activity as an alien activity not belonging to him; it is activity as suffering, strength as weakness, begetting as emasculating, the worker's *own* physical and mental energy, his personal life indeed, what is life but activity?—as an activity which is turned against him, independent of him and not belonging to him. Here we have *self-estrangement,* as previously we had the estrangement of the *thing.*

We have still a third aspect of *estranged labor* to deduce from the two already considered.

Man is a species being,[6] not only because in practice and in theory he adopts the species as his object (his own as well as those of other things), but—and this is only another way of expressing it—also because he treats himself as the actual, living species; because he treats himself as a *universal* and therefore a free being.

The life of the species, both in man and in animals, consists physically in the fact that man (like the animal) lives on inorganic nature; and the more universal man is compared with an animal, the more universal is the sphere of inorganic nature on which he lives. Just as plants, animals, stones, air, light, etc., constitute theoretically a part of human consciousness, partly as objects of natural science, partly as objects of art—his spiritual inorganic nature, spiritual nourishment which he must first prepare to make palatable and digestible—so also in the realm of practice they constitute a part of human life and human activity. Physically man lives only on these products of nature, whether they appear in the form of food, heating, clothes, a dwelling, etc. The universality of man appears in practice precisely in the universality which makes all nature his *inorganic* body—both inasmuch as nature is (1) his direct means of life, and (2) the material, the object, and the instrument of his life activity. Nature is man's *inorganic body*—nature, that is, in so far as it is not itself the human body. Man *lives* on nature—means that nature is his *body,* with which he must remain in continuous interchange if he is not to die. That man's physical and spiritual life is linked to nature means simply that nature is linked to itself, for man is a part of nature.

In estranging from man (1) nature, and (2) himself, his own active functions, his life activity, estranged labor estranges the *species* from man. It changes for him the *life of the species* into a means of individual life. First it estranges the life of the species and individual life, and secondly it makes individual life in its abstract form the purpose of the life of the species, likewise in its abstract and estranged form.

Indeed, labor, *life-activity, productive life* itself, appears in the first place merely as a *means* of satisfying a need—the need to maintain physical existence. Yet the productive life is the life of the species. It is life-engendering life. The whole character of a species—its species character—is contained in the character of its life activity; and free, conscious activity is man's species character. Life itself appears only as a *means to life*.

The animal is immediately one with its life activity. It does not distinguish itself from it. It is *its life activity*. Man makes his life activity itself the object of his will and of his consciousness. He has conscious life activity. It is not a determination with which he directly merges. Conscious life activity distinguishes man immediately from animal life activity. It is just because of this that he is a species being. Or rather, it is only because he is a species being that he is a conscious being, i.e., that his own life is an object for him. Only because of that is his activity free activity. Estranged labor reverses this relationship, so that it is just because man is a conscious being that he makes his life activity, his *essential* being, a mere means to his *existence*.

In creating a *world of objects* [7] by his practical activity, in *his work upon* inorganic nature, man proves himself a conscious species being, i.e., as a being that treats the species as its own essential being, or that treats itself as a species being. Admittedly animals also produce. They build themselves nests, dwellings, like the bees, beavers, ants, etc. But an animal only produces what it immediately needs for itself or its young. It produces one-sidedly, whilst man produces universally. It produces only under the dominion of immediate physical need, whilst man produces even when he is free from physical need and only truly produces in freedom therefrom. An animal produces only itself, whilst man reproduces the whole of nature. An animal's product belongs immediately to its physical body, whilst man freely confronts his product. An animal forms things in accordance with the standard and the need of the species to which it belongs, whilst man knows how to produce in accordance with the standard of every species, and knows how to apply everywhere the inherent standard to the object. Man therefore also forms things in accordance with the laws of beauty.

It is just in his work upon the objective world, therefore, that man first really proves himself to be a *species being*. This production is his active species life. Through and because of this production, nature appears as *his* work and his reality. The object of labor is, therefore, the *objectification of man's species life*: for he duplicates himself not only, as in consciousness, intellectually, but also actively, in reality, and therefore he contemplates himself in a world that he has created. In tearing away from man the object of his production, therefore, estranged labor tears from him his *species life,* his real objectivity as a member of the species and transforms his advantage over animals into the disadvantage that his inorganic body, nature, is taken away from him.

Similarly, in degrading spontaneous, free, activity, to a means, estranged labor makes man's species life a means to his physical existence.

The consciousness which man has of his species is thus transformed by estrangement in such a way that species life becomes for him a means.

Estranged labor turns thus:

(3) *Man's species being,* both nature and his spiritual species property, into a being *alien* to him, into a *means* to his *individual existence*. It estranges from man his own body, as well as external nature and his spiritual essence, his *human* being.

(4) An immediate consequence of the fact that man is estranged from the product of his labor, from his life activity, from his species being is the *estrangement of man* from *man*. When man confronts himself, he confronts the *other* man. What applies to a man's relation to his work, to the product of his labor and to himself, also holds of a man's relation to the other man, and to the other man's labor and object of labor.

In fact, the proposition that man's species nature is estranged from him means that one man is estranged from the other, as each of them is from man's essential nature.

The estrangement of man, and in fact every relationship in

which man stands to himself, is first realized and expressed in the relationship in which a man stands to other men.

Hence within the relationship of estranged labor each man views the other in accordance with the standard and the relationship in which he finds himself as a worker.

We took our departure from a fact of political economy—the estrangement of the worker and his production. We have formulated this fact in conceptual terms as *estranged, alienated* labor. We have analyzed this concept—hence analyzing merely a fact of political economy.

Let us now see, further, how the concept of estranged, alienated labor must express and present itself in real life.

If the product of labor is alien to me, if it confronts me as an alien power, to whom, then, does it belong?

If my own activity does not belong to me, if it is an alien, a coerced activity, to whom, then, does it belong?

To a being *other* than myself.

Who is this being?

The *gods?* To be sure, in the earliest times the principal production (for example, the building of temples, etc., in Egypt, India and Mexico) appears to be in the service of the gods, and the product belongs to the gods. However, the gods on their own were never the lords of labor. No more was *nature.* And what a contradiction it would be if, the more man subjugated nature by his labor and the more the miracles of the gods were rendered superfluous by the miracles of industry, the more man were to renounce the joy of production and the enjoyment of the product in favor of these powers.

The *alien* being, to whom labor and the product of labor belongs, in whose service labor is done and for whose benefit the product of labor is provided, can only be *man* himself.

If the product of labor does not belong to the worker, if it confronts him as an alien power, then this can only be because it belongs to some *other man than the worker.* If the worker's activity is a torment to him, to another it must be *delight* and his life's joy. Not the gods, not nature, but only man himself can be this alien power over man.

We must bear in mind the previous proposition that man's relation to himself only becomes for him *objective* and *actual* [8] through his relation to the other man. Thus, if the product of his labor, his labor *objectified*, is for him an *alien*, hostile, powerful object independent of him, then his position towards it is such that someone else is master of this object, someone who is alien, hostile, powerful, and independent of him. If his own activity is to him related as an unfree activity, then he is related to it as an activity performed in the service, under the dominion, the coercion, and the yoke of another man.

Every self-estrangement of man, from himself and from nature, appears in the relation in which he places himself and nature to men other than and differentiated from himself. For this reason religious self-estrangement necessarily appears in the relationship of the layman to the priest, or again to a mediator, etc., since we are here dealing with the intellectual world. In the real practical world self-estrangement can only become manifest through the real practical relationship to other men. The medium through which estrangement takes place is itself *practical*. Thus through estranged labor man not only creates his relationship to the object and to the act of production as to men that are alien and hostile to him; he also creates the relationship in which other men stand to his production and to his product, and the relationship in which he stands to these other men. Just as he creates his own production as the loss of his reality, as his punishment; his own product as a loss, as a product not belonging to him; so he creates the domination of the person who does not produce over production and over the product. Just as he estranges his own activity from himself, so he confers to the stranger an activity which is not his own.

We have until now only considered this relationship from the standpoint of the worker and later we shall be considering it also from the standpoint of the non-worker.

Through *estranged, alienated labor*, then, the worker produces the relationship to this labor of a man alien to labor and standing outside it. The relationship of the worker to labor creates the relation to it of the capitalist (or whatever one chooses to call the master of labor) . *Private property* is thus the product, the result, the necessary consequence, of *alienated labor,* of the external relation of the worker to nature and to himself.

Private property thus results by analysis from the concept of *alienated labor,* i.e., of *alienated man,* of estranged labor, of estranged life, of *estranged* man.

True, it is as a result of the *movement of private property* that we have obtained the concept of *alienated labor (of alienated life)* from political economy. But on analysis of this concept it becomes clear that though private property appears to be the source, the cause of alienated labor, it is rather its consequence, just as the gods are *originally* not the cause but the effect of man's intellectual confusion. Later this relationship becomes reciprocal.

Only at the last culmination of the development of private property does this, its secret, appear again, namely, that on the one hand it is the *product* of alienated labor, and that on the other it is the *means* by which labor alienates itself, the *realization of this alienation.*

This exposition immediately sheds light on various hitherto unsolved conflicts.

(1) Political economy starts from labor as the real soul of production; yet to labor it gives nothing, and to private property everything. Confronting this contradiction, Proudhon has decided in favor of labor against private property. We understand, however, that this apparent contradiction is the contradiction of *estranged labor* with itself, and that political economy has merely formulated the laws of estranged labor.

We also understand, therefore, that *wages* and *private property* are identical: since the product, as the object of labor pays for labor itself, therefore the wage is but a necessary consequence of labor's estrangement. After all, in the wage of labor, labor does not appear as an end in itself but as the servant of the wage. We shall develop this point later, and meanwhile will only derive some conclusions.[9]

An enforced increase of wages (disregarding all other difficulties, including the fact that it would only be by force, too, that higher wages, being an anomaly, could be maintained) would therefore be nothing but *better payment for the slave,* and would not win either for the worker or for labor their human status and dignity.

Indeed, even the *equality of wages* demanded by Proudhon only transforms the relationship of the present-day worker to his labor into the relationship of all men to labor. Society is then conceived as an abstract capitalist.

Wages are a direct consequence of estranged labor, and estranged labor is the direct cause of private property. The downfall of the one must involve the downfall of the other.

(2) From the relationship of estranged labor to private property it follows further that the emancipation of society from private property, etc., from servitude, is expressed in the *political* form of the *emancipation of the workers*; not that *their* emancipation alone is at stake, but because the emancipation of the workers contains universal human emancipation—and it contains this, because the whole of human servitude is involved in the relation of the worker to production, and every relation of servitude is but a modification and consequence of this relation.

Just as we have derived the concept of *private property* from the concept of *estranged, alienated labor* by *analysis,* so we can develop every *category* of political economy with the help of these two factors; and we shall find again in each category, e.g., trade, competition, capital, money, only a *definite* and *developed expression* of these first elements.

Before considering this aspect, however, let us try to solve two problems.

(1) To define the general *nature of private property,* as it has arisen as a result of estranged labor, in its relation to *truly human* and *social property.*

(2) We have accepted the *estrangement of labor,* its *alienation,* as a fact, and we have analyzed this fact. How, we now ask, does *man* come to *alienate,* to estrange, *his labor*? How is this estrangement rooted in the nature of human development? We have already gone a long way to the solution of this problem by *transforming* the question of the *origin of private property* into the question of the relation of *alienated labor* to the course of humanity's development. For when one speaks of *private property,*

one thinks of dealing with something external to man. When one speaks of labor, one is directly dealing with man himself. This new formulation of the question already contains its solution.

As to (1): The general nature of private property and its relation to truly human property.

Alienated labor has resolved itself for us into two elements which mutually condition one another, or which are but different expressions of one and the same relationship. *Appropriation* appears as *estrangement,* as *alienation*; and *alienation* appears as *appropriation, estrangement* as true introduction into society.[10]

We have considered the one side—*alienated* labor in relation to the *worker* himself, i.e., the *relation of alienated labor to itself.* The *property relation of the non-worker to the worker and to labor* we have found as the product, the necessary outcome of this relationship. *Private property,* as the material, summary expression of alienated labor, embraces both relations—the *relation of the worker to work and to the product of his labor and to the non-worker,* and the relation of the *non-worker to the worker and to the product of his labor.*

Having seen that in relation to the worker who *appropriates* nature by means of his labor, this appropriation appears as estrangement, his own spontaneous activity as activity for another and as activity of another, vitality as a sacrifice of life, production of the object as loss of the object to an alien power, to an *alien* person—we shall now consider the relation to the worker, to labor and its object of this person who is *alien* to labor and the worker.

First it has to be noted that everything which appears in the worker as an *activity of alienation, of estrangement,* appears in the non-worker as a *state of alienation, of estrangement.*

Secondly, that the worker's *real, practical attitude* in production and to the product (as a state of mind) appears in the non-worker confronting him as a *theoretical* attitude.

Thirdly, the non-worker does everything against the worker which the worker does against himself; but he does not do against himself what he does against the worker.

Let us look more closely at these three relations.

[*At this point the first manuscript breaks off unfinished.*]

ANTITHESIS OF CAPITAL AND LABOR. LANDED PROPERTY AND CAPITAL

. . . forms the interest on his capital.[1] The worker is the subjective manifestation of the fact that capital is man wholly lost to himself, just as capital is the objective manifestation of the fact that labor is man lost to himself. But the *worker* has the misfortune to be a *living* capital, and therefore a capital *with needs*—one which loses its interest, and hence its livelihood, every moment it is not working. The *value* of the worker as capital rises according to demand and supply, and even *physically* his *existence*, his *life*, was and is looked upon as a supply of a *commodity* like any other. The worker produces capital, capital produces him—hence he produces himself, and man as *worker*, as a *commodity*, is the product of this entire cycle. To the man who is nothing more than a *worker*—and to him as a worker—his human qualities only exist in so far as they exist for capital *alien* to him. Because man and capital are foreign to each other, however, and thus stand in an indifferent, external and accidental relationship to each other, it is inevitable that this foreignness should also appear as something *real*. As soon, therefore, as it occurs to capital (whether from necessity or caprice) no longer to be for the worker, he himself is no longer for himself: he has *no* work, hence *no* wages, and as he has no existence as a *human being* but only as a *worker*, he can go and bury himself, starve to death, etc. The worker exists as a worker only when he exists *for himself* as capital; and he exists as capital only when some *capital* exists *for him*. The existence of capital is *his* existence, his *life;* as it determines the tenor of his life in a manner indifferent to him.

Political economy, therefore, does not recognize the unoccupied worker, the workingman, in so far as he happens to be outside this

120

labor relationship. The cheat-thief, swindler, beggar, and un-
employed; the starving, wretched and criminal workingman—
these are *figures* who do not exist for *political economy* but only
for other eyes, those of the doctor, the judge, the grave digger,
and bumbailiff, etc.; such figures are specters outside its domain.
For it, therefore, the worker's needs are but the one *need*—to
maintain him *whilst he is working* in so far as may be necessary to
prevent the race of laborers from dying out. The wages of labor
have thus exactly the same significance as the *maintenance* and
servicing of any other productive instrument, or as the *consumption of a capital,* in general, required for its reproduction with
interest; or as the oil which is applied to wheels to keep them
turning. Wages, therefore, belong to capital's and the capitalist's
necessary *costs,* and must not exceed the bounds of this necessity.
It was therefore quite logical for the English factory owners, before the Amendment Bill of 1834, to deduct from the wages of the
worker the public charity which he was rceiving out of the Poor
Rate and to consider this to be an integral part of wage.

Production does not simply produce man as a *commodity,* the
human commodity, man in the role of *commodity;* it produces
him in keeping with this role as a *mentally* and physically *dehu-
manized* being.—Immorality, deformity, and dulling of the workers and the capitalists.—Its product is the *self-conscious and self-
acting commodity.* . . . the human commodity. . . . Great advance of Ricardo, Mill, etc., on Smith and Say, to declare the
existence of the human being—the greater or lesser human productivity of the commodity—to be *indifferent* and even *harmful.*
Not how many workers are maintained by a given capital, but
rather how much interest it brings in, the sum-total of the
annual *savings,* is said to be the true purpose of production.

It was likewise a great and logical advance of the newer English
political economy,[2] that, whilst elevating *labor* to the position of
its *sole* principle, it should at the same time expound with complete clarity the *inverse* relation between wages and interest on
capital, and the fact that the capitalist could normally *only* gain
by pressing down wages, and vice versa. Not the defrauding of the

consumer, but the capitalist and the worker defrauding each other, is shown to be the *normal* relationship.

The relations of private property contain latent within them the relations of private property as *labor*, the relation of private property as *capital*, and the *mutual* relation of these two to one another. There is the production of human activity as *labor*—that is, as an activity quite alien to itself, to man and to nature, and therefore to consciousness and the flow of life—the *abstract* existence of man as a mere *workman* who may therefore daily fall from his filled void into the absolute void—into his social, and therefore actual, non-existence. On the other hand, there is the production of the object of human activity as *capital*—in which all the natural and social characteristic of the object is *extinguished*; in which private property has lost its natural and social quality (and therefore every political and social illusion, and has lost even the *appearance* of human relationships) ; in which the *selfsame* capital remains the *same* in the most diverse social and natural manifestations, totally indifferent to its *real* content. This contradiction, driven to the limit, is of necessity the limit, the culmination, and the downfall of the whole private-property relationship.

It is therefore another great achievement of the newer English political economy to have declared ground rent to be the difference in the interest yielded by the worst and the best land under cultivation; to have exposed the landowner's romantic illusions—his alleged social importance and identity of his interest with the interest of society, a view still maintained by *Adam Smith* after the physiocrats; and to have anticipated and prepared the movement of the real world which will transform the landowner into an ordinary, prosaic capitalist, and thus simplify and sharpen the contradiction between labor and capital and hasten its resolution. *Land as land,* and *ground rent as ground rent,* have lost their *distinction of rank* and become dumb *capital* and *interest*—or rather, become *capital* and *interest* that only talk money.

The *distinction* between capital and land, between profit and ground rent, and between both and wages, and *industry,* and *agriculture,* and *immovable* and *movable* private property—this distinction is not rooted in the nature of things, but is a *historical*

distinction, a *fixed* moment in the formation and development of
the contradiction between capital and labor. In industry, etc., as
opposed to immovable landed property, is only expressed the way
in which industry came into being and the contradiction to agriculture in which industry developed. This distinction of industry
only continues to exist as a *special* sort of work—as an *essential,
important* and *life-embracing* distinction—so long as industry
(town life) develops *over* and *against* landed property (aristocratic feudal life) and itself continues to bear the feudal character of its opposite in the form of monopoly, craft, guild, corpo-
ration, etc., within which labor still has a *seemingly social*
significance, still the significance of *real community life,* and has
not yet reached the stage of *indifference* to its content, of complete
being-for-self,[3] i.e., of abstraction from all other being, and hence
has not yet become *liberated* capital.

But liberated industry, *industry* constituted for itself as such,
and *liberated capital,* are the necessary *development* of labor. The
power of industry over its opposite is at once revealed in the
emergence of *agriculture* as a real industry, while previously it left
most of the work to the soil and to the *slave* of the soil, through
whom the land cultivated itself. With the transformation of the
slave into a *free* worker—i.e., into a *hireling*—the landlord himself
is transformed into a captain of industry, into a capitalist—a
transformation which takes place at first through the intermediacy
of the *tenant farmer.* The tenant *farmer,* however, is the landowner's representative—the landowner's revealed *secret:* it is only
through him that the landowner has his *economic* existence—his
existence as a private proprietor—for the rent of his land only
exists due to the competition between the farmers. Thus, in the
person of the *tenant farmer* the landlord has already become in
essence a *common* capitalist. And thus must work itself out, too, in
actual fact: the capitalist engaged in agriculture—the tenant—
must become a landlord, or vice versa. The tenant's *industrial
trade* is the *landowner's* industrial trade, for the being of the
former postulates the being of the latter.

But mindful of their contrasting origin, of their line of descent
—the landowner knows the capitalist as his insolent, liberated, en-

riched slave of yesterday and sees himself as a *capitalist* who is threatened by him. The capitalist knows the landowner as the idle, cruel and egotistical master of yesterday; he knows that he injures him as a capitalist, and yet that it is to industry that he, the landowner, owes all his present social significance, his possessions and his pleasures; he sees in him a contradiction to *free* industry and to *free* capital—to capital independent of every natural limitation. This contradiction between landowner and capitalist is extremely bitter, and each side tells the truth about the other. One need only read the attacks of immovable on movable property and vice versa to obtain a clear picture of their respective worthlessness. The landowner lays stress on the noble lineage of his property, on feudal momentoes, reminiscences, the poetry of recollection, on his romantic disposition, on his political importance, etc.; and when he talks economics, it is *only* agriculture that he holds to be productive. At the same time he depicts his adversary as a sly, haggling, deceitful, greedy, mercenary, rebellious, heart- and soul-less cheapjack—extorting, pimping, servile, smooth, flattering, fleecing, dried-up rogue without honor, principles, poetry, substance, or anything else—a person estranged from the community who freely trades it away and who breeds, nourishes and cherishes competition, and with it pauperism, crime, and the dissolution of all social bonds. (Amongst others see the physiocrat *Bergasse*, whom Camille Desmoulins flays in his journal, *Révolutions de France et de Brabant* [4]; see von Vincke, Lancizolle, Haller, Leo, Kosegarten [5] and also Sismondi. [6]) *

Movable property for its part, points to the miracles of industry and progress. It is the child of modern times, its legitimate, native-born son. It pities its adversary as a simpleton, *unenlightened* about his own nature (and in this it is completely right), who

---

* See the garrulous, old-Hegelian theologian Funke who tells, after Herr Leo, with tears in his eyes how a slave had refused, when serfdom was abolished, to cease being the *property of the gentry*. See also the *Patriotic Visions* of Justus Möser, which distinguish themselves by the fact that they never for a moment abandon the ingenuous, petty-bourgeois "home-baked," *ordinary*, narrow, horizon of the philistine, and which nevertheless remain *pure* fancy. This contradiction has given him such an appeal to the German heart. [7]

wants to replace moral capital and free labor by brute, immoral force and serfdom. It depicts him as a Don Quixote, who under the guise of *bluntness, decency, the general interest, and stability,* conceals incapacity for progress, greedy self-indulgence, selfishness, sectional interest, and evil intent. It declares him an artful *monopolist*; it pours cold water on his reminiscences, his poetry, and his romanticism by a historical and sarcastic enumeration of the baseness, cruelty, degradation, prostitution, infamy, anarchy and rebellion, of which romantic castles were the workshops.

It claims to have obtained political freedom for the people; to have loosed the chains which fettered civil society; to have linked together different worlds; to have created trade promoting friendship between the peoples; to have created pure morality and an agreeable degree of culture; to have given the people civilized needs in place of their crude wants, and the means of satisfying them. Meanwhile, it claims, the landowner—this idle, troublesome, parasitic grain-jobber—raises the price of the people's basic necessities and so forces the capitalist to raise wages without being able to increase productivity, thus impeding the growth of the nation's annual income, the accumulation of capital, and therefore the possibility of providing work for the people and wealth for the country, eventually canceling it, thus producing a general decline—whilst he parasitically exploits *every* advantage of modern civilization without doing the least thing for it, and without even abating in the slightest his feudal prejudices. Finally, let him—for whom the cultivation of the land and the land itself exist only as a source of money, which comes to him as a present— let him just take a look at his *tenant farmer* and say whether he himself is not a *"naive," deluded, sly* scoundrel who in his heart and in actual fact has for a long time belonged to *free* industry and to *beloved* trade, however much he may protest and prattle about historical memories and ethical or political goals. Everything which he can really advance to justify himself is true only of the *cultivator of the land* (the capitalist and the laborers), of whom the *landowner* is rather the *enemy*. Thus he gives evidence against himself. *Without* capital landed property is dead, worthless matter. It has been exactly movable property's civilized victory to have discovered and made human labor the source of wealth in place of the dead thing. (See Paul Louis Courier, Saint-Simon, Ganilh, Ricardo, Mill, McCulloch and Destutt de Tracy, and Michel Chevalier.) [8]

The *real* course of development (to be inserted at this point) results in the necessary victory of the *capitalist* over the *landowner* —that is to say, of developed over undeveloped immature private property—just as in general, movement must triumph over immobility—open, self-conscious baseness over hidden, unconscious baseness; *greed* over *self-indulgence*; the avowedly restless, adroit self-interest of *enlightenment* over the parochial, worldwise, naive, idle and deluded *self-interest of superstition;* and *money* over the other forms of private property.

Those states which divine something of the danger attaching to fully developed free industry, to fully developed pure morality and to fully developed philanthropic trade, try, but in vain, to hold in check the capitalization of landed property.

Landed property in its distinction from capital is private property—capital—still afflicted with *local* and political prejudices; it is capital which has not yet regained itself from its entanglement with the world—capital not yet *fully developed*. It must achieve its abstract, that is, its *pure,* expression in the course of its *worldwide development*.

The character of *private property* is expressed by labor, capital, and the relations between these two.

The movement through which these constituents have to pass is:

[*First*] *Unmediated* or *mediated unity of the two.*

Capital and labor, at first still united. Then, though separated and estranged, they reciprocally develop and promote each other as *positive* conditions.

[*Second*] *The two in opposition,* mutually excluding each other. The worker knows the capitalist as his own non-existence, and vice versa: each tries to rob the other of his existence.

[*Third*] *Opposition* of each *to* itself. Capital=stored-up labor = labor. Capital as such—splitting into capital *itself* and into its *interest,* and this latter again into *interest* and *profit*. The capitalist completely sacrificed. He falls into the working class, whilst the worker (but only exceptionally) becomes a capitalist. Labor as a moment of capital—its *costs*. Thus the wages of labor —a sacrifice of capital.

Splitting of labor into *labor itself* and the *wages of labor*. The worker himself a capital, a commodity.

Clash of mutual contradictions.

[*The second manuscript ends here.*]

PRIVATE PROPERTY AND LABOR

Re: p. XXXVI.[1] The *subjective essence* of private property—*private property* as activity for itself,[2] *as subject,* as *person*—is *labor.* It is therefore evident that only the political economy which acknowledged *labor* as its principle (Adam Smith), and which therefore no longer looked upon private property as a mere *condition* external to man—that it is this political economy which has to be regarded on the one hand as a product of the real *energy* and the real *movement* of private property*—as a product of modern *industry*—and on the other hand, as a force which has quickened and glorified the energy and development of modern *industry* and made it a power in the realm of *consciousness.*

To this enlightened political economy, which has discovered within private property the *subjective essence* of wealth, the ad-herents of the money and mercantile system, who look upon private property *only as an objective* substance [3] confronting men, seem therefore to be *fetishists,*[4] *Catholics. Engels* was therefore right to call *Adam Smith the Luther of Political Economy.*[5] Just as Luther recognized *religion—faith*—as the substance of the external *world* and in consequence stood opposed to Catholic paganism —just as he superseded [6] *external* religiosity by making religiosity the *inner* substance of man—just as he negated the priests outside the layman because he transplanted the priest into laymen's hearts, just so with wealth: wealth as something outside man and independent of him, and therefore as something to be maintained and asserted only in an external fashion, is done away with; that is, this *external, mindless, objectivity* of wealth is done away with, with private property being incorporated in man himself and with man himself being recognized as its essence. But as a result man is brought within the orbit of private property, just as with Luther he is brought within the orbit of religion. Under the

* It is a movement of private property become independent for itself in consciousness—the modern industry as Self.

semblance of recognizing man, political economy, whose principle is labor, rather carries to its logical conclusion the denial of man, since man himself no longer stands in an external relation of tension to the external substance of private property, but has himself become this essence of private property. What was previously being *external* to oneself—man's externalization in the thing—has merely become the act of externalizing—the process of alienating.[7]

This political economy begins by seeming to acknowledge man (his independence, spontaneity, etc.); then locating private property in man's own being, it can no longer be conditioned by the local, national or other *characteristics of private property* as of *something existing outside itself*. This political economy, consequently, displays a *cosmopolitan,* universal energy which overthrows every restriction and bond so as to establish itself instead as the *sole* politics, the sole universality, the sole limit and sole bond. Hence it must throw aside this *hypocrisy* in the course of its further development and come out *in its complete cynicism.* And this it does—untroubled by all the apparent contradictions in which it becomes involved—by developing the idea of *labor* much *more one-sidedly,* and therefore *more sharply* and *more consistently,* as the sole *essence of wealth;* by proving the implications of this theory to be *anti-human* in character, in contrast to the other, original approach. Finally, by dealing the deathblow to ground rent—that last, *individual, natural* mode of private property and source of wealth existing independently of the movement of labor, that expression of feudal property, an expression which has already become wholly economic in character and therefore incapable of resisting political economy. (The *Ricardo* school.)

There is not merely a relative growth in the *cynicism* of political economy from Smith through Say to Ricardo, Mill, etc., inasmuch as the implications of *industry* appear more developed and more contradictory in the eyes of the last-named; these later economists also advance in a positive sense constantly and consciously further than their predecessors in their estrangement from man. They do so, however, *only* because their science develops more consistently and genuinely. Because they make private property

in its active form the subject, thus simultaneously making man—
and man as something unessential—the essence,[8] the contradiction
of reality corresponds completely to the contradictory essence
which they accept as their principle. Far from refuting it, the
ruptured *world of industry* confirms their *self-ruptured* principle.
Their principle is, after all, the principle of this rupture.

The physiocratic doctrine of Dr. *Quesnay* [9] forms the transition
from the mercantile system to Adam Smith. *Physiocracy* represents
in political economy directly the decomposition of feudal property, but it therefore just as directly represents its *metamorphosis*
and restoration, save that now its language is no longer feudal
but economic. All wealth is resolved into *land* and *cultivation*
(agriculture). Land is not yet *capital*: it is still a *special* mode of
its existence, the validity of which is supposed to lie in, and to
derive from, its natural peculiarity. Yet land is a general natural
element, whilst the mercantile system admits the existence of
wealth only in the form of *precious metal.* Thus the *object* of
wealth—its matter—has straightway obtained the highest degree
of generality within the *bounds of nature,* in so far also as *nature*
it is immediate objective wealth. And land only exists for *man*
through labor, through agriculture.

Thus the subjective essence of wealth has already been trans-
ferred to labor. But at the same time agriculture is the *only productive* labor. Hence, labor is not yet grasped in its generality and
abstraction: it is still bound to a particular *natural element as
its matter,* and it is therefore only recognized in a *particular mode
of existence determined by nature.* It is therefore still only a
specific, particular alienation of man, just as its product is conceived only as a specific form of wealth, due more to nature than
to labor itself. The land is here still recognized as a phenomenon
of nature independent of man—not yet as capital, i.e., as an aspect
of labor itself. Labor appears, rather, as an aspect of the *land.* But
since the fetishism of the old external wealth, of wealth existing
only as an object, has been reduced to a very simple natural element, and since its essence—even if only partially and in a particular form—has been recognized within its subjective existence, the
necessary step forward has been made in revealing the *general*

nature of wealth and hence in the raising of *labor* in its total absoluteness (i.e., its abstraction) as the *principle*. It is argued against physiocracy that *agriculture,* from the economic point of view—that is to say, from the only valid point of view—does not differ from any other industry; and that the *essence* of wealth, therefore, is not a *specific* form of labor bound to a particular element—a particular expression of labor—but *labor in general.*

Physiocracy denies *particular,* external, merely objective wealth by declaring labor to be the *essence* of wealth. But for physiocracy labor is from the outset only the *subjective essence* of landed property. (It takes its departure from the type of property which historically appears as the dominant and acknowledged type.) It only turns landed property into *alienated man.* It annuls its feudal character by declaring *industry* (agriculture) as its *essence.* But its attitude to the world of industry is one of denial; it acknowledges the feudal system by declaring *agriculture* to be the *only* industry.

It is clear that if the *subjective essence* of industry is now grasped (of industry in opposition to landed property, i.e., of industry constituting itself as industry), this essence includes within itself its opposite. For just as industry incorporates annulled landed property, the *subjective essence* of industry at the same time incorporates the subjective essence of *landed property.*

Just as landed property is the first form of private property, with industry at first confronting it historically merely as a special kind of property—or, rather, as landed property's liberated slave—so this process repeats itself in the scientific understanding of the *subjective* essence of private property, *labor.* Labor appears at first only as *agricultural labor;* but then asserts itself as *labor* in general.

All wealth has become *industrial* wealth, the wealth of *labor;* and *industry* is accomplished labor, just as the *factory system* is the essence of *industry*—of labor—brought to its maturity, and just as *industrial capital* is the accomplished objective form of private property.

We can now see how it is only at this point that private property can complete its dominion over man and become, in its most general form, a world-historical power.

PRIVATE PROPERTY AND
COMMUNISM

Re: p. XXXIX.[1] The antithesis between *lack of property* and *property,* so long as it is not comprehended as the antithesis of *labor* and *capital,* still remains an indifferent antithesis, not grasped in its *active connection,* with its *internal* relation—an antithesis not yet grasped as a *contradiction.* It can find expression in this *first* form even without the advanced development of private property (as in ancient Rome, Turkey, etc.). It does not yet *appear* as having been established by private property itself. But labor, the subjective essence of private property as exclusion of property, and capital, objective labor as exclusion of labor, constitute *private property* as its developed state of contradiction— hence a dynamic relationship moving to its resolution.

Re: the same page. The transcendence [2] of self-estrangement follows the same course as self-estrangement. *Private property* is first considered only in its objective aspect—but nevertheless with labor as its essence. Its form of existence is therefore *capital,* which is to be annulled "as such" (Proudhon). Or a *particular form* of labor—labor leveled down, parceled, and therefore unfree—is conceived as the source of private property's *perniciousness* and of its existence in estrangement from men. For instance, *Fourier,* who, like the physiocrats, also conceived *agricultural labor* to be at least the *exemplary* type, whilst *Saint-Simon* declares in contrast that *industrial labor* as such is the essence, and only aspires to the *exclusive* rule of the industrialists and the improvement of the workers' condition. Finally, *communism* is the *positive* expression of annulled private property—at first as *universal* private property. By embracing this relation as a *whole,* communism is:

(1) In its first form only a *generalization* and *consummation* of this relationship. As such it appears in a twofold form: on the one

132

hand, the dominion of *material* property bulks so large that it wants to destroy *everything* which is not capable of being possessed by all as *private property*. It wants to do away *by force* with talent, etc. For it the sole purpose of life and existence is direct, physical *possession*. The task of the *laborer* is not done away with, but extended to all men. The relationship of private property persists as the relationship of the community to the world of things.

Finally, this movement of opposing universal private property to private property finds expression in the animal form of opposing to *marriage* (certainly a *form of exclusive private property*) the *community of women,* in which a woman becomes a piece of *communal* and *common* property. It may be said that this idea of the *community of women* gives away the *secret* of this as yet completely crude and thoughtless communism.[3] Just as woman passes from marriage to general prostitution,* so the entire world of wealth (that is, of man's objective substance) passes from the relationship of exclusive marriage with the owner of private property to a state of universal prostitution with the community. In negating the *personality* of man in every sphere, this type of communism is really nothing but the logical expression of private property, which is its negation. General *envy* constituting itself as a power is the disguise in which *greed* reestablishes itself and satisfies itself, only in *another* way. The thought of every piece of private property—inherent in each piece as such—is *at least* turned against all *wealthier* private property in the form of envy and the urge to reduce things to a common level, so that this envy and urge even constitute the essence of competition. The crude communism is only the culmination of this envy and of this leveling-down proceeding from the *preconceived* minimum. It has a *definite, limited* standard. How little this annulment of private property is really an appropriation is in fact proved by the abstract negation of the entire world of culture and civiliza-

---

* Prostitution is only a *specific* expression of the *general* prostitution of the *laborer*, and since it is a relationship in which falls not the prostitute alone, but also the one who prostitutes—and the latter's abomination is still greater—the capitalist, etc., also comes under this head.

tion, the regression to the *unnatural* simplicity of the *poor and undemanding* man who has not only failed to go beyond private property, but has not yet even reached it.

The community is only a community of *labor*, and of equality of *wages* paid out by communal capital—the *community* as the universal capitalist. Both sides of the relationship are raised to an *imagined* universality—*labor* as a state in which every person is placed, and *capital* as the acknowledged universality and power of the community.

In the approach to *woman* as the spoil and handmaid of communal lust is expressed the infinite degradation in which man exists for himself, for the secret of this approach has its *unambiguous*, decisive, *plain* and undisguised expression in the relation of *man* to *woman* and in the manner in which the *direct* and *natural* species relationship is conceived. This direct, natural, and necessary relation of person to person is the *relation of man to woman*. In this *natural* species relationship man's relation to nature is immediately his relation to man, just as his relation to man is immediately his relation to nature—his own *natural* destination. In this relationship, therefore, is *sensuously manifested*, reduced to an observable *fact*, the extent to which the human essence has become nature to man, or to which nature to him has become the human essence of man. From this relationship one can therefore judge man's whole level of development. From the character of this relationship follows how much *man* as a *species being*, as *man*, has come to be himself and to comprehend himself; the relation of man to woman is *the most natural* relation of human being to human being. It therefore reveals the extent to which man's *natural* behavior has become *human*, or the extent to which the *human* essence in him has become a *natural* essence—the extent to which his *human nature* has come to be *nature to him*. In this relationship is revealed, too, the extent to which man's *need* has become a *human* need; the extent to which, therefore, the *other* person as a person has become for him a need—the extent to which he in his individual existence is at the same time a social being.

The first positive annulment of private property—*crude* communism—is thus merely one *form* in which the vileness of private property, which wants to set itself up as the *positive community, comes to the surface.*

(2) Communism (*a*) still political in nature—democratic or despotic; (*b*) with the abolition of the state, yet still incomplete, and being still affected by private property (i.e., by the estrangement of man). In both forms communism already is aware of being reintegration or return of man to himself, the transcendence of human self-estrangement; but since it has not yet grasped the positive essence of private property, and just as little the *human* nature of need, it remains captive to it and infected by it. It has, indeed, grasped its concept, but not its essence.[4]

(3) *Communism* as the *positive* transcendence of *private property,* as *human self-estrangement,* and therefore as the real *appropriation of the human* essence by and for man; communism therefore as the complete return of man to himself as a *social* (i.e., human) being—a return become conscious, and accomplished within the entire wealth of previous development. This communism, as fully developed naturalism, equals humanism,[5] and as fully developed humanism equals naturalism; it is the *genuine* resolution of the conflict between man and nature and between man and man—the true resolution of the strife between existence and essence, between objectification and self-confirmation, between freedom and necessity, between the individual and the species. Communism is the riddle of history solved, and it knows itself to be this solution.

The entire movement of history is, therefore, both its *actual* act of genesis (the birth act of its empirical existence) and also for its thinking consciousness the *comprehended* and *known* process of its *becoming.* That other, still immature communism, meanwhile, seeks an *historical* proof for itself—a proof in the realm of what already exists—among disconnected historical phenomena opposed to private property, tearing single phases from the historical process and focusing attention on them as proofs of its historical pedigree (a hobbyhorse ridden hard especially by Cabet, Villegardelle, etc.).[6] By so doing it simply makes clear that by far the greater part of this process contradicts its own claim, and that, if it has ever existed, precisely its being in the *past* refutes its pretension to being *essential being.*

It is easy to see that the entire revolutionary movement necessarily finds both its empirical and its theoretical basis in the movement of *private property*—more precisely, in that of the economy.

This *material,* immediately perceptible private property is the material perceptible expression of *estranged human* life. Its movement—production and consumption—is the *perceptible* revelation of the movement of all production until now, i.e., the realization or the reality of man. Religion, family, state, law, morality, science, art, etc., are only *particular* modes of production, and fall under its general law. The positive transcendence of *private property,* as the appropriation of *human* life, is therefore the positive transcendence of all estrangement—that is to say, the return of man from religion, family, state, etc., to his *human,* i.e., *social* existence. Religious estrangement as such occurs only in the realm of *consciousness,* of man's inner life, but economic estrangement is that of *real life;* its transcendence therefore embraces both aspects. It is evident that the *initial* stage of the movement amongst the various peoples depends on whether the true and *authentic* life of the people manifests itself more in consciousness or in the external world—is more ideal or real. Communism begins from the outset (*Owen*) [7] with atheism; but atheism is at first far from being *communism;* indeed, it is still mostly an abstraction.

The philanthropy of atheism is therefore at first only *philosophical,* abstract, philanthropy, and that of communism is at once *real* and directly bent on *action.*

We have seen how on the assumption of positively annulled private property man produces man—himself and the other man; how the object, being the direct embodiment of his individuality, is simultaneously his own existence for the other man, the existence of the other man, and that existence for him. Likewise, however, both the material of labor and man as the subject, are the point of departure as well as the result of the movement (and precisely in this fact, that they must constitute the *point of departure,* lies the historical *necessity* of private property). Thus the *social* character is the general character of the whole movement: *just as* society itself produces *man as man,* so is society *produced* by him. Activity and mind, both in their content and in their *mode of existence,* are *social*: *social* activity and *social* mind. The *human* essence of nature first exists only for *social* man; for only here does nature exist for him as a *bond* with *man* —as his existence for the other and the other's existence for him— as the life-element of human reality. Only here does nature exist as the *foundation* of his own *human* existence. Only here has what is to him his *natural* existence become his *human* existence, and nature become man for him. Thus *society* is the unity of being of man with nature—the true resurrection of nature— the naturalism of man and the humanism of nature both brought to fulfillment.

Social activity and social mind exist by no means *only* in the form of some *directly* communal activity and directly *communal* mind, although *communal* activity and *communial* mind—i.e., activity and mind which are manifested and directly revealed in *real association* with other men—will occur wherever such a *direct* expression of sociability stems from the true character of the activity's content and is adequate to its nature.

But also when I am active *scientifically,* etc.,—when I am engaged in activity which I can seldom perform in direct community with others—then I am *social,* because I am active as a *man.* Not only is the material of my activity given to me as a social product (as is even the language in which the thinker is active): my *own* existence *is* social activity, and therefore that which I make of myself, I make of myself for society and with the consciousness of myself as a social being.

My *general* consciousness is only the *theoretical* shape of that which the *living* shape is the *real* community, the social fabric, although at the present day *general* consciousness is an abstraction from real life and as such confronts it with hostility. The *activity* of my general consciousness, as an activity, is therefore also my *theoretical* existence as a social being.

Above all we must avoid postulating "Society" again as an

abstraction *vis-à-vis* the individual. The individual *is the social being*. His life, even if it may not appear in the direct form of a *communal* life in association with others—is therefore an expression and confirmation of *social life*. Man's individual and species life are not *different*, however much—and this is inevitable —the mode of existence of the individual is a more *particular*, or more *general* mode of the life of the species, or the life of the species is a more *particular* or more *general* individual life.

In his *consciousness of species* man confirms his real *social life* and simply repeats his real existence in thought, just as conversely the being of the species confirms itself in species-consciousness and exists for *itself* in its generality as a thinking being.

Man, much as he may therefore be a *particular* individual (and it is precisely his particularity which makes him an individual, and a real *individual* social being), is just as much the *totality*— the ideal totality—the subjective existence of thought and experienced society for itself; just as he exists also in the real world as the awareness and the real mind of social existence, and as a totality of human manifestation of life.

Thinking and being are thus no doubt *distinct*, but at the same time they are in *unity* with each other.

Death seems to be a harsh victory of the species over the *definite* individual and to contradict their unity. But the particular individual is only a *particular species being*, and as such mortal.

(4) Just as *private property* is only the perceptible expression of the fact that man becomes *objective* for himself and at the same time becomes to himself a strange and inhuman object; just as it expresses the fact that the assertion of his life is the alienation of his life, that his realization is his loss of reality,[8] is an *alien* reality: so, the positive transcendence of private property—i.e., the *perceptible* appropriation for and by man of the human essence and of human life, of objective man, of human *achievements*—should not to be conceived merely in the sense of *immediate,* one-sided *gratification*—merely in the sense of *possessing*, of *having*. Man appropriates his total essence in a total manner, that is to say, as a whole man. Each of his *human* relations to the world—seeing, hearing, smelling, tasting, feeling, thinking, observing, experi-

encing, wanting, acting, loving—in short, all the organs of his individual being, like those organs which are directly social in their form, are in their *objective* orientation or in their *orientation to the object,* the appropriation of that object. The appropriation of *human* reality;* its orientation to the object is the *manifestation of the human reality,* it is human *activity* and human *suffering,* for suffering, humanly considered, is a self-indulgence of man.

Private property has made us so stupid and one-sided that an object is only *ours* when we have it—when it exists for us as capital, or when it is directly possessed, eaten, drunk, worn, inhabited, etc.,—in short, when it is *used* by us. Although private property itself again conceives all these direct realizations of possession only as *means of life,* and the life which they serve as means is the *life of private property*—labor and conversion into capital.

All these physical and mental senses have therefore—the sheer estrangement of *all* these senses—the sense of *having.* The human being had to be reduced to this absolute poverty in order that he might yield his inner wealth to the outer world. (On the category of "*having,*" see Hess in the *Twenty-One Sheets.*[9])

The transcendence of private property is therefore the complete *emancipation* of all human senses and qualities, but it is this emancipation precisely because these senses and attributes have become, subjectively and objectively, *human.* The eye has become a *human* eye, just as its *object* has become a social, *human* object —an object made by man for man. The *senses* have therefore become directly in their practice *theoreticians.* They relate themselves to the *thing* for the sake of the thing, but the thing itself is an *objective human* relation to itself and to man,† and vice versa. Need or enjoyment have consequently lost their *egotistical* nature, and nature has lost its mere *utility* by use becoming *human* use.

In the same way, the senses and minds of other men have

---

* For this reason it is just as highly varied as the *determinations* of human *essence* and *activities.*

† In practice I can relate myself to a thing humanly only if the thing relates itself humanly to the human being.

become my *own* appropriation. Besides these direct organs, therefore, *social* organs develop in the *form* of society; thus, for instance, activity in direct association with others, etc., has become an organ for *expressing* my own *life,* and a mode of appropriating *human* life.

It is obvious that the *human* eye enjoys things in a way different from the crude, non-human eye; the human *ear* different from the crude ear, etc.

To recapitulate: man is not lost in his object only when the object becomes for him a *human* object or objective man. This is possible only when the object becomes for him a *social* object, he himself for himself a social being, just as society becomes a being for him in this object.

On the one hand, therefore, it is only when the objective world becomes everywhere for man in society the world of man's essential powers [10]—human reality, and for that reason the reality of his *own* essential powers—that all *objects* become for him the *objectification of himself,* become objects which confirm and realize his individuality, become *his* objects: that is, *man himself* becomes the object. The manner in which they become *his* depends on the *nature of the objects* and on the nature of the *essential power* corresponding *to it;* for it is precisely the *determinate nature* of this relationship which shapes the particular, *real* mode of affirmation. To the *eye* an object comes to be other than it is to the *ear,* and the object of the eye is another object than the object of the *ear.* The specific character of each essential power is precisely its *specific essence,* and therefore also the specific mode of its objectification, of its *objectively actual* living *being.* Thus man is affirmed in the objective world not only in the act of thinking, but with *all* his senses.

On the other hand, let us look at this in its subjective aspect. Just as music alone awakens in man the sense of music, and just as the most beautiful music has *no* sense for the unmusical ear—is no object for it, because my object can only be the confirmation of one of my essential powers. It can therefore only be so for me as my essential power exists for itself as a subjective capacity, because the meaning of an object for me goes only so far as *my* senses go (has only a meaning for a sense corresponding to that object[11])—for this reason the *senses* of the social man are *other* senses than those of the non-social man. Only through the objectively unfolded richness of man's essential being is the richness of subjective *human* sensibility (a musical ear, an eye for beauty of form—in short, *senses* capable of human gratification, senses affirming themselves as essential powers of *man*) either cultivated or brought into being. For not only the five senses but also the so-called mental senses—the practical senses (will, love, etc.)—in a word, *human* sense—the human nature of the senses—comes to be by virtue of its object, by virtue of *humanized* nature. The *forming* of the five senses is a labor of the entire history of the world down to the present.

The *sense* caught up in crude practical need has only a restricted sense. For the starving man, it is not the human form of food that exists, but only its abstract being as food. It could just as well be there in its crudest form, and it would be impossible to say wherein this feeding activity differs from that of *animals*. The care-burdened man in need has no sense for the finest play; the dealer in minerals sees only the commercial value but not the beauty and the unique nature of the mineral: he has no mineralogical sense. Thus, the objectification of the human essence, both in its theoretical and practical aspects, is required to make man's *sense human*, as well as to create the *human sense* corresponding to the entire wealth of human and natural substance.

Just as through the movement of *private property*, of its wealth as well as its poverty—or of its material and spiritual wealth and poverty—the budding society finds at hand all the material for this *development*, so *established* society produces man in this entire richness of his being—produces the *rich* man *profoundly endowed with all the senses*—as its enduring reality.

We see how subjectivism and objectivism, spiritualism and materialism, activity and suffering, only lose their antithetical character, and thus their existence as such antitheses in social centers; we see how the resolution of the *theoretical* antitheses is *only* possible *in a practical* way, by virtue of the practical energy of man. Their resolution is therefore by no means merely a problem of understanding, but a *real* problem of life, which *philosophy* could not solve precisely because it conceived this problem as *merely* a theoretical one.

We see how the history of *industry* and the established *objective* existence of industry are the *open book* of *man's essential powers*, the exposure to the senses of human *psychology*. Hitherto this was not conceived in its inseparable connection with man's *essential being*, but only in an external relation of utility, because, moving in the realm of estrangement, people could only think of man's general mode of being—religion or history in its abstract-general character as politics, art, literature, etc.—as the reality of man's essential powers and *man's species activity*. We have before us the *objectified essential powers* of man in the form of *sensuous, alien, useful objects,* in the form of estrangement, displayed in *ordinary material industry* (which can be conceived as well as a part of that general movement, just as that movement can be conceived as a *particular* part of industry, since all human activity hitherto has been labor—that is, industry—activity estranged from itself).

A *psychology* for which this, the part of history most contemporary and accessible to sense, remains a closed book, cannot become a genuine, comprehensive and *real* science. What indeed are we to think of a science which *airily* abstracts from this large part of human labor and which fails to feel its own incompleteness, while such a wealth of human endeavor, unfolded before it, means nothing more to it than, perhaps, what can be expressed in one word—*"need," "vulgar need"*?

The *natural sciences* have developed an enormous activity and have accumulated an ever-growing mass of material. Philosophy, however, has remained just as alien to them as they remain to philosophy. Their momentary unity was only a *chimerical illusion*. The will was there, but the means were lacking. Even historiography pays regard to natural science only occasionally, as a factor of enlightenment, utility, and of some special great discoveries. But natural science has invaded and transformed human life all the more *practically* through the medium of industry; and has prepared human emancipation, although its immediate effect had to be the furthering of the dehumanization of man. *Industry* is the *actual*, historical relationship of nature, and therefore of natural science, to man. If, therefore, industry is conceived as the *exoteric* revelation of man's *essential powers*, we also gain an understanding of the *human* essence of nature or the *natural* essence of man. In consequence, natural science will lose its abstractly material—or rather, its idealistic—tendency, and will become the basis of *human* science, as it has already become the basis of actual human life, albeit in an estranged form. *One* basis for life and another basis for *science* is *a priori* a lie. The nature which develops in human history—the genesis of human society—is man's *real* nature; hence nature as it develops through industry, even though in an *estranged* form, is true *anthropological* nature.

Sense-perception (see Feuerbach) must be the basis of all science. Only when it proceeds from sense-perception in the twofold form both of *sensuous* consciousness and of *sensuous* need—that is, only when science proceeds from nature—is it *true* science. All history is the preparation for *"man"* to become the object of *sensuous* consciousness, and for the needs of "man as man" to become [natural, sensuous] needs. History itself is a *real* part of *natural history*—of nature developing into man. Natural science will in time incorporate into itself the science of man, just as the science of man will incorporate into itself natural science: there will be *one* science.

Man is the immediate object of natural science; for immediate, *sensuous nature* for man is, immediately, human sensuousness (the expressions are identical)—presented immediately in the form of the *other* man sensuously present for him. Indeed, his own sensuousness first exists as human sensuousness for himself through the *other* man. But *nature* is the immediate object of the *science of man*: the first object of man—man—is nature, sensuousness; and the particular sensuous human essential powers can only find their self-understanding in the science of the natural world in general, since they can find their objective realization in *natural* objects only. The element of thought itself—the element of thought's living expression—*language*—is of a sensuous nature. The *social* reality of nature, and *human* natural science, or the *natural science about man*, are identical terms.

It will be seen how in place of the *wealth* and *poverty* of political economy comes the *rich human being* and the rich *human* need. The *rich* human being is simultaneously the human being *in need of* a totality of human manifestations of life—the man in whom his own realization exists as an inner necessity, as *need*.[12] Not only *wealth*, but likewise the *poverty* of man—under the assumption of socialism—receives in equal measure a *human* and therefore social significance. Poverty is the passive bond which causes the human being to experience the need of the greatest wealth—the *other* human being. The dominion of the objective being in me, the sensuous outburst of my life activity, is *passion*, which thus becomes here the *activity* of my being.

(5) A *being* only considers himself independent when he stands on his own feet; and he only stands on his own feet when he owes his *existence* to himself. A man who lives by the grace of another regards himself as a dependent being. But I live completely by the grace of another if I owe him not only the maintenance of my life, but if he has, moreover, *created* my *life*—if he is the *source* of my life. When it is not of my own creation, my life has necessarily a source of this kind outside of it. The *Creation* is therefore an idea very difficult to dislodge from popular consciousness. The fact that nature and man exist in their own account is *incomprehensible* to it, because it contradicts everything *tangible* in practical life.

The creation of the *earth* has received a mighty blow from geogeny—i.e., from the science which presents the formation of the earth, the further development of the earth, as a process, as a self-generation. *Generatio aequivoca*[13] is the only practical refutation of the theory of creation.

Now it is certainly easy to say to the single individual what Aristotle has already said: You have been begotten by your father and your mother; therefore in you the mating of two human beings—a species-act of human beings—has produced the human being. You see, therefore, that even physically, man owes his existence to man. Therefore you must not only keep sight of the *one* aspect—the *infinite* progression which leads you further to enquire: "Who begot my father? Who his grandfather?," etc. You must also hold on to the *circular movement* sensuously percep-

tible in that progression, by which man repeats himself in procreation, *man* thus always remaining the subject. You will reply,
however: I grant you this circular movement; now grant me the
progression which drives me ever further until I ask: Who begot
the first man, and nature as a whole? I can only answer you: Your
question is itself a product of abstraction. Ask yourself how you
arrived at that question. Ask yourself whether your question is
not posed from a standpoint to which I cannot reply, because it
is wrongly put. Ask yourself whether that progression as such
exists for a reasonable mind. When you ask about the creation of
nature and man, you are abstracting, in so doing, from man and
nature. You postulate them as *non-existent,* and yet you want me
to prove them to you as *existing.* Now I say to you: Give up your
abstraction and you will also give up your question. Or if you
want to hold on to your abstraction, then be consistent, and if you
think of man and nature as *non-existent,* then think of yourself
as non-existent, for you too are surely nature and man. Don't
think, don't ask me, for as soon as you think and ask, your *abstraction* from the existence of nature and man has no meaning.
Or are you such an egotist that you conceive everything as nothing, and yet want yourself to exist?

You can reply: I do not want to conceive the nothingness of
nature, etc. I ask you about *its genesis,* just as I ask the anatomist
about the formation of bones, etc.

But since for the socialist man the *entire so-called history of
the world* is nothing but the creation of man through human
labor, nothing but the emergence of nature for man, so he has the
visible, irrefutable proof of his *birth* through himself, of the
process of his creation. Since the *real existence* of man and nature
—since man has become for man as the being of nature, and nature for man as the being of man has become practical, sensuous,
perceptible—the question about an *alien* being, about a being
above nature and man—a question which implies the admission
of the unreality of nature and of man—has become impossible in
practice. *Atheism,* as the denial of this unreality, has no longer
any meaning, for atheism is a *negation of God,* and postulates the
existence of man through this negation; but socialism as socialism

no longer stands in any need of such a mediation. It proceeds from the *practically and theoretically sensuous consciousness* of man and of nature as the *essence*. Socialism is man's *positive self-consciousness,* no longer mediated through the annulment of religion, just as *real life* is man's positive reality, no longer mediated through the annulment of private property, through *communism.* Communism is the position as the negation of the negation, and is hence the *actual* phase necessary for the next stage of historical development in the process of human emancipation and rehabilitation. *Communism* is the necessary pattern and the dynamic principle of the immediate future, but communism as such is not the goal of human development—which goal is the structure of human society.[14]

THE MEANING OF HUMAN
REQUIREMENTS

We have seen what significance, given socialism, the *wealth* of human needs has, and what significance, therefore, both a *new mode of production* and a new *object* of production have: a new manifestation of the forces of *human* nature and a new enrichment of *human* nature.[1] Under private property their significance is reversed: every person speculates on creating a *new* need in another, so as to drive him to a fresh sacrifice, to place him in a new dependence and to seduce him into a new mode of *gratification* and therefore economic ruin. Each tries to establish over the other an *alien power,* so as thereby to find satisfaction of his own selfish need. The increase in the quantity of objects is accompanied by an extension of the realm of the alien powers to which man is subjected, and every new product represents a new *possibility* of mutual swindling and mutual plundering. Man becomes ever poorer as man, his need for *money* becomes ever greater if he wants to overpower hostile being. The power of his *money* declines so to say in inverse proportion to the increase in the volume of production: that is, his neediness grows as the *power* of money increases.

The need for money is therefore the true need produced by the modern economic system, and it is the only need which the latter produces. The *quantity* of money becomes to an ever greater degree its sole *effective* quality. Just as it reduces everything to its abstract form, so it reduces itself in the course of its own movement to *quantitative* entity. *Excess* and *intemperance* come to be its true norm. Subjectively, this is partly manifested in that the extension of products and needs falls into *contriving* and ever-*calculating* subservience to inhuman, unnatural and *imaginary* appetites. Private property does not know how to change crude need into *human* need. Its *idealism* is *fantasy,*

147

caprice and *whim*; and no eunuch flatters his despot more basely or uses more despicable means to stimulate his dulled capacity for pleasure in order to sneak a favor for himself than does the industrial eunuch—the producer—in order to sneak for himself a few pennies—in order to charm the golden birds out of the pockets of his dearly beloved neighbors in Christ. He puts himself at the service of the other's most depraved fancies, plays the pimp between him and his need, excites in him morbid appetites, lies in wait for each of his weaknesses—all so that he can then demand the cash for this service of love. (Every product is a bait with which to seduce away the other's very being, his money; every real and possible need is a weakness which will lead the fly to the gluepot. General exploitation of communal human nature, just as every imperfection in man, is a bond with heaven—an avenue giving the priest access to his heart; every need is an opportunity to approach one's neighbor under the guise of the utmost amiability and to say to him: Dear friend, I give you what you need, but you know the *conditio sine qua non*; [2] you know the ink in which you have to sign yourself over to me; in providing for your pleasure, I fleece you.)

This estrangement manifests itself in part in that it produces sophistication of needs and of their means on the one hand, and a bestial barbarization, a complete, unrefined, abstract simplicity of need, on the other; or rather in that it merely resurrects itself in its opposite. Even the need for fresh air ceases for the worker. Man returns to a cave dwelling, which is now, however, contaminated with the pestilential breath of civilization, and which he continues to occupy only *precariously,* it being for him an alien habitation which can be withdrawn from him any day— a place from which, if he does not pay, he can be thrown out any day. For this mortuary he has to *pay.* A dwelling in the *light,* which Prometheus in Aeschylus designated as one of the greatest boons, by means of which he made the savage into a human being,[3] ceases to exist for the worker. Light, air, etc.—the simplest *animal* cleanliness—ceases to be a need for man. *Filth,* this stagnation and putrefaction of man—the *sewage* of civilization (speaking quite literally)—comes to be the *element of life* for him. Utter, *unnatural* neglect, putrefied nature, comes to be his *life-element*. None of his senses exist any longer, and not only in his human fashion, but in an *inhuman* fashion, and therefore not even in an animal fashion. The crudest *methods* (and *instruments*) of human labor are coming back: the *treadmill* of the Roman slaves, for instance, is the means of production, the means of existence, of many English workers. It is not only that man has no human needs—even his *animal* needs cease to exist. The Irishman no longer knows any need now but the need to *eat,* and indeed only the need to eat *potatoes*—and *scabby potatoes* at that, the worst kind of potatoes. But in each of their industrial towns England and France have already a *little* Ireland. The savage and the animal have at least the need to hunt, to roam, etc.—the need of companionship. Machine labor is simplified in order to make a worker out of the human being still in the making, the completely immature human being, the *child*—whilst the worker has become a neglected child. The machine accommodates itself to the *weakness* of the human being in order to make the *weak* human being into a machine.

How the multiplication of needs and of the means of their satisfaction breeds the absence of needs and of means is demonstrated by the political economist (and the capitalist: it should be noted that it is always *empirical* businessmen we are talking about when we refer to political economists, their *scientific* confession and existence). This he shows:

(1) By reducing the worker's need to the barest and most miserable level of physical subsistence, and by reducing his activity to the most abstract mechanical movement, he says: Man has no other need either of activity or of enjoyment. For he calls *even* this life *human* life and existence.

(2) By *counting* the *lowest* possible level of life (existence) as the standard, indeed, as the general standard—general because it is applicable to the mass of men. He changes the worker into an insensible being lacking all needs, just as he changes his activity into a pure abstraction from all activity. To him, therefore, every *luxury* of the worker seems to be reprehensible, and everything that goes beyond the most abstract need—be it in the realm of

passive enjoyment, or a manifestation of activity—seems to him
a luxury. Political economy, this science of *wealth*, is therefore
simultaneously the science of renunciation, of want, of *saving*—
and it actually reaches the point where it *spares* man the *need*
of either fresh *air* or physical *exercise.* This science of marvelous
industry is simultaneously the science of *asceticism,* and its true
ideal is the *ascetic* but *extortionate* miser and the *ascetic* but *productive* slave. Its moral ideal is the *worker* who takes part of his
wages to the savings-bank, and it has even found ready-made an
abject *art* in which to embody this pet idea: they have presented
it, bathed in sentimentality, on the stage. Thus political economy
—despite its worldly and wanton appearance—is a true moral
science, the most moral of all the sciences. Self-renunciation, the
renunciation of life and of all human needs, is its principal thesis.
The less you eat, drink and buy books; the less you go to the
theater, the dance hall, the public house; the less you think, love,
theorize, sing, paint, fence, etc., the more you *save*—the *greater*
becomes your treasure which neither moths nor dust will devour—
your *capital.* The less you *are,* the less you express your own life,
the greater is your *alienated* life, the more you *have,* the greater
is the store of your estranged being. Everything which the political
economist takes from you in life and in humanity, he replaces for
you in *money* and in *wealth*; and all the things which you cannot do, your money can do. It can eat and drink, go to the dance
hall and the theater; it can travel, it can appropriate art, learning, the treasures of the past, political power—all this it *can* appropriate for you—it can buy all this for you: it is the true *en-
dowment.* Yet being all this, it is *inclined* to do nothing but create
itself, buy itself; for everything else is after all its servant. And
when I have the master I have the servant and do not need his
servant. All passions and all activity must therefore be submerged
in *greed.* The worker may only have enough for him to want to
live, and may only want to live in order to have that.

It is true that a controversy now arises in the field of political
economy. The one side (Lauderdale, Malthus, etc.) recommends
luxury and execrates thrift. The other (Say, Ricardo, etc.) recommends thrift and execrates luxury. But the former admits that it

wants luxury in order to produce *labor* (i.e., absolute thrift); and the latter admits that it recommends thrift in order to produce *wealth* (i.e., luxury).[4] The Lauderdale-Malthus school has the *romantic* notion that greed alone ought not to determine the consumption of the rich, and it contradicts its own laws in advancing *extravagance* as a direct means of enrichment. Against it, therefore, the other side very earnestly and circumstantially proves that I do not increase but reduce my *possessions* by being extravagant. The Say-Ricardo school, however, is hypocritical in not admitting that it is precisely whim and caprice which determine production. It forgets the "refined needs"; it forgets that there would be no production without consumption; it forgets that as a result of competition production can only become more extensive and luxurious. It forgets that it is use that determines a thing's value, and that fashion determines use. It wishes to see only "useful things" produced, but it forgets that production of too many useful things produces too large a *useless* population. Both sides forget that extravagance and thrift, luxury and privation, wealth and poverty are equal.

And you must not only stint the immediate gratification of your senses, as by stinting yourself on food, etc.: you must also spare yourself all sharing of general interest, all sympathy, all trust, etc.; if you want to be economical, if you do not want to be ruined by illusions.

You must make everything that is yours *saleable,* i.e., useful. If I ask the political economist: Do I obey economic laws if I extract money by offering my body for sale, by surrendering it to another's lust? (The factory workers in France call the prostitution of their wives and daughters the Xth working hour, which is literally correct.)—Or am I not acting in keeping with political economy if I sell my friend to the Moroccans? (And the direct sale of men in the form of a trade in conscripts, etc., takes place in all civilized countries.)[5]—Then the political economist replies to me: You do not transgress my laws; but see what Cousin Ethics and Cousin Religion have to say about it. My *political economic* ethics and religion have nothing to reproach you with, but—But whom am I now to believe, political economy or ethics? The ethics of political economy is *acquisition,* work, thrift, sobriety—but political economy promises to satisfy my needs. The political economy of ethics is the opulence of a good conscience, of virtue, etc.; but how can I live virtuously if I do not live? And how can I have a good conscience if I am not conscious of anything? It stems from the very nature of estrangement that each sphere applies to me a different and opposite yardstick—ethics one and political economy another; for each is a specific estrangement of many and focuses attention on a particular round of estranged essential activity, and each stands in an estranged relation to the other. Thus M. *Michel Chevalier* reproaches Ricardo with having abstracted from ethics.[6] But Ricardo is allowing political economy to speak its own language, and if it does not speak ethically, this is not Ricardo's fault. M. Chevalier abstracts from political economy in so far as he moralizes, but he really and necessarily abstracts from ethics in so far as he practices political economy. The relationship of political economy to ethics, if it is other than an arbitrary, contingent and therefore unfounded and unscientific relationship, if it is not being put up as a *sham* but is meant to be *essential,* can only be the relationship of the laws of political economy to ethics. If there is no such connection, or if the contrary is rather the case, can Ricardo help it? Moreover, the opposition between political economy and ethics is only a *sham* opposition and just as much no opposition as it is an opposition. All that happens is that political economy expresses moral laws *in its own way.*

Needlessness as the principle of political economy is *most brilliantly* shown in its *theory of population.* There are *too many* people. Even the existence of men is a pure luxury; and if the worker is *"ethical,"* he will be *sparing* in procreation. (Mill suggests public acclaim for those who prove themselves continent in their sexual relations, and public rebuke for those who sin against such barrenness of marriage. . . . Is not this the ethics, the teaching of asceticism?)[7] The production of people appears as public misery.

The meaning which production has in relation to the rich is seen *revealed* in the meaning which it has for the poor. At the top the manifestation is always refined, veiled, ambiguous—a sham; lower, it is rough, straightforward, frank—the real thing. The worker's *crude* need is a far greater source of gain than the *refined* need of the rich. The cellar dwellings in London bring more to those who let them than do the palaces; that is to say, with reference to the landlord they constitute *greater wealth,* and thus (to speak the language of political economy) greater *social* wealth.

Industry speculates on the refinement of needs, but it speculates just as much on their *crudeness,* but on their artificially produced crudeness, whose true enjoyment, therefore, is *self-stupefaction*— this *illusory* satisfaction of need—this civilization contained *within* the crude barbarism of need; the English gin shops are therefore the *symbolical representations* of private property. Their *luxury* reveals the true relation of industrial luxury and wealth to man. They are therefore rightly the only Sunday pleasures of the people, treated at least mildly by the English police.

We have already seen how the political economist establishes the unity of labor and capital in a variety of ways: (1) Capital is *accumulated labor.* (2) The purpose of capital within production —partly, reproduction of capital with profit, partly, capital as raw material (material of labor), and partly, as itself a *working instrument* (the machine is capital directly equated with labor)— is *productive labor.* (3) The worker is a capital. (4) Wages belong to costs of capital. (5) In relation to the worker, labor is the reproduction of his life-capital. (6) In relation to the capitalist, labor is an aspect of his capital's activity.

Finally, (7) the political economist postulates the original unity of capital and labor as the unity of the capitalist and the worker; this is the original state of paradise. The way in which these two aspects, as two persons, leap at each other's throats is for the political economist an *accidental* event, and hence only to be explained by reference to external factors. (See Mill.)

The nations which are still dazzled by the sensuous glitter of precious metals, and are therefore still fetish-worshippers of metal money, are not yet fully developed money-nations.—Contrast of France and England. The extent to which the solution of theoretical riddles is the task of practice and effected through practice, just as true practice is the condition of a real and positive theory, is shown, for example, in *fetishism*. The sensuous consciousness of the fetish-worshipper is different from that of the Greek, because his sensuous existence is still different. The abstract enmity between sense and spirit is necessary so long as the human feeling for nature, the human sense of nature, and therefore also the *natural* sense of *man*, are not yet produced by man's own labor.

Equality is nothing but a translation of the German "Ich=Ich" into the French, i.e., political form. Equality as the basis of communism is its *political* justification, and it is the same as when the German justifies it by conceiving man as *universal self-consciousness*.[8] Naturally, the transcendence of the estrangement always proceeds from that form of the estrangement which is the *dominant* power: in Germany, *self-consciousness;* in France, *equality*, because of politics; in England, real, material, *practical* need taking only itself as its standard. It is from this standpoint that Proudhon is to be criticized and appreciated.

If we characterize *communism* itself because of its character as negation of the negation, as the appropriation of the human essence through the intermediary of the negation of private property—as being not yet the *true*, self-originating position but rather a position originating from private property.[9]

... the real estrangement of the life of man remains, and remains all the more, the more one is conscious of it as such, hence it may be accomplished solely by putting communism into operation.

In order to abolish the *idea* of private property, the *idea* of communism is completely sufficient. It takes *actual* communist action to abolish actual private property. History will come to it; and this movement, which in *theory* we already know to be a self-transcending movement, will constitute *in actual fact* a very severe and protracted process. But we must regard it as a real advance to have gained beforehand a consciousness of the limited character as well as of the goal of this historical movement—and a consciousness which reaches out beyond it.

When communist *artisans* associate with one another, theory, propaganda, etc., is their first end. But at the same time, as a result of this association, they acquire a new need—the need for society—and what appears as a means becomes an end. In this practical process the most splendid results are to be observed whenever French socialist workers are seen together. Such things as smoking, drinking, eating, etc., are no longer means of contact or means that bring together. Company, association, and conversation, which again has society as its end, are enough for them; the brotherhood of man is no mere phrase with them, but a fact of life, and the nobility of man shines upon us from their work-hardened bodies.

When political economy claims that demand and supply always balance each other, it immediately forgets that according to its own claim (theory of population) the supply of *people* always exceeds the demand, and that, therefore, in the essential result of the whole production process—the existence of man—the disparity between demand and supply gets its most striking expression.

The extent to which money, which appears as a means, constitutes true *power* and the sole *end*—in general *that* means which gives me essence, which gives me possession of alien objective essence, is an *end in itself*—can be clearly seen from the fact that landed property, wherever land is the source of life, *horse* and *sword*, wherever these are the *true means of life*, are also acknowledged as the true political powers in life. In the Middle Ages a social class is emancipated as soon as it is allowed to carry the *sword*. Amongst nomadic peoples it is the *horse* which makes me a free man and a participant in the life of the community.

We have said above that man is regressing to the *cave dwelling*, etc.—but that he is regressing to it in an estranged, malignant form. The savage in his cave—a natural element which freely offers itself for his use and protection—feels himself no more a stranger, or rather feels himself to be just as much at home as a *fish* in water. But the cellar dwelling of the poor man is a hostile dwelling, "an alien, restraining power which only gives itself up to him in so far as he gives up to it his blood and sweat"—a dwelling which he cannot regard as his own home where he might at last exclaim, "Here I am at home," but where instead he finds

himself in *someone else's* house, in the house of a *stranger* who
daily lies in wait for him and throws him out if he does not pay
his rent. He is also aware of the contrast in quality between his
dwelling and a human dwelling—a residence in that *other* world,
the heaven of wealth.

Estrangement is manifested not only in the fact that *my* means
of life belong to *someone else,* that *my* desire is the inaccessible
possession of *another,* but also in the fact that eveything is itself
something *different* from itself—that my activity is *something else*
and that, finally (and this applies also to the capitalist), all is under
the sway of *inhuman* power. There is a form of inactive, extravagant wealth given over wholly to pleasure, the enjoyer of which
on the one hand *behaves* as a mere *ephemeral* individual franti-
cally spending himself to no purpose, knows the slave-labor of
others (human *sweat and blood*) as the prey of his cupidity, and
therefore knows man himself, and hence also his own self, as a
sacrificed and empty being. With such wealth contempt of man
makes its appearance, partly as arrogance and as squandering of
what can give sustenance to a hundred human lives, and partly
as the infamous illusion that his own unbridled extravagance and
ceaseless, unproductive consumption is the condition of the other's
labor and therefore of his *subsistence*. He knows the realization
of the *essential powers* of many only as the realization of his own
excesses, his whims and capricious, bizarre notions. This wealth
which, on the other hand, again knows wealth as a mere means,
as something that is good for nothing but to be annihilated and
which is therefore at once slave and master, at once generous and
mean, capricious, presumptuous, conceited, refined, cultured and
witty—this wealth has not yet experienced *wealth* as an utterly
alien power over itself: it sees in it, rather, only its own power,
and not wealth but *gratification* [is its] final aim and end.[10]

This bright illusion about the nature of wealth, blinded by
sensuous appearances, is confronted by the *working, sober, economical, prosaic* industrialist who is quite enlightened about the
nature of wealth, and who, while providing a wider sphere for the
other's self-indulgence and paying fulsome flatteries to him in his
products (for his products are just so many base compliments to

the appetites of the spendthrift), knows how to appropriate for himself in the only *useful* way the other's waning power. If, therefore, industrial wealth appears at first to be the result of extravagant fantastic wealth, yet its motion, the motion inherent in it, ousts the latter also in an active way. For the fall in the *interest on money* is a necessary consequence and result of industrial development. The extravagant rentier's means therefore dwindle day by day in *inverse* proportion to the increasing possibilities and pitfalls of pleasure. Consequently, he must either consume his capital himself, thus ruining himself, or must become an industrial capitalist. . . . On the other hand, there is a direct, constant rise in the *rent of land* as a result of the course of industrial development; nevertheless, as we have already seen [11] there must come a time when landed property, like every other kind of property, is bound to fall within the category of profitably self-reproducing capital—and this in fact results from the same industrial development. Thus the extravagant landowner, too, must either consume his capital, and thus be ruined, or himself become the tenant of his own estate—an agricultural industrialist.

The diminution in the interest on money, which Proudhon regards as the annulling of capital and as a tendency to socialize capital, is therefore rather only an immediate symptom of the total victory of working capital over extravagant wealth—i.e., the transformation of all private property into industrial capital. It is a total victory of private property over all those of its qualities which are still in *appearance* human, and the complete subjection of the owner of private property to the essence of private property—*labor*. To be sure, the industrial capitalist also takes *his* pleasures. He does not by any means return to the unnatural simplicity of need; but his pleasure is only a side-issue—recreation—something subordinated to production; at the same time it is a *calculated* and, therefore, itself an *economical* pleasure. For he debits it to his capital's expense account, and what is squandered on his pleasure must therefore amount to no more than will be replaced with profit through the reproduction of capital. Pleasure is therefore subsumed under capital, and the pleasure-taking individual under the capital-accumulating individual, whilst formerly the contrary was the case. The decrease in the interest rate is therefore a symptom of the annulment of capital only inasmuch as it is a symptom of the rule of capital in the process of perfecting itself—of the estrangement in this process of becoming fully developed and therefore of hastening to its annulment. This is indeed the only way in which that which exists affirms its opposite.

The quarrel between the political economists about luxury and thrift is, therefore, only the quarrel between that political economy which has achieved clarity about the nature of wealth, and that political economy which is still afflicted with romantic, anti-industrial memories. Neither side, however, knows how to reduce the subject of the controversy to its simple terms, and neither therefore can make short work of the other.

Moreover, *rent of land qua* rent of land has been overthrown, since, contrary to the argument of the physiocrats which maintains that the landowner is the only true producer, modern political economy has proved that the landowner as such is rather the only completely unproductive rentier. According to this theory, agriculture is the business of the capitalist, who invests his capital in it provided he can expect the usual profit. The claim of the physiocrats that landed property, as the sole productive property, should alone pay state taxes and therefore should alone sanction them and participate in the affairs of state, is transformed into the opposite position that the tax on the rent of land is the only tax on unproductive income, and is therefore the only tax not detrimental to national production. It goes without saying that from this point of view the political privilege of landowners no longer follows from their position as principal tax-payers.

Everything which Proudhon conceives as a movement of labor against capital is only the movement of labor in the form of capital, of *industrial capital,* against capital not consumed *as* capital, i.e., not consumed industrially. And this movement is proceeding along its triumphant road—the road to the victory of *industrial* capital. It is clear, therefore, that only when *labor* is grasped as the essence of private property, can the economic process as such be analyzed in its real concreteness.

Society, as it appears to the political economist, is *civil society,*[12] in which every individual is a totality of needs and only exists for the other person, as the other exists for him, in so far as each becomes a means for the other. The political economist reduces everything (just as does politics in its *Rights of Man*) to man, i.e., to the individual whom he strips of all determinateness so as to class him as capitalist or worker.

The *division of labor* is the economic expression of the *social character of labor* within the estrangement. Or, since *labor* is only an expression of human activity within alienation, of the living of life as the estrangement of life,[13] *the division of labor,* too, is therefore nothing else but the *estranged, alienated* positioning of human activity as *a real activity of the species* or as *activity of man as a species being.*

As for *the essence of the division of labor*—and of course the division of labor had to be conceived as a major driving force in the production of wealth as soon as *labor* was recognized as *the essence c; private property*—i.e., about *the estranged and alienated form of human activity as an activity of the species*—the political economists are very unclear and self-contradictory about it.

Adam Smith:[14] "The *division of labour* is not originally the effect of any human wisdom. It is the necessary, slow and gradual consequence of the propensity to exchange and barter one product for another. This propensity to trade is probably a necessary consequence of the use of reason and of speech. It is common to all men, and to be found in no animal. The animal, when it is grown up, is entirely independent. Man has constant occasion for the help of others, and it is in vain for him to expect it from their benevolence only. He will be more likely to prevail if he can appeal to their personal interest and show them that it is for their own advantage to do for him what he requires of them. We address ourselves not to other men's *humanity* but to their *self-love,* and never talk to them of our *own necessities* but of *their advantages.*

"As it is by treaty, by barter, and by purchase that we obtain from one another the greater part of those mutual good offices which we stand in need of, so it is this same *trucking* disposition which originally gives occasion to the *division of labour.* In a tribe of hunters or shepherds a particular person makes bows and arrows, for example, with more readiness and dexterity than any other. He frequently exchanges them for cattle or for venison with his companions; and he finds at last that he can in this manner get more cattle and venison than if he himself went to the field to catch them. From a regard to his own interest, therefore, the making of bows, etc., grows to be his chief business.

"The difference of *natural talents* in different individuals is not so much the *cause* as the *effect* of the division of labour. . . . Without the disposition to truck and exchange, every man must have procured to himself every necessary and conveniency of life. All must have had the *same work* to do, and there could have been no such *difference of employment* as could alone give occasion to any great difference of talents.

"As it is this disposition which forms that difference of talents among men, so it is this same disposition which renders that difference useful. Many tribes of animals of the same species derive from nature a much more remarkable distinction of genius than what, antecedent to custom and education, could be observed among men. By nature a philosopher is not in talent and in intelligence half so different from a street-porter, as a mastiff is from a greyhound, or a greyhound from a spaniel, or this last from a shepherd's dog. Those different tribes of animals, however, though all of the same species, are of scarce any use to one another. The mastiff cannot add to the advantages of his strength by making use of the swiftness of the greyhound, etc. The effects of these different talents or grades of intelligence, for want of the power or disposition to barter and exchange, cannot be brought into a common *stock*, and do not in the least contribute to the better *accommodation and conveniency of the species*. Each animal is still obliged to support and defend itself, separately and independently, and derives no sort of advantage from that variety of talents with which nature has distinguished its fellows. Among men, on the contrary, the most dissimilar geniuses are of use to one another; the *different produces* of their respective talents, by the general disposition to truck, barter and exchange, being brought, as it were, into a common stock, where every man may purchase whatever part of the produce of other men's industry he has occasion for.

"As it is the power of *exchanging* that gives occasion to the *division of labour*, so the *extent* of this *division* must always be limited by the *extent of that power*, or in other words, by the *extent of the market*. When the market is very small, no person can have any encouragement to dedicate himself entirely to one employment, for want of the power to exchange all that surplus part of the produce of his own labour, which is over and above his own consumption, for such parts of the produce of other men's labour as he has occasion for. . . ."

In an *advanced* state of society "Every man lives by exchanging and becomes in some measure a *merchant*, and the *society itself* grows to be what is properly a *commercial* society."[15] (See Destutt de Tracy:[16] "Society is a series of reciprocal exchanges; *commerce* contains the whole essence of society.") The accumulation of capitals mounts with the division of labour, and vice versa. So much for *Adam Smith*.

"If every family produced all that it consumed, society could keep going although no exchange of any sort took place; without being *fundamental*, exchange is indispensable in our advanced state of society. The division of labour is a skilful deployment of man's powers; it increases society's production—its power and its pleasures—but it plunders and reduces the ability of every person taken individually. Production cannot take place without exchange." Thus *J. B. Say*.[17]

"The powers inherent in man are his intelligence and his physical capacity for work. Those which arise from the condition of society consist of the capacity to *divide up labour* and to *distribute different jobs amongst different people* required to obtain means of subsistence, and the *power* to exchange *mutual services* and the products which constitute these means. The motive which impels a man to give his services to another is self-interest—he requires a reward for the services rendered. The right of exclusive private property is indispensable to the establishment of exchange amongst men." "Exchange and division of labour reciprocally condition each other." Thus Skarbek.[18]

Mill presents developed exchange—*trade*—as a *consequence of the division of labor.*

"The agency of man can be traced to very simple elements. He can, in fact, do nothing more than produce motion. He can move things towards one another, and he can separate them from one another: the properties of matter perform all the rest." "In the employment of labour and machinery, it is often found that the effects can be increased by skilful distribution, by separating all those operations which have any tendency to impede one another, and by bringing together all those operations which can be made in any way to aid one another. As men in general cannot perform many different operations with the same quickness and dexterity with which they can by practice learn to perform a few, it is always an advantage to limit as much as possible the number of operations imposed upon each. For dividing labour, and distributing the powers of men and machinery, to the greatest advantage, it is in most cases necessary to operate upon a large scale; in other words, to produce the commodities in greater masses. It is this advantage which gives existence to the great manufactories; a few of which, placed in the most convenient situations, frequently supply not one country, but many countries, with as much as they desire of the commodity produced." Thus Mill.[19]

The whole of modern political economy agrees, however, that division of labor and wealth of production, division of labor and accumulation of capital, mutually determine each other; just as it agrees that *liberated* private property alone—private property left to itself—can produce the most useful and comprehensive division of labor.

Adam Smith's argument can be summarized as follows: Division of labor bestows on labor infinite productive capacity. It stems from the *propensity to exchange* and *barter,* a specifically human propensity which is probably not accidental, but is conditioned by the use of reason and speech. The motive of those who engage in exchange is not *humanity* but *egoism.* The diversity of human talents is more the effect than the cause of the division of labor, i.e., of exchange. Besides, it is only the latter which makes such diversity useful. The particular attributes of the different breeds within a species of animal are by nature much more marked than the degrees of difference in human aptitude and activity. But because animals are unable to engage in *exchange,* no individual animal benefits from the difference in the attributes of animals of the same species but of different breeds. Animals are unable to combine the different attributes of their species, and are unable to contribute anything to the *common* advantage and comfort of the species. It is otherwise with *men,* amongst whom the most dissimilar talents and forms of activity are of use to one another, *because* they can bring their *different* products together into a common stock, from which each can purchase. As the division of labor springs from the propensity to *exchange,* so it grows and is limited by the *extent of exchange*—by the *extent of the market.* In advanced conditions, every man is a *merchant,* and society is a *commercial society. Say* regards *exchange* as accidental and not fundamental. Society could exist without it. It becomes indispensable in the advanced state of society. Yet *production* cannot take place *without it.* Division of labor is a *convenient, useful* means—a skilful deployment of human powers for social wealth; but it reduces the *ability of each person* taken *individually.* The last remark is a step forward on the part of Say.

Skarbek distinguishes the *individual powers inherent in man*—

intelligence and the physical capacity for work—from the powers *derived* from society—*exchange* and *division of labor*, which mutually condition one another. But the necessary premise of exchange is *private property*. Skarbek here expresses in an objective form what Smith, Say, Ricardo, etc., say when they designate *egoism* and *self-interest* as the basis of exchange, and *buying and selling* as the *essential* and *adequate* form of exchange.

Mill presents *trade* as the consequence of the *division of labor*. With him *human* activity is reduced to *mechanical motion*. Division of labor and use of machinery promote wealth of production. Each person must be entrusted with as small a sphere of operations as possible. Division of labor and use of machinery, for their part, require the production of wealth, and therefore of the product, in large quantities. This is the reason for large manufactories.

The examination of *division of labor* and *exchange* is of extreme interest, because these are *perceptibly alienated* expressions of human *activity* and of *essential human power* as a *species* activity and power.

To assert that *division of labor* and *exchange* rest on *private property* is nothing but asserting that *labor* is the essence of private property—an assertion which the political economist cannot prove and which we wish to prove for him. Precisely in the fact that *division of labor* and *exchange* are embodiments of private property lies the twofold proof, on the one hand that *human* life required *private property* for its realization, and on the other hand that it now requires the supersession of private property.

Division of labor and *exchange* are the two *phenomena* which lead the political economist to boast of the social character of his science, while in the same breath he gives expression to the contradiction in his science—the establishment of society through unsocial, particular interests.

The factors we have to consider are: the *propensity to exchange* —the basis of which is found in egoism—regarded as the cause or reciprocal effect of the division of labor. Say regards exchange as not *fundamental* to the nature of society. Wealth—production— is explained by division of labor and exchange. The impoverishment of individual activity, and its loss of character as a result of the division of labor, are admitted. Exchange and division of labor are acknowledged as the sources of the great *diversity of human talents*—a diversity which in its turn becomes *useful* as a result of exchange. Skarbek divides man's essential powers of production—or productive powers—into two parts: (1) those which are individual and inherent in him—his intelligence and his special disposition, or capacity, for work; and (2) those *derived from* society and not from the actual individual—division of labor and exchange. Furthermore, the division of labor is limited by the *market*. Human labor is simple *mechanical motion:* the main work is done by the material properties of the objects. The fewest possible operations must be apportioned to any one individual. Splitting up of labor and concentration of capital; the nothingness of individual production and the production of wealth in large quantities. Meaning of free private property within the division of labor.[20]

THE POWER OF MONEY IN
BOURGEOIS SOCIETY

If man's *feelings*, passions, etc., are not merely anthropological phenomena in the [narrower][1] sense, but truly *ontological* affirmations of being (of nature),[2] and if they are only really affirmed because their *object* exists for them as a sensual object, then it is clear:

(1) That they have by no means merely one mode of affirmation, but rather that the distinct character of their existence, of their life, is constituted by the distinct mode of their affirmation. In what manner the object exists for them, is the characteristic mode of their *gratification*.

(2) Wherever the sensuous affirmation is the direct annulment of the object in its independent form (as in eating, drinking, working up of the object, etc.), this is the affirmation of the object.

(3) In so far as man, and hence also his feeling, etc., are *human*, the affirmation of the object by another is likewise his own gratification.

(4) Only through developed industry—i.e., through the medium of private property—does the ontological essence of human passion come into being, in its totality as in its humanity; the science of man is therefore itself a product of man's establishment of himself by practical activity.

(5) The meaning of private property—apart from its estrangement—is the *existence of essential objects* for man, both as objects of gratification and as objects of activity.

By possessing the *property* of buying everything, by possessing the property of appropriating all objects, *money* is thus the *object* of eminent possession. The universality of its *property* is the omnipotence of its being. It therefore functions as almighty being. Money is the *pimp* between man's need and the object, between his life and his means of life. But *that which* mediates *my* life for me, also *mediates* the existence of other people *for me*. For me it is the *other* person.

> What, man! confound it, hands and feet
> And head and backside, all are yours!
> And what we take while life is sweet,
> Is that to be declared not ours?
>   Six stallions, say, I can afford,
>   Is not their strength my property?
>   I tear along, a sporting lord,
>   As if their legs belonged to me.
>   (Goethe: *Faust*—Mephistopheles.[3]

Shakespeare in *Timon of Athens:*

> Gold? Yellow, glittering, precious gold? No, Gods,
> I am no idle votarist! . . . Thus much of this will
>   make black white, foul fair,
> Wrong right, base noble, old young, coward valiant.
> . . . Why, this
> Will lug your priests and servants from your sides,
> Pluck stout men's pillows from below their heads:
> This yellow slave
> Will knit and break religions, bless the accursed;
> Make the hoar leprosy adored, place thieves
> And give them title, knee and approbation
> With senators on the bench: This is it
> That makes the wappen'd widow wed again;
> She, whom the spital-house and ulcerous sores
> Would cast the gorge at, this embalms and spices
> To the April day again. Come, damned earth,
> Thou common whore of mankind, that putt'st odds
> Among the rout of nations.[4]

And also later:

> O thou sweet king-killer, and dear divorce
> Twixt natural son and sire! thou bright defiler
> Of Hymen's purest bed! thou valiant Mars!
> Thou ever young, fresh, loved and delicate wooer,
> Whose blush doth thaw the consecrated snow
> That lies on Dian's lap! Thou *visible God!*
> That solder'st *close impossibilities,*
> And makest them kiss! That speak'st with every tongue,
> To every purpose! O thou touch of hearts!

> Think, thy slave man rebels, and by thy virtue
> Set them into confounding odds, that beasts
> May have the world in empire![4]

Shakespeare excellently depicts the real nature of *money*. To understand him, let us begin, first of all, by expounding the passage from Goethe.

That which is for me through the medium of *money*—that for which I can pay (i.e., which money can buy) —that am *I*, the possessor of the money. The extent of the power of money is the extent of my power. Money's properties are my properties and essential powers—the properties and powers of its possessor. Thus, what I *am* and *am capable* of is by no means determined by my individuality. I *am* ugly, but I can buy for myself the most *beautiful* of women. Therefore I am not *ugly*, for the effect of *ugliness*—its deterrent power—is nullified by money. I, as an individual, am *lame*, but money furnishes me with twenty-four feet. Therefore I am not lame. I am bad, dishonest, unscrupulous, stupid; but money is honored, and hence its possessor. Money is the supreme good, therefore its possessor is good. Money, besides, saves me the trouble of being dishonest: I am therefore presumed honest. I am *stupid*, but money is the *real mind* of all things and how then should its possessor be stupid? Besides, he can buy talented people for himself, and is he who has power over the talented not more talented than the talented? Do not I, who thanks to money am capable of *all* that the human heart longs for, possess all human capacities? Does not my money, therefore, transform all my incapacities into their contrary?

If *money* is the bond binding me to *human* life, binding society to me, binding me and nature and man, is not money the bond of all *bonds*? Can it not dissolve and bind all ties? Is it not, therefore, the universal *agent of separation*? It is the true *agent of separation* as well as the true *binding agent—the* [universal] [5] *galvano-chemical* power of society.

Shakespeare stresses especially two properties of money:

(1) It is the visible divinity—the transformation of all human and natural properties into their contraries, the universal confounding and overturning of things: it makes brothers of impos-

sibilities. (2) It is the common whore, the common pimp of people and nations.

The overturning and confounding of all human and natural qualities, the fraternization of impossibilities—the *divine* power of money—lies in its *character* as men's estranged, alienating and self-disposing *species nature*. Money is the alienated *ability of mankind*.

That which I am unable to do as a *man*, and of which therefore all my individual essential powers are incapable, I am able to do by means of *money*. Money thus turns each of these powers into something which in itself it is not—turns it, that is, into its *contrary*.

If I long for a particular dish or want to take the mailcoach because I am not strong enough to go by foot, money fetches me the dish and the mailcoach: that is, it converts my wishes from something in the realm of imagination, translates them from their meditated, imagined or willed existence into their *sensuous, actual* existence—from imagination to life, from imagined being into real being. In effecting this mediation, money is the *truly creative* power.

No doubt *demand* also exists for him who has no money, but his demand is a mere thing of the imagination without effect or existence for me, for a third party, for the others, and which therefore remains for me *unreal* and *objectless*. The difference between effective demand based on money and ineffective demand based on my need, my passion, my wish, etc., is the difference between *being* and *thinking*, between that which *exists* merely within me as imagination and the imagined as it exists as a *real object* outside of me.

If I have no money for travel, I have no *need*—that is, no real and self-realizing need—to travel. If I have the *vocation* for study but no money for it, I have *no* vocation for study—that is, no *effective*, no *true* vocation. On the other hand, if I have really *no* vocation for study but have the will *and* the money for it, I have an *effective* vocation for it. Being the external, common *medium* and *faculty* for turning an *image* into *reality* and *reality* into a mere *image* (a faculty not springing from man as man or from human society as society), *money* transforms the *real essential powers of man and nature* into what are merely abstract conceits and therefore *imperfections*—into tormenting chimeras—just as it transforms *real imperfections and chimeras*— essential powers which are really impotent, which exist only in the imagination of the individual—into *real powers* and *faculties*.

In the light of this characteristic alone, money is thus the general overturning of *individualities* which turns them into their contrary and adds contradictory attributes to their attributes.

Money, then, appears as this *overturning* power both against the individual and against the bonds of society, etc., which claim to be *essences* in themselves. It transforms fidelity into infidelity, love into hate, hate into love, virtue into vice, vice into virtue, servant into master, master into servant, idiocy into intelligence, and intelligence into idiocy.

Since money, as the existing and active concept of value, confounds and exchanges all things, it is the general *confounding* and *compounding* of all things—the world upside-down—the confounding and compounding of all natural and human qualities.

He who can buy bravery is brave, though he be a coward. As money is not exchanged for any one specific quality, for any one specific thing, or for any particular human essential power, but for the entire objective world of man and nature, from the standpoint of its possessor it therefore serves to exchange every property for every other, even contradictory, property and object: it is the fraternization of impossibilities. It makes contradictions embrace.

Assume *man* to be *man* and his relationship to the world to be a human one: then you can exchange love only for love, trust for trust, etc. If you want to enjoy art, you must be an artistically cultivated person; if you want to exercise influence over other people, you must be a person with a stimulating and encouraging effect on other people. Every one of your relations to man and to nature must be a *specific expression*, corresponding to the object of your will, of your *real individual* life. If you love without evoking love in return—that is, if your loving as loving does not produce reciprocal love; if through a *living expression* of yourself as a loving person you do not make yourself a *loved person*, then your love is impotent—a misfortune.

CRITIQUE OF THE HEGELIAN
DIALECTIC AND PHILOSOPHY
AS A WHOLE

This is perhaps the place [1] at which, by way of explaining and justifying the ideas here presented, we might offer some considerations in regard to the Hegelian dialectic generally and especially its exposition in the *Phenomenology* and *Logic,* and also, lastly, the relation to it of the modern critical movement.

So powerful was modern German criticism's preoccupation with the past—so completely was it possessed in its development by its subject matter—that there prevailed a completely uncritical attitude to the method of criticizing, together with a complete lack of awareness about the *partly formal,* but really *vital* question: how do we now stand as regards the Hegelian *dialectic?* This lack of awareness about the relationship of modern criticism to the Hegelian philosophy as a whole and especially to the Hegelian dialectic has been so great that critics like *Strauss* and *Bruno Bauer* still remain wholly within the confines of the Hegelian Logic; the former completely so and the latter at least implicitly so in his *Synoptics* [2] (where, in opposition to Strauss, he replaces the substance of "abstract nature" by the "self-consciousness" of abstract man), and even in *Christianity Discovered.* [3] Thus in *Christianity Discovered,* for example, you get:

"As though in positing the world, self-consciousness posits that which is different from itself, and in what it posits it posits itself, because it in turn annuls the difference between what it has posited and itself, inasmuch as it itself has being only in the positing and the movement.—How then can it not have its purpose in this movement?" etc.; or again: "They [the French materialists] have not yet been able to see that it is only as the movement of self-consciousness that the movement of the universe has actually come to be for itself, and achieved unity with itself."

170

Such expressions do not even show any verbal divergence from the Hegelian approach, but on the contrary repeat it word for word.

How little consciousness there was in relation to the Hegelian dialectic during the act of criticism (Bauer, *The Synoptics*), and how little this consciousness came into being even after the act of material criticism, is proved by Bauer when, in his *The Good of Freedom* [4] he dismisses the brash question put by Herr Gruppe— "What about logic now?"—by referring him to future critics.[5]

But even now—now that *Feuerbach* both in his *Theses* in the *Anekdota* and, in detail, in *The Philosophy of the Future*,[6] has in principle overthrown the old dialectic and philosophy; now that that school of criticism, on the other hand, which was incapable of accomplishing this has all the same seen it accomplished and has proclaimed itself pure, resolute, absolute criticism—criticism that has come into the clear with itself; now that this criticism, in its spiritual pride, has reduced the whole process of history to the relation between the rest of the world and itself (the rest of the world, in contrast to itself, falling under the category of "the masses") and dissolved all dogmatic antitheses into the *single* dogmatic antithesis of its own cleverness and the stupidity of the world—the antithesis of the critical Christ and Mankind, the *rabble*; now that daily and hourly it has demonstrated its own excellence against the dullness of the masses; now, finally, that it has proclaimed the critical *Last Judgement* in the shape of an announcement that the day is approaching when the whole of expiring humanity will assemble before it and be sorted by it into groups, each particular mob receiving its *testimonium paupertatis*; [7] now that it has made known in print [8] its superiority to human feelings as well as its superiority to the world, over which it sits enthroned in sublime solitude, only letting fall from time to time from its sarcastic lips the ringing laughter of the Olympian Gods—even now, after all these delightful antics of idealism expiring in the guise of criticism (i.e., of Young Hegelianism) — even now it has not expressed the suspicion that the time was ripe for a critical settling of accounts with the mother of Young Hegelianism—the Hegelian dialectic—and even had [nothing]

to say about its critical attitude towards the Feuerbachian dialectic. Criticism with a completely uncritical attitude to itself!

Feuerbach is the only one who has a *serious, critical* attitude to
the Hegelian dialectic and who has made genuine discoveries in
this field. He is in fact the true conqueror of the old philosophy.
The extent of his achievement, and the unpretentious simplicity
with which he, Feuerbach, gives it to the world, stand in striking
contrast to the opposite attitude of the others.

Feuerbach's great achievement is:

(1) The proof that philosophy is nothing else but religion
rendered into thought and expounded by thought, hence equally
to be condemned as another form and manner of existence of the
estrangement of the essence of man;

(2) The establishment of *true materialism* and of *real science,*
since Feuerbach also makes the social relationship "of man to
man" the basic principle of the theory;

(3) His opposing to the negation of the negation, which claims
to be the absolute positive, the self-supporting positive, positively
based on itself.

Feuerbach explains the Hegelian dialectic (and thereby justifies
starting out from the positive facts which we know by the senses)
as follows:

Hegel sets out from the estrangement of substance (in logic,
from the infinite, the abstractly universal) —from the absolute and
fixed abstraction; which means, but popularly, that he sets out
from religion and theology.

Secondly, he annuls the infinite, and establishes the actual,
sensuous, real, finite, particular (philosophy—annulment of
religion and theology).

Thirdly, he again annuls the positive and restores the abstraction, the infinite—restoration of religion and theology.

Feuerbach thus conceives the negation of the negation *only* as a
contradiction of philosophy with itself—as the philosophy which
affirms theology (the transcendent, etc.) after having denied it,
and which it therefore affirms in opposition to itself.

The position or self-affirmation and self-confirmation contained
in the negation of the negation is taken to be a position which is

not yet sure of itself, which is therefore burdened with its opposite, which is doubtful of itself and therefore in need of proof, and which, therefore, is not a position demonstrating itself by its existence—not a position that justifies itself; hence it is directly and immediately confronted by the position of sense-certainty based on itself.[9]

But because Hegel has conceived the negation of the negation, from the point of view of the positive relation inherent in it, as the true and only positive, and from the point of view of the negative relation inherent in it as the only true act and self-realizing act of all being, he has only found the *abstract, logical, speculative* expression for the movement of history; which is not yet the *real* history of man—of man as a given subject, but only man's *act of creation*—the *story* of man's *origin*. We shall explain both the abstract form of this process and the difference between this process as it is in Hegel in contrast to modern criticism, that is, in contrast to the same process in Feuerbach's *Essence of Christianity*, or rather the *critical* form of this in Hegel still uncritical process.

Let us take a look at the Hegelian system. One must begin with Hegel's *Phenomenology*, the true point of origin and the secret of the Hegelian philosophy.

PHENOMENOLOGY [10]

A. *Self-consciousness*
I. *Consciousness.* (a) Certainty at the level of sense-experience; or the "This" and *Meaning.* (b) *Perception*, or the Thing with Its Properties, and *Deception.* (c) Force and Understanding, Appearance and the Supersensible World.

II. *Self-consciousness.* The Truth of Certainty of Self. (a) Independence and Dependence of Self-consciousness; Lordship and Bondage. (b) Freedom of Self-consciousness: Stoicism, Scepticism, the Unhappy Consciousness.

III. *Reason.* Reason's Certainty and Reason's Truth. (a) Observation as a Process of Reason. Observation of Nature and of Self-consciousness. (b) Realization of Rational Self-consciousness through its own Activity. Pleasure and Necessity. The Law of the

174ECONOMIC AND PHILOSOPHIC MANUSCRIPTS

Heart and the Frenzy of Self-conceit. Virtue and the Course of the World. (c) The Individuality Which is Real In and For Itself. The Spiritual Animal Kingdom and the Deception, or the Real Fact. Reason as Lawgiver. Reason Which Tests Laws.

B. *Mind*
    I. *True* Mind; the Ethical Order.
    II. Mind in Self-Estrangement—Culture.
    III. Mind Certain of Itself, Morality.

C. *Religion*
Natural Religion; *Religion in the Form of Art*; *Revealed* Religion.

D. *Absolute Knowledge*

Hegel's *Encyclopaedia*,[11] beginning as it does with Logic, with *pure speculative thought,* and ending with *Absolute Knowledge*— with the self-consciousness, self-comprehending, philosophic or absolute (i.e., superhuman) abstract mind—is in its entirety nothing but the *display,* the self-objectification, of the *essence* of the philosophic mind, and the philosophic mind is nothing but the estranged mind of the world thinking within its self-estrangement—i.e., comprehending itself abstractly. *Logic* (mind's *coin of the realm,* the speculative or *thought-value* of man and nature— their essence grown totally indifferent to all real determinateness, and hence their unreal essence) is *alienated thinking,* and therefore thinking which abstracts from nature and from real man: *abstract* thinking. Then: *The externality of this abstract thinking* . . . *nature,* as it is for this abstract thinking. Nature is external to it—its self-loss; and it apprehends nature also in an external fashion, as abstract thinking—but as alienated abstract thinking. Finally, *Mind,* this thinking returning home to its own point of origin—the thinking which, as the anthropological, phenomenological, psychological, ethical, artistic and religious mind is not valid for itself, until ultimately it finds itself, and relates itself to itself, as *absolute* knowledge in the hence absolute, i.e., abstract mind, and so receives its conscious embodiment in the mode of being corresponding to it. For its real mode of being is *abstraction.*

There is a double error in Hegel.

The first emerges most clearly in the *Phenomenology*, the birth-place of the Hegelian philosophy. When, for instance, wealth, state power, etc., are understood by Hegel as entities estranged from the *human* being, this only happens in their form as thoughts. . . . They are thought-entities, and therefore merely an estrangement of *pure*, i.e., abstract, philosophical thinking. The whole process therefore ends with Absolute Knowledge. It is precisely abstract thought from which these objects are estranged and which they confront with their presumption of reality. The *philosopher* sets up himself (that is, one who is himself an abstract form of estranged man) as the *measuring rod* of the estranged world. The whole *history of the alienation process* and the whole *process of the retraction* of the alienation is therefore nothing but the *history of the production* of abstract (i.e., absolute) thought— of logical, speculative thought. The *estrangement,* which there-fore forms the real interest of this alienation and of the tran-scendence of this alienation, is the opposition of *in itself and for itself,*[12] of *consciousness* and *self-consciousness,* of *object* and *sub-ject*—that is to say, it is the opposition, within thought itself, between abstract thinking and sensuous reality or real sensuous-ness. All other oppositions and movements of these oppositions are but the *semblance, the cloak, the esoteric* shape of these oppo-sitions which alone matter, and which constitute the *meaning* of these other, profane oppositions. It is not the fact that the human being *objectifies himself inhumanly,* in opposition to himself, but the fact that he *objectifies himself* in *distinction* from and in *opposition* to abstract thinking, that constitutes the posited essence of the estrangement and the thing to be superseded.

The appropriation of man's essential powers, which have be-come objects—indeed, alien objects—is thus in the *first place* only an *appropriation* occurring in *consciousness,* in *pure thought,* i.e., in *abstraction*: it is the appropriation of these objects as *thoughts* and as *movements of thought.* Consequently, despite its thor-oughly negative and critical appearance and despite the genuine criticism contained in it, which often anticipates far later devel-opment, there is already latent in the *Phenomenology* as a germ, a potentiality, a secret, the uncritical positivism and the equally uncritical idealism of Hegel's later works—that philosophic dissolution and restoration of the existing empirical world.

In the *second place:* the vindication of the objective world for man—for example, the realization that *sensuous* consciousness is not an *abstractly* sensuous consciousness but a *humanly* sensuous consciousness—that religion, wealth, etc., are but the estranged world of *human* objectification, of *man's* essential powers put to work and that they are therefore but the *path* to the true *human* world—this appropriation or the insight into this process appears in Hegel therefore in this form, that *sense, religion,* state power, etc., are *spiritual* entities; for only *mind* is the *true* essence of man, and the true form of mind is thinking mind, the logical, speculative mind. The *human character* of nature and of the nature created by history—man's products—appears in the form that they are *products* of abstract mind and as such, therefore, phases of *mind—thought entities.* The *Phenomenology* is, therefore, a hidden and mystifying criticism—still to itself obscure; but inasmuch as it grasps steadily man's *estrangement,* even though man appears only in the shape of mind, there lie concealed in it *all* the elements of criticism, already *prepared* and *elaborated* in a manner often rising far above the Hegelian standpoint. The "Unhappy Consciousness," the "Honest Consciousness," the struggle of the "Noble and Base Consciousness," [13] etc., etc.—these separate sections contain, but still in an estranged form, the *critical* elements of whole spheres such as religion, the state, civil life, etc. Just as *entities, objects,* appear as *thought entities,* so the *subject* is always *consciousness* or *self-consciousness*; or rather the object appears only as *abstract* consciousness, man only as *self-consciousness*: the distinct forms of estrangement which make their appearance are, therefore, only various forms of consciousness and self-consciousness. Just as *in itself* abstract consciousness (the form in which the object is conceived) is merely a moment of distinction of self-consciousness, what appears as the result of the movement is the identity of self-consciousness with consciousness —absolute knowledge—the movement of abstract thought no longer directed outwards but proceeding now only within its own self: that is to say, the dialectic of pure thought is the result.

The outstanding achievement of Hegel's *Phenomenology* and of its final outcome, the dialectic of negativity as the moving and generating principle, is thus first that Hegel conceives the self-creation of man as a process, conceives objectification as loss of the object, as alienation and as transcendence of this alienation; that he thus grasps the essence of *labor* and comprehends objective man—true, because real man—as the outcome of man's *own* labor. The *real*, active orientation of man to himself as a species being, or his manifestation as a real species being (i.e., as a human being), is only possible by the utilization of all the *powers* he has in himself and which are his as belonging to the *species*—something which in turn is only possible through the cooperative action of all of mankind, as the result of history—is only possible by man's treating these generic powers as objects: and this, to begin with, is again only possible in the form of estrangement.

We shall now demonstrate in detail Hegel's one-sidedness and limitations as they are displayed in the final chapter of the *Phenomenology*, "Absolute Knowledge"—a chapter which contains the concentrated spirit of the *Phenomenology*, the relationship of the *Phenomenology* to speculative dialectic, and also Hegel's *consciousness* concerning both and their relationship to one another.

Let us provisionally say just this much in advance: Hegel's standpoint is that of modern political economy.[14] He grasps *labor* as the *essence* of man—as man's essence in the act of proving itself: he sees only the positive, not the negative side of labor.[15] Labor is man's *coming-to-be for himself* within *alienation,* or as *alienated* man. The only labor which Hegel knows and recognizes is *abstractly mental* labor. Therefore, that which constitutes the *essence* of philosophy—the *alienation of man in his knowing of himself*, or *alienated* science *thinking itself*—Hegel grasps as its essence; and he is therefore able to gather together the separate elements and phases of previous philosophy, and to present his philosophy as *the* philosophy. What the other philosophers did— that they grasped separate phases of nature and of human life as phases of self-consciousness, and indeed of abstract self-consciousness—is *known* to Hegel from the *doings* of philosophy. Hence his science is absolute.

Let us now turn to our subject.

Absolute Knowledge. The last chapter of the "Phenomenology."

The main point is that the *object of consciousness* is nothing else but *self-consciousness,* or that the object is only *objectified self-consciousness*—self-consciousness as object.

(Positing of man = self-consciousness.)

The issue, therefore, is to surmount the *object of consciousness. Objectivity* as such is regarded as an *estranged* human relationship which does not correspond to the *essence of man,* to self-consciousness. The *reappropriation* of the objective essence of man, begotten in the form of estrangement as something alien, therefore not only as the annulment of *estrangement,* but of *objectivity* as well. Man, that is to say, is regarded as a *non-objective, spiritual* being.

The movement of *surmounting the object of consciousness* is now described by Hegel in the following way:

The *object* reveals itself not merely as *returning into the self*—for Hegel that is the *one-sided* way of apprehending this movement, the grasping of only one side. Man is equated with self. The self, however, is only the *abstractly* conceived man—man begotten by abstraction. Man *is* egotistic. His eye, his ear, etc., are *egotistic*. In him every one of his essential powers has the quality of *selfhood*.[16] But it is quite false to say on that account *"self-consciousness* has eyes, ears, essential powers." Self-consciousness is rather a quality of human nature, of the human eye, etc.; it is not human nature that is a quality of *self-consciousness*.

The self-abstracted entity, and fixed for itself, is man as *abstract egoist*—egoism raised in its pure abstraction to the level of thought. (We shall return to this point later.)

For Hegel the *essence of man*—*man*—equals *self-consciousness.* All estrangement of the human essence is therefore *nothing but estrangement of self-consciousness.* The estrangement of self-consciousness is not regarded as an *expression* of the *real* estrangement of the human being—its expression reflected in the realm of knowledge and thought. Instead, the *real* estrangement—that which appears real—is according to its *innermost,* hidden nature (a nature first brought to light by philosophy) nothing but the *manifestation* of the estrangement of the real essence of man, of *self-consciousness*. The science which comprehends this is therefore called *Phenomenology*.[17] All reappropriation of the estranged objective essence appears, therefore, as a process of incorporation into self-consciousness: The man who takes hold of his essential being is *merely* the self-consciousness which takes hold of objective essences. Return of the object into the self is therefore the reappropriation of the object.

Expressed in *all* its aspects, the *surmounting of the object of consciousness* means: [18]

(1) That the object as such presents itself to consciousness as something vanishing. (2) That it is the alienation of self-consciousness which establishes thinghood.[19] (3) That this externalization [20] of self-consciousness has not merely a *negative* but a *positive* significance. (4) That it has this meaning not merely *for us* or *intrinsically*, but *for self-consciousness itself*. (5) For *self-consciousness*, the negative of the object, its annulling of itself, has *positive* significance—self-consciousness itself alienates itself; for in this alienation it establishes *itself* as object, or, for the sake of the indivisible unity of *being-for-self*, establishes the object as itself. (6) On the other hand, there is also this other moment in the process, that self-consciousness has also just as much annulled and superseded this alienation and objectivity and resumed them into itself, being thus at home with *itself* in *its* other-being as such. (7) This is the movement of *consciousness* and this is therefore the totality of its moments. (8) Consciousness must similarly have taken up a relation to the object in the totality of its determinations and have comprehended it in terms of each of them. This totality of its determinations makes the object *intrinsically a spiritual being*; and it becomes so in truth for consciousness through the apprehending of each single one of them as *self* or through what was called above the *spiritual* attitude to them.

As to (1): That the object as such presents itself to consciousness as something vanishing—this is the above-mentioned *return of the object into the self.*

As to (2): The alienation of self-consciousness establishes *thing-*

hood. Because man equals self-consciousness, his alienated, objective essence, or *thinghood,* equals *alienated self-consciousness,* and *thinghood* is thus established through this alienation (thinghood being *that* which is an *object for man* and an object for him is really only that which is to him an essential object, therefore his *objective* essence. And since it is not *real Man,* nor therefore *Nature*—Man being *human Nature*—who as such is made the subject, but only the abstraction of man—self-consciousness—thinghood cannot be anything but alienated self-consciousness). It is only to be expected that a living, natural being equipped and endowed with objective (i.e., material) essential powers should have *real natural objects* of his essence; as is the fact that his self-alienation should lead to the establishing of a *real,* objective world, therefore, not belonging to his own essential being, and an overpowering objective world. There is nothing incomprehensible or mysterious in this. It would be mysterious, rather, if it were otherwise. But it is equally clear that a *self-consciousness* (i.e. its alienation) can only establish *thinghood* (i.e., establish something which itself is only an abstract thing, a thing of abstraction and not a *real* thing). It is clear, further, that thinghood is therefore utterly without any *independence,* any *essentiality vis-à-vis* self-consciousness; that on the contrary it is a mere creature—something *posited* by self-consciousness. And what is posited, instead of confirming itself, is but confirmation of the act of positing which for a moment but only for a moment, fixes its energy as the product, and *seems* to give it the character of an independent, real substance.[21]

Whenever real, corporeal *man,* man with his feet firmly on the solid ground, man exhaling and inhaling all the forces of nature, *establishes* his real, objective *essential powers* as alien objects by his externalization, it is not the *act of positing* which is the subject in this process: it is the subjectivity of *objective* essential powers, whose action, therefore, must also be something *objective.* An objective being acts objectively, and he would not act objectively if the objective did not reside in the very nature of his being. He creates or establishes only *objects, because* he is established by objects—because at bottom he is *nature.* In the act of establishing, therefore, this objective being does not fall from his state of "pure activity" into a *creating of the object*; on the contrary, his *objective* product only confirms his *objective* activity, establishing his activity as the activity of an objective, natural being.

Here we see how consistent naturalism or humanism distinguishes itself both from idealism and materialism, constituting at the same time the unifying truth of both. We see also how only naturalism is capable of comprehending the act of world history.

Man is directly a *natural being*. As a natural being and as a living natural being he is on the one hand endowed with *natural powers of life*—he is an *active* natural being. These forces exist in him as tendencies and abilities—as *instincts*. On the other hand, as a natural, corporeal, sensuous, objective being he is a *suffering*, conditioned and limited creature, like animals and plants. That is to say, the *objects* of his instincts exist outside him, as *objects* independent of him; yet these objects are *objects* that he *needs*—essential *objects*, indispensable to the manifestation and confirmation of his essential powers. To say that man is a *corporeal*, living, real, sensuous, objective being full of natural vigor is to say that he has *real, sensuous, objects* as the objects of his being or of his life, or that he can only *express* his life in real, sensuous objects. *To be* objective, natural and sensuous, and at the same time to have object, nature and sense outside oneself, or oneself to be object, nature and sense for a third party, is one and the same thing. *Hunger* is a natural *need;* it therefore needs a *nature* outside itself, an *object* outside itself, in order to satisfy itself, to be stilled. Hunger is an acknowledged need of my body for an *object* existing outside it, indispensable to its integration and to the expression of its essential being. The sun is the *object* of the plant —an indispensable object to it, confirming its life—just as the plant is an object of the sun, being an *expression* of the life-awakening power of the sun, of the sun's *objective* essential power.

A being which does not have its nature outside itself is not a *natural* being, and plays no part in the system of nature. A being which has no object outside itself is not an objective being. A being which is not itself an object for some third being has no being for its *object;* i.e., it is not objectively related. Its be-ing is not objective.[22]

An unobjective being is a *nullity*—an *un-being.*

Suppose a being which is neither an object itself, nor has an object. Such a being, in the first place, would be the *unique* being: there would exist no being outside it—it would exist solitary and alone. For as soon as there are objects outside me, as soon as I am not *alone,* I am *another—another reality* than the object outside me. For this third object I am thus an *other reality* than itself; that is, I am *its* object. Thus, to suppose a being which is not the object of another being is to presuppose that *no* objective being exists. As soon as I have an object, this object has me for an object. But a *non-objective* being is an unreal, nonsensical [23] thing—a product of mere thought (hence of mere imagination)— a creature of abstraction. To be *sensuous* is to be an object of sense, to be a *sensuous* object, and thus to have sensuous objects outside oneself—objects of one's sensuousness. To be sensuous is to *suffer.*[24]

Man as an objective, sensuous being is therefore a *suffering* being—and because he feels what he suffers, a *passionate* being. Passion is the essential force of man energetically bent on its object.

But man is not merely a natural being: he is a *human* natural being. That is to say, he is a being for himself. Therefore he is a *species being,* and has to confirm and manifest himself as such both in his being and in his knowing. Therefore, *human* objects are not natural objects as they immediately present themselves, and neither is *human sense* as it immediately *is*—as it is objectively—*human* sensibility, human objectivity. Neither nature objectively nor nature subjectively is directly given in a form adequate to the *human* being. And as everything natural has to have its *beginning, man* too has his act of origin—*history*—which, however, is for him a known history, and hence as an act of origin it is a conscious self-transcending act of origin. History is the true natural history of man (on which more later).

Thirdly, because this establishing of thinghood is itself only a sham, an act contradicting the nature of pure activity, it has to be canceled again and thinghood denied.

Re, 3, 4, 5 and 6. (3) This externalization of consciousness has not merely a *negative* but a *positive* significance, and (4) it has this meaning not merely *for us* or intrinsically, but for consciousness itself.[25] (5) *For consciousness* the negative of the object, its annulling of itself, has *positive* significance—consciousness *knows* this nullity of the object because it alienates *itself*; for in this alienation it *knows* itself as object, or, for the sake of the indivisible unity of *being-for-itself,* the object as itself. (6) On the other hand, there is also this other moment in the process, that consciousness has also just as much annulled and superseded this alienation and objectivity and resumed them into itself, being thus *at home with itself* in its *other-being as such.*

As we have already seen, the appropriation of what is estranged and objective, or the annulling of objectivity in the form of *estrangement* (which has to advance from indifferent foreignness to real, antagonistic estrangement) means equally or even primarily for Hegel that it is *objectivity* which is to be annulled, because it is not the *determinate* character of the object, but rather its *objective* character that is offensive and constitutes estrangement for self-consciousness. The object is therefore something negative, self-annulling—a *nullity.* This nullity of the object has not only a negative but a *positive* meaning for consciousness, for such a *nullity* of the object is precisely the *self-confirmation* of the non-objectivity, of the *abstraction* of itself. For *consciousness itself* this nullity of the object has a positive meaning because it *knows* this nullity, the objective being, as its *self-alienation*; because it knows that it exists only as a result of its own *self-alienation.* . . .

The way in which consciousness is, and in which something is for it, is *knowing.* Knowing is its sole act. Something therefore comes to be for consciousness in so far as the latter *knows* this *something.* Knowing is its sole objective relation. Consciousness, then, knows the nullity of the object (i.e., knows the non-existence of the distinction between the object and itself, the non-existence of the object for it) because it knows the object as its *self-alienation*; that is, it knows itself—knows knowing as the object—because the object is only the *semblance* of an object, a piece of mystification, which in its essence, however, is nothing else but knowing itself, which has confronted itself with itself and in so doing has confronted itself with a *nullity*—a something which has *no* objectivity outside the knowing. Or: knowing knows that in relating itself to an object it is only *outside* itself—that it only externalizes itself; that *it itself appears* to itself only *as an object* —or that that which appears to it as an object is only itself.

On the other hand, says Hegel, there is here at the same time this other moment, that consciousness has just as much annulled and reabsorbed this externalization and objectivity, being thus *at home* in its *other-being as such.*

In this discussion are brought together all the illusions of speculation.

First of all: consciousness—self-consciousness—is *at home in its other-being as such.* It is therefore—or if we here abstract from the Hegelian abstraction and put the self-consciousness of man instead of Self-consciousness—*it is at home in its other-being as such.* This implies, for one thing that consciousness (knowing as knowing, thinking as thinking) pretends to be directly the *other* of itself—to be the world of sense, the real world, life—thought over-reaching itself in thought (Feuerbach).[26] This aspect is contained herein, inasmuch as consciousness as mere consciousness takes offense not at estranged objectivity, but at *objectivity as such.*

Secondly, this implies that self-conscious man, in so far as he has recognized and annulled and superseded the spiritual world (or his world's spiritual, general mode of being) as self-alienation, nevertheless again confirms this in its alienated shape and passes it off as his true mode of being—reestablishes it, and pretends to be *at home in his other-being as such.* Thus, for instance, after annulling and superseding religion, after recognizing religion to be a product of self-alienation, he yet finds confirmation of himself in *religion as religion.* Here *is* the root of Hegel's *false* positivism, or of his merely *apparent* criticism: this is what Feuerbach designated as the positing, negating and reestablishing of religion or theology—but it has to be grasped in more general terms. Thus reason is at home in unreason as unreason. The man who has recognized that he is leading an alienated life in politics, law, etc., is leading his true human life in this alienated life as such. Self-affirmation, *in contradiction* with itself—in contradiction both with the knowledge of and with the essential being of the object —is thus true *knowledge* and *life*.

There can therefore no longer be any question about an act of accommodation on Hegel's part *vis-à-vis* religion, the state, etc., since this lie is the lie of his principle.

If I *know* religion as *alienated* human self-consciousness, then what I know in it as religion is not my self-consciousness, but my alienated self-consciousness confirmed in it. I therefore know my own self, the self-consciousness that belongs to its very nature, confirmed not in *religion* but rather in *annihilated* and *superseded* religion.

In Hegel, therefore, the negation of the negation is not the confirmation of the true essence, effected precisely through negation of the pseudo-essence. With him the negation of the negation is the confirmation of the pseudo-essence, or of the self-estranged essence in its denial; or it is the denial of this pseudo-essence as an objective being dwelling outside man and independent of him, and its transformation into the subject.

A peculiar role, therefore, is played by the act of *superseding* in which denial and preservation—denial and affirmation—are bound together.

Thus, for example, in Hegel's *Philosophy of Right, Private Right* superseded equals *Morality,* Morality superseded equals the *Family*, the Family superseded equals *Civil Society*, Civil Society superseded equals the *State,* the State superseded equals *World History*. In the *actual world* private right, morality, the family, civil society, the state, etc., remain in existence, only they have become *moments* of man—state of his existence and being—which have no validity in isolation, but dissolve and engender one another, etc. They have become *moments of motion*.

In their actual existence this *mobile* nature of theirs is hidden. It first appears and is made manifest in thought, in philosophy. Hence my true religious existence is my existence in the *philosophy of religion*; my true political existence is my existence within the *philosophy of right*; my true natural existence, existence in the *philosophy of nature*; my true artistic existence, existence in the *philosophy of art*; my true *human* existence, my existence in *philosophy*. Likewise the true existence of religion, the state, nature, art, is the *philosophy* of religion, of nature, of the state and of art. If, however, the philosophy of religion, etc., is for me the sole true existence of religion, then, too, it is only as a *philosopher of religion* that I am truly religious, and so I deny *real* religious sentiment and the really *religious* man. But at the same time I *assert* them, in part within my own existence or within the alien existence which I oppose to them—for this *is* only their *philosophic* expression—and in part I assert them in their own original shape, for they have validity for me as merely the *apparent* other-being, as allegories, forms of their own true existence (i.e., of my *philosophical* existence) hidden under sensuous disguises.

In just the same way, *Quality* superseded equals *Quantity*, Quantity superseded equals *Measure*, Measure superseded equals *Essence*, Essence superseded equals *Appearance*, Appearance superseded equals *Actuality*, Actuality superseded equals the *Concept*, the Concept superseded equals *Objectivity*, Objectivity superseded equals the *Absolute Idea*, the Absolute Idea superseded equals *Nature*, Nature superseded equals *Subjective* Mind, Subjective Mind superseded equals *Ethical* Objective Mind, Ethical Mind superseded equals *Art*, Art superseded equals *Religion*, Religion superseded equals *Absolute Knowledge*.[27]

On the one hand, this act of superseding is a transcending of the thought entity; thus, private property *as a thought* is transcended in the *thought* of morality. And because thought imagines itself to be directly the other of itself, to be *sensuous reality*—and therefore takes its own action for *sensuous, real action*—this superseding in thought, which leaves its object standing in the real world, believes that it has really overcome it. On the other hand, because the object has now become for it a moment of thought, thought takes it in its reality too to be self-confirmation of itself—of self-consciousness of abstraction.

From the one point of view the entity which Hegel *supersedes* in philosophy is therefore not *real* religion, the *real* state, or *real* nature, but religion itself already as an object of knowledge, i.e., *Dogmatics;* the same with *Jurisprudence, Political Science* and *Natural Science.* From the one point of view, therefore, he stands in opposition both to the *real* thing and to immediate, unphilosophic *science* or the unphilosophic *conceptions* of this thing. He therefore contradicts their conventional conceptions.[28]

On the other hand, the religious man, etc., can find in Hegel his final confirmation.

It is now time to grasp the *positive* aspects of the Hegelian dialectic within the realm of estrangement,

(a) Supersession as an objective movement of *retracting* the alienation *into self.* This is the insight, expressed within the estrangement, concerning the *appropriation* of the objective essence through the supersession of its estrangement; it is the estranged insight into the *real objectification* of man, into the real appropriation of his objective essence through the annihilation of the *estranged* character of the objective world, through the supersession of the objective world in its estranged mode of being. In the same way atheism, being the supersession of God, is the advent of theoretic humanism, and communism, as the supersession of private property, is the vindication of real human life as man's possession and thus the advent of practical humanism (or just as atheism is humanism mediated with itself through the supersession of religion, whilst communism is humanism mediated with itself through the supersession of private property). Only through the supersession of this mediation—which is itself, however, a necessary premise—does positively self-deriving humanism, *positive humanism,* come into being.

But atheism and communism are no flight, no abstraction; no loss of the objective world created by man—of man's essential powers born to the realm of objectivity; they are not a returning in poverty to unnatural, primitive simplicity. On the contrary, they are but the first real emergence, the actual realization for man of man's essence and of his essence as something real.

Thus, by grasping the *positive* meaning of self-referred negation (although again in estranged fashion) Hegel grasps man's self-estrangement, the alienation of man's essence, man's loss of objectivity and his loss of realness as self-discovery, change of his nature, objectification and realization.[29] In short, within the sphere of abstraction, Hegel conceives labor as man's act of *self-genesis*—conceives man's relation to himself as an alien being and the manifestation of himself as an alien being to be the emergence of *species consciousness* and *species life*.

(b) However, apart from, or rather in consequence of, the reversal already described, this act appears in Hegel:

First of all as a merely formal, because abstract, act, because the human essence itself is taken to be only an *abstract, thinking essence*, conceived merely as self-consciousness. And,

Secondly, because the exposition is *formal* and *abstract*, the supersession of the alienation becomes a confirmation of the alienation; or again, for Hegel this movement of *self-genesis* and *self-objectification* in the form of *self-alienation* and *self-estrangement* is the *absolute*, and hence final, *expression of human life*—of life with itself as its aim, of life at peace with itself, and in unity with its essence.

This movement, in its abstract form as dialectic, is therefore regarded as *truly human life*, and because it is nevertheless an abstraction—an estrangement of human life—it is regarded as a *divine process*, but as the divine process of man, a process traversed by man's abstract, pure, absolute essence that is distinct from himself.

Thirdly, this process must have a bearer, a subject. But the subject first emerges as a result. This result—the subject knowing itself as absolute self-consciousness—is therefore *God*—*absolute Spirit—the self-knowing and self-manifesting Idea*. Real man and real nature become mere predicates—symbols of this esoteric, unreal man and of this unreal nature. Subject and predicate are therefore related to each other in absolute reversal—a *mystical subject-object* or a *subjectivity reaching beyond* the *object*—the *absolute subject* as a *process*, as *subject alienating* itself and returning from alienation into itself, but at the same time retracting this alienation into itself, and the subject as this process; a pure, *restless* revolving within itself.

A *formal and abstract* conception of man's act of self-creation or self-objectification remains.

Hegel having posited man as equivalent to self-consciousness, the estranged object—the estranged essential reality of man—is nothing but *consciousness*, the thought of estrangement merely —estrangement's *abstract* and therefore empty and unreal expression, *negation*. The supersession of the alienation is therefore likewise nothing but an abstract, empty supersession of that empty abstraction—the *negation of the negation*. The rich, living, sensuous, concrete activity of self-objectification is therefore reduced to its mere abstraction, *absolute negativity*—an abstraction which is again fixed as such and considered as an independent activity— as sheer activity. Because this so-called negativity is nothing but the *abstract, empty* form of that real living act, its content can in consequence be merely a *formal* content begotten by abstraction from all content. As a result there are general, abstract *forms of abstraction* pertaining to every content and on that account indifferent to, and, consequently, valid for, all content—the thought-forms or logical categories torn from *real* mind and from *real* nature. (We shall unfold the *logical* content of absolute negativity further on.)

Hegel's positive achievement here, in his speculative logic, is that the *definite concepts*, the universal *fixed thought-forms* in their independence *vis-à-vis* nature and mind are a necessary result of the general estrangement of the human essence and therefore also of human thought, and Hegel has therefore brought these together and presented them as moments of the abstraction-process. For example, superseded Being is Essence, superseded Essence is Concept, the Concept superseded is . . . the Absolute Idea. But what, then, is the Absolute Idea? It supersedes its own self again, if it does not want to traverse once more from the beginning the whole act of abstraction, and to satisfy itself by being a totality of abstractions or the self-comprehending abstraction. But abstraction comprehending itself as abstraction knows itself to be nothing: it must abandon itself—abandon abstraction —and so it arrives at an entity which is its exact opposite—at *nature*. Thus, the entire *Logic* is the demonstration that abstract thought is nothing in itself; that the Absolute Idea is nothing for itself; that only *Nature* is something.

The absolute idea, the *abstract* idea, which "*considered* with regard to its unity with itself is *intuiting*," [30] (Hegel's *Encyclopaedia,* 3rd edition, p. 222), and which "in its own absolute truth *resolves* to let the moment of its particularity or of initial characterization and other-being—the *immediate idea,* as its reflection, *go forth freely from itself as nature" (l.c.)*—this whole idea which behaves in such a strange and grotesque way, and which has given the Hegelians such terrible headaches, is from beginning to end nothing else but *abstraction* (i.e., the abstract thinker)—abstraction which, made wise by experience and enlightened concerning its truth, resolves under various (false and themselves still abstract) conditions to *abandon itself* and to replace its self-absorption, nothingness, generality and indeterminateness by its other-being, the particular, and the determinate; resolves to let *nature,* which it held hidden in itself only as an abstraction, as a thought-entity, *go forth freely from itself:* that is to say, abstraction resolves to forsake abstraction and to have a look at nature *free* of abstraction. The abstract idea, which without mediation becomes *intuiting,* is indeed nothing else but abstract thinking that gives itself up and resolves on *intuition.* This entire transition from Logic to Natural Philosophy is nothing else but the transition— so difficult to effect for the abstract thinker, who therefore describes it in such an adventurous way—from *abstracting* to *intuiting.* The *mystical* feeling which drives the philosopher forward from abstract thinking to intuiting is *boredom*—the longing for a content.

(The man estranged from himself is also the thinker estranged from his *essence*—that is, from the natural and human essence. His thoughts are therefore fixed mental shapes or ghosts dwelling outside nature and man. Hegel has locked up all these fixed mental forms together in his *Logic,* laying hold of each of them first as negation—that is, as an *alienation* of *human* thought—and then as negation of the negation—that is, as a superseding of this alienation, as a *real* expression of human thought. But as even this still takes place within the confines of the estrangement, this negation of the negation is in part the restoring of these fixed forms in their estrangement; in part a stopping-short at the last act—the act of self-reference in alienation—as the true mode of being of these fixed mental forms; * and in part, to the extent that this abstraction apprehends itself and experiences an infinite weariness with itself, there makes its appearance in Hegel, in the form of the resolution to recognize *nature* as the essential being and to go over to intuition, the abandonment of abstract thought—the abandonment of thought revolving solely within the orbit of thought, of thought sans eyes, sans teeth, sans ears, sans everything.)

But *nature* too, taken abstractly, for itself—nature fixed in isolation from man—is *nothing* for man. It goes without saying that the abstract thinker who has committed himself to intuiting, intuits nature abstractly. Just as nature lay enclosed in the thinker in the form of the absolute idea, in the form of a thought-entity —in a shape which is his and yet is esoteric and mysterious even to him—so what he has really let emerge from himself is only this *abstract nature*, only nature as a *thought-entity*—but now with the significance that it is the other-being of thought, that it is real, intuited nature—nature distinguished from abstract thought. Or, to talk in human language, the abstract thinker learns in his intuition of nature that the entities which he thought to create from nothing, from pure abstraction—the entities he believed he was producing in the divine dialectic as pure products of the labor of thought, forever shuttling back and forth in itself and never looking outward into reality—are nothing else but *abstractions* from *characteristics of nature*. To him, therefore, the whole of nature merely repeats the logical abstractions in a sensuous, external form. He *analyzes* nature and these abstractions over

* This means that what Hegel does is to put in place of these fixed abstractions the act of abstraction which revolves in its own circle. In so doing, we must give him the credit for having indicated the source of all these inappropriate concepts which, as originally presented, belonged to philosophies; for having brought them together; and for having created the entire compass of abstraction as the object of criticism, instead of some specific abstraction. (Why Hegel separates thought from the *subject* we shall see later: at this stage it is already clear, however, that when man is not his characteristic expression he also cannot be human, and so neither could thought be grasped as an expression of man as a human and natural subject endowed with eyes, ears, etc., and living in society, in the world, and in nature.)

again. Thus, his intuition of nature is only the act of confirming his abstraction from the intuition of nature—is only the conscious repetition by him of the process of creating his abstraction. Thus, for example, Time equals Negativity referred to itself (*l.c.*, p. 238): to the superseded Becoming as Being there corresponds, in natural form, superseded Movement as Matter. Light is *Reflection-in-Itself*, in *natural* form. Body as *Moon* and *Comet* is the *natural* form of the *antithesis* which according to the *Logic* is on the one side the *Positive resting on itself* and on the other side the *Negative* resting on itself. The Earth is the *natural* form of the logical *Ground*, as the negative unity of the antithesis, etc.[31]

Nature as nature—that is to say, in so far as it is still sensuously distinguished from that secret sense hidden within it—nature isolated, distinguished from these abstractions, is *nothing*—a nothing *proving itself to be nothing*—is *devoid of sense*, or has only the sense of being an externality which has to be annulled.

"In the finite-*teleological* position is to be found the correct premise that nature does not contain within itself the absolute purpose." (p. 225).

Its purpose is the confirmation of abstraction.

"Nature has shown itself to be the Idea in the *form* of *other-being*. Since the *Idea* is in this form the negative of itself or *external to itself*, nature is not just relatively external *vis-à-vis* this idea, but *externality* constitutes the form in which it exists as nature" (p. 227).[32]

Externality here is not to be understood as the *self-externalizing world of sense* open to the light, open to the man endowed with senses. It is to be taken here in the sense of alienation, of a mistake, a defect, which ought not to be. For what is true is still the Idea. Nature is only the *form of the Idea's other-being*. And since abstract thought is the *essence*, that which is external to it is by its essence something merely *external*. The abstract thinker recognizes at the same time that *sensuousness—externality* in contrast to thought shuttling back and forth *within itself*—is the essence of nature. But he expresses this contrast in such a way as to make this *externality of nature*, its *contrast* to thought, its *defect*, so that inasmuch as it is distinguished from abstraction, nature is

something defective. Something which is defective not merely for
me or in my eyes but in itself—intrinsically—has something outside itself which it lacks. That is, its being is something other
than it itself. Nature has therefore to supersede itself for the
abstract thinker, for it is already posited by him as a potentially
superseded being.

"*For us*, Mind has *nature* for its *premise*, being nature's *truth* and
for that reason its *absolute prius*. In this truth nature *has vanished*,
and mind has resulted as the Idea arrived at being-for-itself, the
object of which, as well as the *subject*, is the *concept*. This identity is
absolute negativity, for whereas in nature the concept has its perfect
external objectivity, this its alienation has been superseded, and in
this alienation the concept has become identical with itself. But it is
this identity, therefore, only in being a return out of nature" (p. 392).

"As the *abstract* idea, *revelation* is unmediated transition to, the
coming-to-be of, nature; as the revelation of the mind, which is free,
it is the *establishing* of nature as the *mind's* world—an establishing
which at the same time, being reflection, is a *presupposing* of the
world as independently-existing nature. Revelation in conception is
the creation of nature as the mind's being, in which the mind procures
the *affirmation* and the *truth* of its freedom."[33] "*The absolute is mind.*
This is the highest definition of the absolute."

APPENDIX

OUTLINES OF A CRITIQUE OF POLITICAL ECONOMY[1]

By FREDERICK ENGELS

Political economy came into being as a natural result of the expansion of trade and with its appearance elementary, unscientific huckstering was replaced by a developed system of licensed fraud—a complete get-rich economy.

This political economy or science of enrichment born of the merchants' mutual envy and greed, bears on its brow the mark of the most loathsome selfishness. People still lived in the naïve belief that gold and silver were wealth, and considered nothing more urgent than the prohibition everywhere of the export of the "precious" metals. The nations faced each other like misers, each clasping to himself with both arms his precious moneybag, eyeing his neighbors with envy and distrust. Every conceivable means was employed to lure from the nations with whom one had commerce as much ready cash as possible, and to retain snugly within the customs boundary all which had happily been gathered in.

A rigorously consistent pursuit of this principle would have killed trade. People therefore began to go beyond this first stage. They came to appreciate that capital locked up in a chest was dead capital, while capital in circulation multiplied itself continuously. They then became more philanthropic, sent off their ducats as call-birds to bring others back with them, and recognized that there is no harm in paying A too much for his commodity so long as it can be disposed of to B at a higher price.

On this basis the *mercantile system was built*. The greedy character of trade was hidden to some extent; the nations drew slightly nearer to one another, concluded trade and friendship agreements, did business together and, for the sake of larger profits,

197

treated one another with all possible love and kindness. But basically there was still the old rage for money and selfishness which from time to time erupted in wars, which in that day were all based on trade jealousy. In these wars it also became evident that trade, like robbery, is based on the law of the strong hand. No scruples whatever were felt about exacting by cunning or violence such treaties as were held to be the most advantageous.

The cardinal point in the whole mercantile system is the theory of the balance of trade. For as they still subscribed to the dictum that gold and silver were wealth, only such transactions as would finally bring ready cash into the country were considered profitable. To ascertain this, exports were compared with imports. When more had been exported than imported, it was believed that the difference had come into the country in ready cash, and that the country was richer by that difference. The art of the economists, therefore, consisted in ensuring that at the end of each year exports should show a favorable balance over imports; and for the sake of this ridiculous illusion thousands of men have been slaughtered! Trade, too, has had its crusades and inquisitions.

The eighteenth century, the century of revolution, also revolutionized economics. But just as all the revolutions of this century were one-sided and bogged down in antitheses—just as abstract materialism was set in opposition to abstract spiritualism, the republic to monarchy, the social contract to divine right—so did the economic revolution not get beyond antithesis. The premises remained everywhere in force: materialism did not contend with the Christian contempt for and humiliation of Man, and merely posited Nature instead of the Christian God as the Absolute facing Man. In politics no one dreamt of examining the premises of the state as such. It did not occur to economics to question *the validity of private property*. Therefore, the new economics was only half an advance. It was obliged to betray and to disavow its own premises, to have recourse to sophistry and hypocrisy so as to cover up the contradictions in which it became entangled, so as to reach the conclusions to which it was driven not by its premises but by the humane spirit of the century. Thus economics took on a philanthropic character. It withdrew its favor from the producers and bestowed it on the consumers. It affected a solemn abhorrence of the bloody ᵗerror of the mercantile system, and proclaimed trade to be a bond of friendship and union among nations as among individuals. All was pure splendor and magnificence—yet the premises reasserted themselves soon enough, and in contrast to this sham philanthropy produced the Malthusian population theory—the crudest, most barbarous theory that ever existed, a system of despair which struck down all those beautiful phrases about love of neighbor and world citizenship. The premises begot and reared the factory system and modern slavery, which yields nothing in inhumanity and cruelty to ancient slavery. Modern economics—the system of free trade based on Adam Smith's *Wealth of Nations*—reveals itself to be that same hypocrisy, inconsistency and immorality which now confront free humanity in every sphere.

But was Smith's system, then, not an advance? Of course it was, and a necessary advance at that. It was necessary to overthrow the mercantile ssytem with its monopolies and hindrances to trade, so that the true consequences of private property could come to light. It was necessary for all these petty, local and national considerations to recede into the background, so that the struggle of our time could become a universal human struggle. It was necessary for the theory of private property to leave the purely empirical path of merely objective enquiry and to acquire a more scientific character which would also make it responsible for the consequences, and thus transfer the matter to a universally human sphere. It was necessary to carry the immorality contained in the old economics to its highest pitch, by attempting to deny it and by veiling it in hypocrisy (a necessary result of that attempt). All this lay in the nature of the matter.

We gladly concede that it is only thanks to the establishment and development of free trade that we were placed in a position from which we can go beyond the economics of private property; but we must at the same time have the right to demonstrate the utter theoretical and practical nullity of this free trade.

The nearer to our time the economists whom we have to judge, the more severe must our judgment become. For while Smith and

Malthus only had scattered fragments to go by, the modern economists had the whole system complete before them: the consequences had all been drawn; the contradictions came clearly enough to light; yet they did not think of examining the premises, while at the same time assuming responsibility for the whole system. The nearer the economists come to the present time, the further they depart from honesty. With every advance of time, sophistry necessarily increases, so as to prevent economics from lagging behind the times. This is why *Ricardo,* for instance, is more guilty than *Adam Smith,* and *McCulloch* and *Mill* more guilty than *Ricardo.*

Modern economics cannot even judge the mercantile system correctly, since it is itself one-sided and as yet fenced in by that very system's premises. Only that view which rises above the opposition of the two systems, which criticizes the premises common to both and proceeds from a purely human, universal basis, can assign to both their proper position.

It will become evident that the protagonists of free trade are more inveterate monopolists than the old mercantilists themselves. It will become evident that the sham humanity of the modern economists hides a barbarism of which their predecessors knew nothing; that the predecessors' conceptual confusion is simple and consistent compared with the double-tongued logic of their attackers, and that neither of the two can reproach the other with anything which would not recoil upon himself.

This is why modern liberal economics cannot comprehend the restoration of the mercantile system by List,[2] whilst for us the matter is quite simple. The inconsistency and two-faced nature of liberal economics must of necessity dissolve again into its basic components. Just as theology must either regress to blind faith or progress towards free philosophy, so must free trade produce the restoration of monopolies on the one hand and the abolition of private property on the other.

The only *positive* advance which liberal economics has made is the unfolding of the laws of private property. These are contained in it, at any rate, although not yet unfolded fully and expressed clearly. It follows that on all points where it is a question of deciding which is the shortest road to wealth—i.e., in all strictly economic controversies—the protagonists of free trade have right on their side. That is, needless to say, in controversies with the monopolists—not with the opponents of private property, for the English Socialists have long since proved both practically and theoretically that the latter are in a position to settle economic questions more correctly even from an economic point of view.

In the critique of political economy, therefore, we shall examine the basic categories, uncover the contradiction introduced by the free-trade system, and bring out the consequences of both sides of the contradiction.

The term "national wealth" has only arisen as a result of the liberal economists' passion for generalization. As long as private property exists, this term has no meaning. The "national wealth" of the English is very great and yet they are the poorest people under the sun. One either dismisses this term completely, or one accepts such premises as give it meaning. Similarly with the terms "national economy" and "political or public economy." In the present circumstances that science ought to be called *private* economy, for its public connections exist only for the sake of private property.

The immediate consequence of private property is *trade*— exchange of reciprocal demand—buying and selling. This trade, like every activity, must under the dominion of private property become a direct source of gain for the trader, i.e., each must seek to sell as dear as possible and buy as cheap as possible. In every purchase and sale, therefore, two men with diametrically opposed interests confront each other. The confrontation is decidedly antagonistic, for each knows the intentions of the other—knows that they are opposed to his own. Therefore, the first consequence is mutual mistrust, on the one hand, and the justification of this mistrust—the application of immoral means to attain an immoral end—on the other. Thus, the first maxim in trade is "discretion" —the concealment of everything which might reduce the value of the article in question. The result is that in trade it is permitted to take the utmost advantage of the ignorance or the trust of the opposing party, and likewise to bestow qualities on one's commodity which it does not possess. In a word, trade is legalized fraud. Any merchant who wants to give truth its due can bear me witness that actual practice conforms with this theory.

The mercantile system still had a certain artless Catholic candor and did not in the least conceal the immoral nature of trade. We have seen how it openly paraded its mean greed. The mutually hostile attitude of the nations in the eighteenth century, loathsome envy and trade jealousy, were the logical consequences of trade as such. Public opinion had not yet become humanized. Why, therefore, conceal things which resulted from the inhuman, hostile nature of trade itself?

But when the *economic Luther*, Adam Smith, criticized past economics things had changed considerably.[3] The century had been humanized; reason had asserted itself; morality began to claim its eternal right. The extorted trade treaties, the commercial wars, the surly isolation of the nations, offended too greatly against advanced consciousness. Protestant hypocrisy took the place of Catholic candor. Smith proved that humanity, too, was rooted in the nature of trade; that trade, instead of being "the most fertile source of discord and animosity" must become a "bond of union and friendship among nations as among individuals" (*Wealth of Nations*, Bk. 4, ch. 3, §2); that after all it lay in the nature of things for trade, taken as a whole, to be profitable to *all* parties concerned.

Smith was right to eulogize trade as humane. There is nothing absolutely immoral in the world. Trade, too, has an aspect wherein it pays homage to morality and humanity. But what homage! The law of the strong hand, the open highway robbery of the Middle Ages, became humanized when it passed over into trade; and trade became humanized when, in its first stage characterized by the prohibition to export money, it passed over into the mercantile system. Now the mercantile system itself was humanized. Naturally, it is in the interest of the trader to be on good terms with the one from whom he buys cheap as well as with the other to whom he sells dear. A nation therefore acts very imprudently if it fosters feelings of animosity in its suppliers and customers. The more friendly, the more profitable. Such is the humanity of trade. And this hypocritical way of misusing morality for immoral purposes is the pride of the free-trade system.

"Have we not overthrown the barbarism of the monopolies?" exclaim the hypocrites. "Have we not carried civilization to distant parts of the world? Have we not brought about the fraternization of the peoples, and reduced the number of wars?" Yes, all this you have done—but *how!* You have destroyed the small monopolies so that the *one* great basic monopoly, property, may function the more freely and unrestrictedly. You have civilized the ends of the earth to win new terrain for the deployment of your vile greed. You have brought about the fraternization of the peoples—but the fraternity is the fraternity of thieves. You have reduced the number of wars—to earn all the bigger profits in peace, to intensify to the utmost the enmity between individuals, the ignominious war of competition! When have you done anything out of pure humanity, from consciousness of the nullity of the opposition between the general and individual interest? When have you been moral without being interested, without harboring at the back of your mind immoral, egoistical motives?

After liberal economics had done its best to universalize enmity by dissolving nationalities so as to transform mankind into a horde of ravenous beasts (for what else are competitors?) who devour one another just *because* each has identical interest with all the others—after this preparatory work there remained but one step to take before the goal was reached, the dissolution of the family.

To accomplish this, economy's own beautiful invention, the factory system, came to its aid. The last vestige of common interests, the community of possessions constituted by the family, is being undermined by the factory system and—at least here in England—is already in the process of dissolution. It is a common practice for children, as soon as they are capable of work (i.e., as soon as they reach the age of nine), to spend their wages themselves, to look upon their parental home as a mere boarding house, and to make their parents an allowance of a certain sum for food and lodging. How can it be otherwise? What else can result from the separation of interests, such as forms the basis of the free-trade system? Once a principle is set in motion, it works by its own impetus through all its consequences, whether the economists like it or not.

But the economist does not know himself what cause he serves. He does not know that with all his egoistical reasoning he nevertheless forms but a link in the chain of mankind's universal progress. He does not know that by his dissolution of all sectional interests he merely paves the way for the great transformation to which the century is moving—the reconciliation of mankind with nature and with itself.

The next category established by trade is *value*. There is no quarrel between the modern economists and their predecessors over this category, just as there is none over all the others, since the monopolists in their obsessive mania for getting rich had no time left to concern themselves with categories. All controversies over such points stem from the modern economists.

The economist who lives by antitheses has also of course a *double* value—abstract or real, and exchange value. There was a protracted quarrel over the nature of real value between the English, who defined the costs of production as the expression of real value, and the Frenchman, Say, who claimed to measure this value by the utility of an object. The quarrel hung in doubt from the beginning of the century, then became dormant without a decision having been reached. The economists cannot decide anything.

The English—McCulloch and Ricardo in particular—thus claim that the abstract value of a thing is determined by the costs of production. The abstract value, of course, not the exchange value, the "exchangeable value," [4] value in trade—that, they say, is something quite different. Why are the costs of production the measure of value? Because—listen to this!—because no one in ordinary conditions, and leaving aside the circumstance of competition, would sell an object for less than the cost to him of its production. Would sell—? What have we to do with "selling" here, where it is not a question of *trade* value? So we find trade again, which we are specifically supposed to leave aside—and what trade! A trade in which the cardinal factor, the circumstance of competition, is not to be taken into account! First, an abstract value; now also an abstract trade—a trade without competition, i.e., a man without a body, a thought without a brain to produce thoughts. And does the economist never stop to think that as soon as competition is left out of account there is no guarantee at all that the producer will sell his commodity just at the cost of production? What confusion!

Furthermore: Let us concede for a moment that everything is as the economist says. Supposing someone were to make something utterly useless with tremendous exertion and at enormous cost—were to make something which no one desires: is that also worth its production costs? Certainly not, says the economist: Who will want to buy it? So we suddenly have not only Say's despised utility but alongside it—with "buying"—the circumstance of competition. It can't be done—the economist cannot for one moment hold on to his abstraction. Not only what he painfully seeks to remove—competition—but also what he attacks—utility—crops up at every moment. Abstract value and its determination by the costs of production are, after all, only abstractions, nonentities.

But let us suppose once more for a moment that the economist is correct—how then will he determine the costs of production without taking account of competition? When examining the costs of production we shall see that this category too is based on competition, and here once more it becomes evident how little the economist is able to substantiate his claims.

If we turn to Say, we find the same abstraction. The utility of an object is something purely subjective, something which cannot be decided absolutely, and certainly something not to be decided, anyway, so long as one still roams about in antitheses. According to this theory, the necessities of life ought to possess more value than luxury articles. The only possible way to arrive at a more or less objective, *apparently* general decision on the greater or lesser utility of an object is, under the dominion of private property, by the circumstance of competition; and yet it is precisely that circumstance which is to be left aside. But if the circumstance of competition is admitted, production costs enter it as well; for no one will sell for less than what he has himself invested in production. Thus, here, too, the one side of the opposition passes over involuntarily into the other.

Let us try to introduce clarity into this confusion. The value of an object includes both factors, which the contending parties so rudely separate—and, as we have seen, without success. Value is the relation of production costs to utility. The first application of value is the decision as to whether a thing ought to be produced at all, i.e., as to whether utility counterbalances production costs. Only then can one talk of the application of value to exchange. The production costs of two objects being equal, the deciding factor determining their comparative value will be utility.

This basis is the only just basis of exchange. But if one proceeds from the basis, who is to decide the utility of the object? The mere opinion of the parties concerned? Then in any event *one* will be cheated. Or is this decision a determination grounded in the inherent utility of the object independent of the parties concerned, and not apparent to them? If so, the exchange can only be effected *by coercion*, and each party considers itself cheated. The opposition between the real inherent utility of the thing and the determination of that utility, between the determination of utility and the freedom of those who exchange, cannot be superseded without superseding private property; and once this is superseded, there can no longer be any question of exchange as it exists at present. The practical application of the concept of value will then be increasingly confined to the decision about production, and that is its proper sphere.

But how do matters stand at present? We have seen how the concept of value is violently torn asunder, and how the detached sides are each substituted for the whole. Production costs, distorted from the outset by competition, are supposed to be value itself. So is mere subjective utility—since no other kind of utility can exist at this stage. To help these lame definitions on to their feet, we must in both cases have recourse to competition; and the best of it is that with the English competition represents utility, in contrast to the costs of production, whilst inversely with Say it introduces the costs of production in contrast to utility. But what kind of utility, what kind of production costs, does it introduce? Its utility depends on chance, on fashion, on the whim of the rich; its production costs fluctuate with the accidental relationship of demand and supply.

The difference between real value and exchange value is based on the fact, namely, that the value of a thing differs from the so-called equivalent given for it in trade; i.e., that this equivalent is not an equivalent. This so-called equivalent is the *price* of the thing, and if the economist were honest, he would employ this term for trade value. But he has still to keep up some sort of pretense that price is somehow bound up with value, lest the immorality of trade become too obvious. It is, however, quite correct, and a fundamental law of private property, that *price* is determined by the reciprocal action of production costs and competition. This purely empirical law was the first to be discovered by the economist; and from this law he then abstracted his "real value," i.e., the price at the time when competition is in a state of equilibrium, when demand and supply cover each other. Then, of course, what remains over are the costs of production and it is these which the economist proceeds to call "real value," whilst they are merely the determinateness of price. Thus everything in economics stands on its head. Value, the origin or source of price, is made dependent on that which is its own product. As is well known, this inversion is the essence of abstraction; on which see Feuerbach.

According to the economists, the production costs of a commodity consist of three elements: the rent for the piece of land required to produce the raw material; the capital with its profit; and the wages for the labor required for production and manufacture. But it becomes immediately evident that capital and labor are identical, since the economists themselves confess that capital is "stored-up labor." We are therefore left with only two sides—the natural objective side, land; and the human, subjective side, labor, which includes capital and, besides capital, a third factor which the economist does not think about—I mean the spiritual element of invention, of thought, alongside the physical element of sheer labor. What has the economist to do with the spirit of invention? Have not all inventions come flying to him without any effort on his part? Has *one* of them cost him anything? Why then should he bother about them in the calculation of production costs? Land, capital and labor are for him the conditions of wealth, and he requires no more. Science is no concern of his. What does it matter to him that he has received its gifts through Berthollet, Davy, Liebig, Watt, Cartwright, etc.—gifts which have benefited him and his production immeasurably? He does not know how to calculate such things; the advances of science go beyond his figures. But in a rational order which has gone beyond the division of interests as it is found with the economist, the spiritual element certainly belongs among the elements of production and will find its place, too, in economics among the costs of production. And here it is certainly gratifying to know that the promotion of science also brings its material reward; to know that a single achievement of science like James Watt's steam engine has brought in more for the world in the first fifty years of its existence than the world has spent on the promotion of science since the beginning of time.

We have, then, two elements of production in operation—nature and man, with man again active physically and spiritually, and can go back to the economist and his production costs.

What cannot be monopolized has no value, says the economist—a proposition which we shall examine more closely later. If we say "has no *price*," then the proposition is valid for the order which rests on private property. If land could be had as easily as air, no one would pay rent. Since this is not the case, but since, rather, the extent of a piece of land to be acquired is limited in any particular case, one pays rent for the acquired, i.e., the monopolized land, or one pays down a purchase price for it. After this enlightenment about the origin of ground rent it is, however, very strange to have to hear from the economist that the rent of land is the difference between the yield from the rented land and from the worst land worth cultivating at all. As is well known, this is the definition of rent fully developed for the first time by Ricardo. This definition is no doubt correct in practice if one presupposes that a fall in demand reacts *instantaneously* on rent, and at once puts a corresponding amount of the worst cultivated land out of cultivation. This, however, is not the case, and the definition is therefore inadequate. Moreover, it does not cover the origin of rent, and must therefore be dismissed for that reason alone. In opposition to this definition, Col. T. P. Thompson, the champion of the Anti-Corn Law League,[5] revived Adam Smith's definition, and consolidated it. According to him, rent is the relation between the competition of those striving for the use of the land and the limited quantity of available land. Here, at least is a return to the origin of rent; but this explanation does not take into account the varying fertility of the soil, just as the previous explanation leaves out competition.

Once more, therefore, we have two one-sided and hence only imperfect definitions of a single object. As in the case of the concept of value, we shall again have to bring together these two definitions so as to find the correct definition which will follow from the development of the thing itself and thus embrace all practice. Rent is the relation between the productivity of the land—between the natural side (which in turn consists of *natural* fertility and *human* cultivation—labor applied to effect improvement), and the human side, competition. The economists may shake their heads over this "definition"; they will discover to their horror that it embraces everything relevant to this matter.

The *landowner* has nothing with which to reproach the merchant.

He practices robbery in monopolizing the land. He practices robbery in exploiting for his own benefit the increase in population which increases competition and thus the value of his estate; in turning into a source of personal advantage that which has not been his own doing—that which is his by sheer accident. He practices robbery in *leasing his land,* when he eventually seizes for himself the improvements effected by his tenant. This is the secret of the ever-increasing wealth of the great landowners.

The axioms which qualify as robbery the landowner's method of deriving an income—namely, that each has a right to the product of his labor, or that no one shall reap where he has not sown—are not something *we* have invented. The first excludes the duty of feeding children; the second deprives each generation of the right to live, since each generation starts with what it inherits from the preceding generation. These axioms are, rather, implications of private property. Either one implements its implications or one abandons private property as a premise.

Indeed, the original act of appropriation itself is justified by the assertion of the still earlier *common* property right. Thus, wherever we turn, private property leads us into contradictions.

To make earth an object of huckstering—the earth which is our one and all, the first condition of our existence—was the last step toward making oneself an object of huckstering. It was and is to this very day an immorality surpassed only by the immorality of self-alienation. And the original appropriation—the monopolization of the earth by a few, the exclusion of the rest from that which is the condition of their life—yields nothing in immorality to the subsequent huckstering of the earth.

If here again we abandon private property, rent is reduced to its truth, to the rational notion which essentially lies at its root. The value of the land divorced from it as rent then reverts to the land itself. This value, to be measured by the productivity of equal acres of land subjected to equal applications of labor, should, however, be taken into account as part of the production costs when determining the value of products; and like rent, it is the relation of productivity to competition—but to *true* competition, such as will be developed when its time comes.

We have seen how capital and labor are initially identical; we see further from the explanations of the economist himself, how, in the process of production, capital, the result of labor, is immediately transformed again into the substratum, into the material of labor; and how therefore the momentarily established separation of capital from labor immediately gives way to the unity of both. And yet the economist separates capital from labor, and still insists on the division without giving any other recognition to their unity than by his defining capital as "stored-up labor." The split between capital and labor resulting from private property is nothing but the inner dichotomy of labor corresponding to this divided condition and arising out of it. And after this separation is accomplished, capital divides itself once more into the original capital and profit—the increment of capital, which it receives in the process of production; although in practice profit is immediately lumped together with capital and set into motion with it. Indeed, even profit is in its turn split into interest and profit proper. In the case of interest, the absurdity of these splits is carried to the extreme. The immorality of interest-loans, of receiving without working, for merely lending, though already inherent in private property, is only too obvious, and has long ago been recognized for what it is by unsophisticated popular consciousness, which in such matters is usually right. All these minute splits and divisions stem from the original separation of capital from labor and from the culmination of this separation— the division of mankind into capitalists and workers—a division which daily becomes ever more acute, and which, as we shall see, is *bound* to deepen. This separation, however, like the separation already considered of land from capital and labor, is in the final analysis an impossible separation. What share land, capital and labor each have in any particular product cannot be determined. The three magnitudes are incommensurable. The soil creates the raw material, but not without capital and labor. Capital presupposes land and labor. And labor presupposes *at least* land, and usually also capital. The functions of these three elements are completely different, and are not to be measured by a fourth common standard. Therefore, when it comes to dividing the proceeds among the three elements under existing conditions, there is no inherent standard; it is an entirely alien and to them fortuitous standard that decides—competition, the slick right of the stronger. Rent implies competition; profit on capital is solely determined by competition; and the position with regard to wages we shall see presently.

If we abandon private property, then all these unnatural divi-

sions disappear. The difference between interest and profit disappears; capital is nothing without labor, without movement.
The significance of profit is reduced to the weight which capital
carries in the determination of the costs of production; and profit
thus remains inherent in capital, in the same way as capital itself
reverts to its original unity with labor.

Labor—the main factor in production, the "source of wealth,"
free human activity—comes off badly with the economist. Just
as capital was previously separated from labor, likewise labor is
now in turn split for a second time: the product of labor confronts labor as wages, is separated from it, and is as usual once
more determined by competition—there being, as we have seen,
no firm standard determining labor's share in production. If we
do away with private property, this unnatural separation also
disappears. Labor becomes its own reward, and the true significance of the wages of labor, hitherto alienated, comes to light—
namely, the significance of labor for the determination of the
production costs of a thing.

We have seen that in the end everything comes down to competition, so long as private property exists. It is the economist's
principal category—his most beloved daughter, whom he cease-
lessly caresses—and look out for the Medusa's head which she will
show you!
The immediate consequence of private property was the split
of production into two opposing sides—the natural and the
human sides, the soil which without fertilization by man is dead
and sterile, and human activity, whose first condition is that very
soil. Furthermore we have seen how human activity in its turn
was dissolved into labor and capital, and how these two sides
antagonistically confronted each other. Thus already we had the
struggle of the three elements against one another, instead of their
mutual support; and to make matters worse, private property
brings in its wake the splintering of each of these elements. One
estate stands confronted by another, one piece of capital by another, one unit of labor power by another. In other words, because

private property isolates everyone in his own crude solitariness, and because, nevertheless, everyone has the same interest as his neighbor, one landowner stands antagonistically confronted by another, one capitalist by another, one worker by another. In this discord of identical interests resulting precisely from this identity is consummated the immorality of mankind's condition until now; and this consummation is competition.

The opposite of *competition* is *monopoly*. Monopoly was the war cry of the mercantilists; competition the battle cry of the liberal economists. It is easy to see that this antitheses is again quite hollow. Every competitor *cannot but* desire to have the monopoly, be he worker, capitalist or landowner. Each smaller group of competitors cannot but desire to have the monopoly for itself against all others. Competition is based on self-interest, and self-interest in turn breeds monopoly. In short, competition passes over into monopoly. On the other hand, monopoly cannot stem the tide of competition—indeed, it itself breeds competition; just as high tariffs, for instance, or a prohibition of imports positively breed the competition of smuggling. The contradiction of competition is exactly the same as that of private property. It is in the interest of each to possess everything, but in the interest of the whole that each possesses an equal amount. Thus, the general and the individual interest are diametrically opposed to each other. The contradiction of competition is that each cannot but desire the monopoly, whilst the whole as such is bound to lose by monopoly and must therefore remove it. Moreover, competition already presupposes monopoly—namely, the monopoly of property (and here the hypocrisy of the liberals comes once more to light); and so long as the monopoly of property exists, for just so long the possession of monopoly is equally justified—for monopoly, once it exists, is also property. What a pitiful half-measure, therefore, to attack the small monopolies, and to leave untouched the basic monopoly! And if we here bring in the above-mentioned proposition of the economist, that nothing has value which cannot be monopolized—that nothing, therefore, which does not permit of such monopolization can enter this arena of competition—then our assertion that competition presupposes monopoly is completely justified.

The law of competition is that demand and supply always strive to complement each other, and therefore never do so. The two sides are torn apart again and transformed into flat opposition. Supply always follows close on demand without ever quite covering it. It is either too big or too small, never corresponding to demand; because in this unconscious condition of mankind no one knows how big supply or demand is. If demand is greater than supply the price rises and, as a result, supply is to a certain degree stimulated. As soon as it comes on to the market, prices fall; and if it becomes greater than demand, then the fall in prices is so significant that demand is once again stimulated. So it goes on unending—a permanently unhealthy state of affairs—a constant alternation of over-stimulation and collapse which precludes all advance—a state of perpetual fluctuation perpetually unresolved. This law with its constant balancing, in which whatever is lost here is gained there, seems to the economist marvelous. It is his chief glory—he cannot see enough of it, and considers it in all its possible and impossible applications. Yet it is obvious that this law is a purely natural law, and not a law of the mind. It is a law which produces revolution. The economist comes along with his lovely theory of demand and supply, proves to you that "one can never produce too much," and practice replies with trade crises, which reappear as regularly as the comets, and of which we have now on the average one every five to seven years. For the last eighty years these trade crises have come just as regularly as the great plagues did in the past—and they have brought in their train more misery and more immorality than the latter. (Compare Wade: *History of the Middle and Working Classes*, London, 1835, p. 211.) [6] Of course, these trade crises confirm the law, confirm it exhaustively—but in a manner different from that which the economist would have us believe to be the case. What are we to think of a law which can only assert itself through periodic crises? It is just a natural law based on the unconsciousness of the participants. If the producers as such knew how much the consumers required, if they were to organize production, if they were to share it out amongst themselves, then the fluctuations of competition and its tendency to crisis would be impossible. Produce with consciousness, as human beings, not as dispersed atoms without consciousness of your species, and you are beyond all these artificial and untenable antitheses. But as long as you continue to produce in the present unconscious, thoughtless manner, at the mercy of chance, for just so long trade crises will remain; and each successive crisis is bound to become more universal and therefore worse than the preceding one; is bound to impoverish a larger body of small capitalists, and to augment in increasing proportion the numbers of that class who live by labor alone, thus visibly enlarging the mass of labor to be employed (the major problem of our economists) and finally causing a social revolution such as has never been dreamt of by the school wisdom of the economists.

The perpetual fluctuation of prices such as is created by the condition of competition completely deprives trade of its last vestige of morality. *Value* is no longer even mentioned; the same system which appears to attach such importance to value, which confers on the abstraction of value in money form the honor of having an existence of its own—this very system destroys by means of competition the inherent value of all things, and daily and hourly changes the value relationship of all things to one another. Where does there remain any possibility of an exchange based on a moral foundation in this whirlpool? In this continuous up-and-down, every one *must* seek to hit upon the most favorable moment for purchase and sale; every one must become a speculator—that is to say, must reap where he has not sown; must enrich himself at the expense of others, must calculate on the misfortune of others, or let chance win for him. The speculator always counts on disasters, particularly on bad harvests. He utilizes everything —for instance, the New York fire in its time [7]—and immorality's culminating point is the speculation on the Stock Exchange, where history, and with it mankind, is demoted to a means of gratifying the avarice of the calculating and gambling speculator. And let not the honest "respectable" merchant rise above the gambling on the Stock Exchange with a Pharisaic "I thank thee, O Lord. . ." etc. He is as bad as the speculators in stocks and shares. He speculates just as much as they do. He has to: competition compels him. And his trading activity therefore implies the same immorality as theirs. The truth of the relationship of competition is the relationship of the power of consumption to the power of production. In a world worthy of mankind there will be no other competition than this. The community will have to calculate what it can produce with the means at its disposal; and in the light of the relationship of this productive power to the mass of consumers it will determine how far it has to raise or lower production, how far it has to give way to, or curtail, luxury. But so that they may be able to pass a correct judgment on this relationship and on the increase in productive power to be expected from a rational state of affairs within the community, I invite my readers to consult the writings of the English Socialists, and partly also those of Fourier.

Subjective competition—the contest of capital against capital, of labor against labor, etc.—will under these conditions be reduced to the spirit of emulation grounded in human nature (a concept tolerably developed so far only by Fourier), which after the elimination of opposing interests will be confined to its proper and rational sphere.

The struggle of capital against capital, of labor against labor, of land against land, drives production to a fever pitch at which production turns all natural and rational relations upside down. No capital can stand the competition of another if it is not brought to the highest pitch of activity. No estate can be profitably cultivated if it does not continuously increase its productive power. No worker can hold his own against his competitors if he does not devote all his powers to labor. No one at all who becomes involved in the struggle of competition can stand the strain without the utmost exertion of his powers, without renouncing every truly human purpose. The consequence of this over-exertion on the one side is, inevitably, collapse on the other. When the fluctuation of competition is small, when demand and supply, consumption and production, are almost equal, a stage must be reached in the development of production where there is so much superfluous productive power that the great mass of the nation has nothing to live on, that the people starve from sheer abundance. For some considerable time England has found herself in this crazy position, in this living absurdity. When, as a necessary consequence of such a situation, production is subject to greater fluctuations, then the alternation of boom and crisis, overproduction and slump, sets in. The economist has never been able to explain to himself this mad situation. In order to explain it, he invented the Population Theory, which is just as senseless—indeed even more senseless—than the contradiction of coexisting wealth and poverty. The economist *could not afford* to see the truth; he could not afford to admit that this contradiction is a simple consequence of competition; for otherwise his entire system would have fallen to bits.

For us the matter is easy to explain. The productive power at mankind's disposal is immeasurable. The productivity of the soil can be increased *ad infinitum* by the application of capital, labor and science. According to the most able economists and statisticians (Alison's *Principles of Population*, Vol. 1, chs. 1 and 2),[3] "overpopulated" Great Britain can be brought within ten years to produce a corn yield sufficient for a population of six times its present size. Capital increases daily; the power of labor grows with population; and day by day science increasingly makes the power of nature subject to man. This immeasurable productive capacity, handled with consciousness and in the interest of all, would soon reduce to a minimum the labor falling to the share of mankind. Left to competition, it does the same, but within a context of antitheses. One part of the land is cultivated in the best possible manner, whilst another part—in Great Britain and Ireland thirty million acres of good land—lies barren. One part of capital circulates with amazing speed; another lies dead in the chest. One part of the workers works fourteen to sixteen hours a day, whilst another part stands idle and inactive, and starves. Or the division leaves this realm of simultaneousness: today trade is good; demand is very considerable; everyone works; capital is turned over with

miraculous speed; farming flourishes; the workers work themselves sick. Tomorrow, a slump sets in. The cultivation of the
land is not worth the effort; entire stretches of land remain un-
tilled; the flow of capital freezes; the workers have no employment, and the whole country labors under surplus wealth and
surplus population.

The economist cannot afford to accept this exposition of the
subject as correct; otherwise, as has been said, he would have to
give up his whole system of competition. He would have to recognize the hollowness of his antitheses of production and consumption, or surplus population and surplus wealth. To bring fact and
theory into conformity with each other—since this fact just could
not be denied— the Population Theory was invented.

Malthus,[9] the originator of this doctrine, maintains that population is always pressing on the means of subsistence; that as soon
as production increases, population increases in the same proportion; and that the inherent tendency of the population to
multiply in excess of the available means of subsistence is the
root of all misery and all vice. Indeed, when there are too many
people, they have to be disposed of in one way or another; either
they must be killed by violence or they must starve. But when
this has happened, there is once more a gap which other multi-
pliers of the population immediately start to fill up once more:
and so the old misery begins all over again. What is more, this
is the case in all circumstances—not only in civilized, but also in
primitive, conditions. In New Holland,[10] with a population
density of one per square mile, the savages suffer just as much
from over-population as England. In short, if we want to be consistent, we must admit that *the earth was already over-populated
when only one man existed.* The implications of this line of
thought are that since it is just the poor who are the surplus,
nothing should be done for them except to make their starvation
as easy as possible, to convince them that it cannot be helped and
that there is no other salvation for their whole class than keeping propagation down to the absolute minimum. Or if this does
not work, then it is always better to establish a state institution
for the painless killing of the children of the poor, such as

"Marcus" [11] has suggested, whereby each working-class family would be allowed to have two and a half children, any excess being painlessly killed. Charity would be a crime, since it supports the augmentation of the surplus population. Indeed, it will be very advantageous to declare poverty a crime and to turn poorhouses into prisons, as has already happened in England as a result of the new "liberal" Poor Law.[12] Admittedly it is true that this theory ill conforms with the Bible's doctrine of the perfection of God and of His creation; but "it is a poor refutation to enlist the Bible against facts."

Am I to go on any longer elaborating this vile, infamous theory, this revolting blasphemy against nature and mankind? Am I to pursue its consequences any further? Here at last we have the immorality of the economist brought to its highest pitch. What are all the wars and horrors of the monopoly system compared with this theory! And it is precisely this theory which is the keystone of the liberal system of free trade, whose fall entails the downfall of the entire edifice. For if here competition is proved to be the root cause of misery, poverty and crime, who then will still dare to speak up for it?

In his above-mentioned work, Alison has shaken the Malthusian theory by invoking the productive power of the earth, and by opposing to the Malthusian principle the fact that each adult can produce more than he himself needs—a fact without which mankind could not multiply, indeed could not even exist; for what else could those still growing up live on? But Alison does not go to the root of the matter, and therefore in the end reaches the same conclusion as Malthus. True enough, he proves that Malthus' principle is incorrect, but cannot gainsay the facts which have impelled Malthus to his principle.

If Malthus had not considered the matter so one-sidedly, he could not have failed to see that surplus population or labor power is invariably tied up with surplus wealth, surplus capital and surplus landed property. The population is only too large where the productive power as a whole is too large. The condition of every over-populated country, particularly England, since the time when Malthus wrote, makes this abundantly clear. These were the facts which Malthus ought to have considered in their totality, and whose consideration was bound to have led to the correct conclusion. Instead, he selected one fact, gave no consideration to the others, and therefore arrived at his crazy conclusion.

The second error he committed was to confuse means of subsistence with means of employment. That population is always pressing on the means of employment—that the number of people produced varies with the number of people who can be employed —in short, that the production of labor power has been regulated so far by the law of competition and is therefore also exposed to periodic crises and fluctuations—this is a fact whose establishment constitutes Malthus' merit. But the means of employment are not the means of subsistence. Only in their end-result are the means of employment increased by the increase in machine power and capital. The means of subsistence increase as soon as productive power increases even slightly.

Here a new contradiction in economics comes to light. The economist's "demand" is not the real demand; his "consumption" is an artificial consumption. For the economist, only that person really demands, only that person is a real consumer, who has an equivalent to offer for what he receives. But if it is a fact that every adult produces more than he himself can consume, that children are like trees which give superabundant returns on the outlays invested in them—and these certainly are facts, are they not?—then one ought to believe that each worker should be able to produce far more than he needs and that the community, therefore, should be very glad to provide him with everything he needs; one ought to believe that a large family should be looked upon by the community as a very welcome gift. But the economist, with his crude outlook, knows no other equivalent than that which is paid to him in tangible ready cash. He is firmly set in his antitheses that the most striking facts are of as little concern to him as the most scientific principles.

We destroy the contradiction simply by transcending it. With the fusion of the interests now opposed to each other there disappears the opposition between excess population here and excess wealth there; there disappears the miraculous fact (more miraculous than all the miracles of all the religions put together) that a nation has to starve from sheer wealth and plenty; and there disappears the crazy assertion that the earth lacks the power to feed men. This assertion is the pinnacle of Christian economics —and that our economics is essentially Christian I could have proved from every proposition, from every category, and shall in fact do so when the time comes The Malthusian theory is but the economic expression of the religious dogma concerning the contradiction of spirit and nature and the resulting corruption of both. So far as religion is concerned, this contradiction has been resolved long ago. I hope that in the sphere of economics I have equally demonstrated the utter emptiness of this contradiction. Moreover, I shall not accept as competent any defense of the Malthusian theory which does not from the outset explain to me on the basis of its own principles how a people can starve from sheer plenty and bring this into harmony with reason and fact.

At the same time, the Malthusian theory has been an absolutely necessary point of transition which has taken us infinitely further. Thanks to this theory, as to economics as a whole, our attention has been drawn to the productive power of the earth and of mankind; and after overcoming this economic despair we have been made for ever secure against the fear of over-population. We derive from it the most powerful economic arguments for a social transformation. For even if Malthus were completely right, this transformation would have to be undertaken on the spot; for only this transformation, and the education of the masses which it alone provides, makes possible that moral restraint of the propagative instinct which Malthus himself presents as the most effective and easiest remedy for over-population. Through this theory we have come to know the deepest degradation of man, his dependence on the realm of competition. It has shown us how in the last instance private property has turned man into a com modity whose production and destruction also depend solely on demand; how the system of competition has thus slaughtered, and daily continues to slaughter, millions of men. All this we have seen, and all this drives us to the abolition of this degradation of mankind through the abolition of private property, competition and the opposing interests.

Yet, so as to deprive the universal fear of over-population of any possible basis, let us once more return to the relationship of productive power to population. Malthus establishes a formula on which he bases his entire system: population is said to increase in a geometrical progression. $1 + 2 + 4 + 8 + 16 + 32$, etc.; the productive power of the land in an arithmetical progression: $1 + 2 + 3 + 4 + 5 + 6$. The difference is obvious, is terrifying; but is it correct? Where has it been proved that the productivity of the land increases in an arithmetical progression? The extent of land is limited. All right! The labor power to be employed on this land surface increases with population. Let us even assume that the increase in yield due to increase in labor does not always rise in proportion to the labor: there still remains a third element which, of course, never means anything to the economist—science —whose progress is as unceasing and at least as rapid as that of population. What progress does the agriculture of this century owe to chemistry alone—indeed, to two men alone, Sir Humphry Davy and Justus Liebig! [13] But science increases at least as much as population. The latter increases in proportion to the size of the previous generation, science advances in proportion to the knowledge bequeathed to it by the previous generation, and thus under the most ordinary conditions also in geometrical progression. And what is impossible to science? But it is absurd to talk of over-population so long as "there is enough waste land in the valley of the Mississippi for the whole population of Europe to be transplanted there" [14]; so long as no more than one-third of the earth can be considered cultivated, and so long as the production of this third itself can be raised sixfold and more by the application of improvements already known.

Thus, competition sets capital against capital, labor against labor, landed property against landed property; and likewise each of these elements against the other two. In the struggle the stronger wins: and in order to predict the outcome of the struggle, we shall have to investigate the strength of the contestants. At first, land and capital are stronger than labor, for the worker must work to live, whilst the landowner can live on his rents, and the capitalist on his interest, or if the need arises, on his capital or on capitalized property in land. The result is that only the very barest necessities, the mere means of subsistence, fall to the lot of labor; whilst the largest part of the product is shared between capital and landed property. Moreover, the stronger worker drives the weaker out of the market, just as larger capital drives out smaller capital, and larger landed property drives out smaller landed property. Practice confirms this conclusion. The advantages which the larger manufacturer and merchant enjoy over the smaller, and the big landowner over the owner of a single acre, are well known. The result is that already under ordinary conditions, in accordance with the law of the stronger, large capital and large landed property swallow small capital and small landed property—i.e., centralization of property. In crises of trade and agriculture, this centralization proceeds much more rapidly. Large property increases in general much more rapidly than small property, since a much smaller portion is deducted from its proceeds as property expenses. This law of the centralization of private property is as immanent in private property as all the others. The middle classes must increasingly disappear until the world is divided into millionaires and paupers, into large landowners and poor farm laborers. All the laws, all the dividing of landed property, all the possible splitting-up of capital, are of no avail: this result must and will come, unless it is anticipated by a total transformation of social conditions, a fusion of opposed interests, a transcendence of private property.

Free competition, the key word of our present-day economists, is an impossibility. Monopoly at least intended to protect the consumer against counterfeit, even if it could not in fact do so. The abolition of monopoly, however, opens the door wide to counterfeit. You say that competition carries with it the remedy for counterfeit, since no one will buy bad articles. But that means that everyone has to be an expert in every article, which is impossible. Hence the necessity for monopoly, which many articles in fact reveal. Apothecaries, etc., *must* have a monopoly. And the most important article—money—requires a monopoly most of all. Whenever the circulating medium has ceased to be a state monopoly it has invariably produced a trade crisis; and the English economists, Dr. Wade among them, do concede in this case the necessity for monopoly. But even monopoly is no protection against counterfeit money. One can take one's stand on either side of the question: the one is as difficult as the other. Monopoly produces free competition, and the latter, in turn, produces monopoly. Therefore, both must fall, and these difficulties must be resolved through the transcendence of the principles which gives rise to them.

Competition has penetrated all the relationships of our life and completed the reciprocal bondage in which men now hold themselves. Competition is the great mainspring which again and again jerks into activity our aging and withering social order, or rather disorder; but with each new exertion it also saps a part of this order's waning strength. Competition governs the numerical advance of mankind; it likewise governs its moral advance. Anyone who has any knowledge of the statistics of crime must have been struck by the peculiar regularity with which crime advances year by year, and with which certain causes produce certain crimes. The extension of the factory system is followed everywhere by an increase in crime. The number of arrests, of criminal cases— indeed, the number of murders, robberies, petty thefts, etc., for a large town or for a district—can be predicted year by year with unfailing precision, as has been done often enough in England. This regularity proves that crime, too, is governed by competition; that society creates a *demand* for crime which is met by a corresponding *supply;* that the gap created by the arrest, transportation or execution of a certain number is at once filled by others, just as every gap in population is at once filled by new arrivals; in other words, this regularity proves that crime presses on the means of punishment just as the people press on the means of employment. How just it is to punish criminals under these circumstances, quite apart from any other considerations, I leave to the judgment of my readers. Here I am merely concerned with demonstrating the extension of competition into the moral sphere, and to show to what deep degradation private property has brought man.

In the struggle of capital and land against labor, the first two elements enjoy yet another special advantage over labor—the assistance of science; for in present conditions science, too, is directed against labor. Almost all mechanical inventions, for instance, have been occasioned by the lack of labor power; especially Hargreaves', Crompton's and Arkwright's cotton-spinning machines. There has never been an intense demand for labor which did not result in an invention that increased labor productivity considerably, thus diverting demand away from human labor. The history of England from 1770 until now is one long proof of this. The last great invention in cotton spinning, the self-acting mule, was occasioned simply and solely by the demand for labor, and rising wages. It doubled machine labor, and thereby cut down hand labor by half; it threw half the workers out of employment, and thereby depressed the wages of the other half; it crushed a joint scheme of the workers against the factory owners, and destroyed the last vestige of strength with which labor had still held out in the unequal struggle against capital. (See Dr. Ure, *Philosophy of Manufactures*, Vol. 2.)[15]

The economist now says, however, that in its final result machinery is favorable to the workers, since it makes production cheaper and thus creates a new and larger market for its products, and since in so doing it ultimately reemploys the workers put out of work. Quite right. But is the economist forgetting, then, that the production of labor power is regulated by competition; that labor-power is always pressing on the means of employment, and that, therefore, when these advantages are due to become operative, a surplus of competitors for work is already waiting for them, and will thus render these advantages illusory; whilst the disadvantages—the sudden withdrawal of the means of subsistence from one half of the workers and the fall in wages for the other half—are not illusory? Is the economist forgetting that the progress of invention never stands still, and that these disadvantages, therefore, perpetuate themselves? Is he forgetting that with the division of labor, developed to such a degree by our civilization, a worker can only live if he can be used at this particular machine for this particular detailed operation; that the change-over from one type of employment to another newer type is almost invariably an absolute impossibility for the adult worker?

In turning my attention to the effects of machinery, I am brought to another subject less directly relevant—the factory system; and I have neither the inclination nor the time to treat this here. Besides, I hope to have an early opportunity to expound in detail the despicable immorality of this system, and to expose mercilessly the economist's hypocrisy which here appears in all its glitter.[16]

EXPLANATORY AND
REFERENCE NOTES

INTRODUCTION BY D. J. STRUIK

1. PRELUDE, 1818-43

1. The best biography of Marx in English is F. Mehring, *Karl Marx: The Story of His Life* (New York, 1935) ; the original German edition was published in Leipzig, 1918. The formative years of Marx and Engels are the subject of A. Cornu, *Karl Marx et Friedrich Engels* (3 vols., Paris, 1955-62), also in German. Cornu uses material to which Mehring had no access.

The published and unpublished writings of Marx and Engels up to March 1848 are to be found in Marx-Engels, *Gesamtausgabe, Abt. I,* in 6 vols., Frankfurt and Berlin, 1927-32, hereafter quoted as MEGA. Section III of MEGA, consisting of 4 vols., contains the lifelong correspondence of Marx and Engels. The advent of Hitler to power forced the suspension of MEGA in Germany, but an additional special volume on the occasion of the 40th commemoration of Engels' death was issued in Moscow-Leningrad, 1935, which includes *Anti-Dühring* and *Dialectics of Nature.* The new edition of the complete writings of Marx and Engels (Dietz, Berlin, 1955) does not include the *Manuscripts of 1844*; these are included in Marx-Engels, *Kleine ökonomische Studien* (Dietz, Berlin, 1955). This edition of the *Manuscripts* corrects errors found in MEGA. The earliest edition of the *Manuscripts* are in Russian, *Arkhiv K. Marksa i F. Engels'a* (Moscow, 1927), but was incomplete; the latest Russian edition (1956) has a complete and improved text.

2. *Grundlagen der Philosophie des Rechts* (1821), arts. 257, 258.

3. Letter of Hegel to his friend Immanuel Niethammer (1808). "Theoretical work, as I convince myself more every day, accomplishes more in the world than practical work, when the empire of the mind *(Vorstellung)* is revolutionized, then reality must follow."

4. The principal one is on censorship, signed only "by a Rhinelander." For *Anekdota, see* Note 3, Marx's Preface.

5. *See* H. F. Mins, *Science and Society,* 12 (1948), pp. 157-69, B. Farrington, *ibid.,* 17 (1953), pp. 326-39.

6. This is not as strange as it looks; as a matter of fact, it sounds quite modern. We explain at present statistical phenomena by the cumulative effect of small deviations, and there exist modern philosophical schools which base themselves on statistical considerations to explain freedom of choice in man. Examples can be found in the extensive literature on the so-called principle of indetermination in physics.

7. Letter to the writer Berthold Auerbach, Sept. 2, 1841, see *Briefwechsel*, quoted below.

8. M. Hess, *Philosophische und sozialistische Schriften, 1837-50*, A. Cornu and W. Mönke, eds. (Berlin, 1961). M. Hess, *Briefwechsel*, E. Silberner, ed. (Gravenhage, 1959).

9. Feuerbach's book exists in many editions, among them an English translation (of the second edition of 1843), *The Essence of Christianity*, M. Evans, transl. (London, 1854). Feuerbach's works have been collected in *Sämtliche Werke* (Stuttgart, 1903-11).

10. F. Engels, *Ludwig Feuerbach and the Outcome of Classical German Philosophy* (New York, 1935), p. 28. The German edition appeared in 1888.

2. SELF-CLARIFICATION, 1843-44

1. The *Jahrbücher* have been reproduced in facsimile (Leipzig, 1925).

2. This Introduction can be found in English in Marx-Engels, *On Religion* (Moscow, 1957).

3. K. Marx, *Zur Kritik der Politischen Ökonomie* (1859), Preface: in English, the Preface is to be found in the Appendix of K. Marx, *The Poverty of Philosophy* (New York, 1963).

4. The best biography of Engels (unfinished) is G. Mayer, *Friedrich Engels: Eine Biographie* (Berlin, 1920), English translation, New York, 1936. *See* also A. Cornu, *op. cit.*

5. F. Engels, "The History of the Communist League," in Marx and Engels, *Selected Works*, vol. II (New York, n.d.), p. 11.

6. Books of more than 20 sheets (each sheet 20 pages) were not subject to censorship. The editor of this periodical, which appeared in Switzerland, was the poet George Herwegh.

7. These papers have been republished; *see* Note 8, previous section.

8. MEGA, *Abt. I, Bd. 5* (1932). Some sections had been published before. Parts I and III are in English: Marx and Engels, *The German Ideology* (New York, 1939 and 1962, paperback edition).

3. FRENCH SOCIALISM

1. *See* e.g. MEGA, I, 4, pp. 409, 451; 5, pp. 109, 436.

2. *Vorwärts*, Aug. 10, 1844; MEGA, I, 3, p. 18.

3. *Le Globe*, at that time edited by Saint-Simonians. *See* also *Neue Zeit*, 14 I (1896) pp. 283. Leroux also introduced the term *Solidarité* (1839). The term "socialism" caught on; we find it in England first in 1839. On Saint-Simon and Fourier see F. Engels, *Socialism, Utopian and Scientific* (New York, 1935).

4. *"A chacun selon sa capacité, à chaque capacité selon ses oeuvres"* (*Le Globe*, 1831); a similar slogan appeared earlier in *L'Organisateur*, 1829.

5. The term "communist" appeared also in those days. The British socialist, John Goodwin Barmby (1820-81), claimed that he heard it in Paris during his visit in 1840, among the followers of Babeuf (*See* Dict. Nat. Biography). It must have been used more widely, since Lorenz Stein uses it freely.

6. On Babeuf see S. Bernstein, *Essays in Political and Intellectual History* (New York, 1955), Ch. V. On Buonarotti see S. Bernstein, *Buonarotti* (Paris, 1949).

7. MEGA, I, 3, pp. 294-95; In English, *The Holy Family, or Critique of Critical Critique,* (Moscow, 1956). On French Socialism of this period see further R. Garaudy, *Les Sources françaises du Socialisme Scientifique* (Paris, 1948).

4. HEGEL

1. Hegel's main works are: *Phenomenologie des Geistes* (1806), *Wissenschaft der Logik* (1812-16), *Encyclopaedie der philosophischen Wissenschaften* (1817), *Grundlinien der Philosophiè des Rechts* (1820), *Vorlesungen über die Philosophie der Geschichte* (1837, posthumously edited). In 1832-40 the collected works appeared in 18 volumes, which were therefore available to Marx. Many writings of Hegel in his younger days have only been published in the present century. G. Lukacz, in *Der junge Hegel* (Zürich, 1948) has observed that there are traits in the development of the young Hegel which have some analogy in the development of young Marx, notably in their common study of Adam Smith—but Hegel studied him around 1800 when there was hardly any industrial capital in Germany.

The literature on Hegel is enormous. In English we have H. Marcuse, *Reason and Revolution* (2nd ed., N.Y., 1954; paperback 1960), which also describes Hegel's relation to Marx; further, e.g., W. T. Stace, *The Philosophy of Hegel* (London, 1924, reprint New York, 1955), and J. N. Findlay, *Hegel, A Reexamination* (London, New York, 1958). Of the English translations of Hegel's works, we use J. B. Bailie's, *The Phenomenology of Mind* (London, New York, 1920, 1931); W. H. Johnston and L. G. Struthers, transl., *Hegel's Science of Logic* (New York, 2 vols., 1929); also W. Wallace's translation of the sections on logic in the Encyclopaedia: *The Logic of Hegel* (Oxford, 1873, 1892); T. M. Knox, transl., *Hegel's Philosophy of Right* (Oxford, 1942); G. E. Mueller, transl., *Hegel, Encyclopaedia of Philosophy* (New York, 1959).

2. Introduction to the *Phenomenology.* In the same period, in which Hegel was writing, mathematics was overcoming to a certain extent these defects in its dialectics. In projective geometry, theory of invariants and other fields new at that time there exists, as a rule, an organic connection between theorem and proof.

3. *Encycl.* 13.

4. *Logic,* Wallace transl. 81, p. 148.

5. *Ibid.* pp. 150, 151, 147. Neither is Dialectics a play on the theme "thesis," "antithesis," "synthesis," as is sometimes argued. Hegel (as well as Marx) occasionally uses this form of reasoning, but the wealth of conceptual relationships that occur in the mind on its road to understanding the world precludes the possibility of using such a catch-all in the form of trichotomies, which soon become stale and wooden. Marx uses this trichotomy in his polemic against Proudhon, in the second section of *La misère de la philosophie* (1847), but only to show Proudhon's misuse of the scheme. It is also true that Hegel had a preference for trichotomies in the division of his books into sections and chapters.

6. *Logic,* Wallace transl. 88, p. 163.

7. *Lenin,* "On Dialectics" (c. 1913), in Lenin, *Collected Works,* vol. XIII (New York, 1927), p. 323.

8. Engels, *Anti-Dühring,* (New York, 1939), Ch. XII.

9. Inaugural Address, Berlin, 1818, Mueller ed. *Encycl.* p. 61.

10. *Logic,* Johnston-Struthers transl. p. 59.

11. An understandable paraphrase of the *Phenomenology* in English (as well as of the *Economic and Philosophic Manuscripts*) can be found in H. Marcuse, *Reason and Revolution.* Helpful are also the summaries in the Bailie translation. A readable paraphrase in German can be found in G. Lukacz, *op. cit.,* and in E. Bloch, *Subjekt-Object* (Berlin, 1951).

12. In the *Encycl.,* Mueller ed., p. 207.

13. The only specific reference is to Diderot's *Neveu de Rameau* (Rameau's Nephew), that magnificent piece of social satire, written c 1760 (in *Diderot: Interpreter of Nature,* J. Kemp, Ed., New York, 1963). Goethe had translated it into German; Marx enjoyed the "unique masterpiece" and quoted Hegel's opinion in his letter to Engels of April 15, 1869.

14. The quotation is from the Bailie transl.

15. Where did Hegel's ideas on the relation of lord and servant originate? It is an interesting fact that the mathematician Gauss, who had no use for Hegel, in an article on the mutual influence of the planets (1813) inserts the remark: "Simple pure domination does not occur in the world of bodies; the dominator feels every time more or less the reaction of the dominated." Was it a reaction to the Napoleonic conquests? Or had both Gauss and Hegel seen "The Marriage of Figaro"?

16. "Alienacioun of God is to men worckynge wickidnesse" (Wyclif, 1388).

17. It is here that Hegel quotes *Rameau's Nephew.*

18. When Feuerbach (and young Marx) use the term anthropology (literally, knowledge of man), they do not mean it in the sense of our

present-day college course, which may deal with such subjects as the Indians of New Mexico or the denizens of Middletown. Feuerbach uses the term in the meaning it had obtained in German philosophy, especially since Kant (who wrote an *Anthropologic in pragmatischer Hinsicht,* 1798), where it denotes the most general study of human nature, questions concerning religion, conscience, and morals, as well as material needs. It is an abstract doctrine, like the anthropology of the theologians, which is the science of the divine in human nature. Marx, in his *Manuscripts,* was struggling against this anthropology, replacing it by sociology.

19. Feuerbach, *Vorläufige Thesen, Werke,* F. Jodl, ed. II (1904). It has been remarked that in Hegel human history has been three times discussed, on different levels, on the subjective, the objective, and the absolute; *see* Bloch, *op. cit.,* p. 63.

5. THE MANUSCRIPTS

1. In the *Theses on Feuerbach,* H. Selsam and H. Martel, eds., *Reader in Marxist Philosophy* (New York, 1963) pp. 316-17. On the term *sinnlich,* translated *sensuous,* see Note on Terminology. The term *Sinnlichkeit,* sensuousness, was a standard term in classical German philosophy. Feuerbach wrote "For the *senses* not only 'external' things are the object. Man himself is given to himself only through the senses —he is object to himself as object of the senses. The identity of subject and object, which is only an abstract thought in self-consciousness, is truth and reality only in the sensuous perception of man by man." (*Werke,* II, p. 303). Such ideas of Feuerbach were very important to Marx in the formative period, and influenced his style.

2. As to *The Holy Family,* written after the *Manuscripts,* but before *The German Ideology,* Marx in a letter to Engels (April 24, 1867) from Hannover reported that he had discovered in his friend Kugelmann's house a copy of *The Holy Family:* "I was pleasantly surprised to discover that we have not to be ashamed of the work, although the Feuerbach cult now makes a very humoristic impression." The considered opinion of Marx and Engels on Feuerbach was later laid down in Engels' essay, *Ludwig Feuerbach* (1888); *see* also *The German Ideology,* Ch. I.

3. As we have seen, Marx had already written his critique of Hegel's *Philosophy of Right.* He never undertook the critique of the *Logic;* however, in a famous passage in the Preface to the second edition of *Capital* (1873) he avowed himself "openly the pupil of that mighty thinker, and even here and there, in the chapter on the theory of value, I have coquetted with the modes of expression peculiar to him." Lenin, who in his *Filosofskie tetradi* (*Philosophical Notebooks,* 1914) did undertake the critique of the *Logic,* added in his notes to Book III,

Part 1: "It is impossible completely to understand Marx's *Capital*, and especially its first chapter, without having thoroughly studied and understood the *whole* of Hegel's *Logic*. Consequently, half a century later none of the Marxists understood Marx!" In English, Lenin, *Collected Works*, vol. 38 (Moscow, 1961), p. 180; *see* also Selsam and Martel, eds. *Reader in Marxist Philosophy*, Appendix II.

4. In MEGA.

5. See A. Cornu, *op. cit.*, III, p. 108.

6. REACTION TO MARX'S MANUSCRIPTS

1. See Note 1, sect. 1.

2. M. Friedrich, *Philosophie und Ökonomie beim jungen Marx* (Berlin, 1960), p. 9.

3. See Note 2, sect. 5.

4. The reluctance of Engels to present his and Marx's early Hegelized work to the public can also be seen in his letter of Feb. 25, 1886, to Florence Kelley Wischnewetzky (Marx and Engels, *Letters to Americans*, New York, 1953, p. 151). See also a discussion of 1893 with Alexis Voden, reported by D. Bell, *Soviet Survey*, 32 (London, 1960), pp. 21-31.

5. An extensive bibliography is in J.-Y. Calvez, *La pensée de Karl Marx* (Paris, 1956). This erudite book of 664 pages, written by a Jesuit father, devotes hundreds of pages to the subject of alienation alone. Other bibliographies in F. Pappenheim, *The Alienation of Modern Man* (New York, 1959); R. C. Tucker, *Philosophy and Myth in Karl Marx* (Cambridge, 1961). Further orientation on the discussion can be found in D. Bell, *loc. cit.*, and I. Fetcher, *Soviet Survey*, 33 (1960), pp. 84-92. A Protestant approach in *Marxismus-studien* (Tübingen, 2 vols., 1954, 1957), a Catholic one in Calvez and the book by P. Bigo, quoted later.

6. *See* D. I. Rosenberg, *Die Entwicklung der ökonomischen Lehre von Marx und Engels in den vierziger Jahren des 19tzen Jahrhunderts* (Berlin, 1958).

7. *See* e.g. F. Pappenheim, *op. cit.*, who compares Marx' ideas with those of the German sociologist, F. Tönnies (1855-1939), also E. and M. Josephson, *Man Alone* (New York, 1962), a collection of essays, and L. Feuer, *New Politics* (New York, 1962), pp. 116-134, who treats us also to a curious theory, modern style, on the relation of Marx's analysis of alienation to sex.

8. Marxist writings on the *Manuscripts* and young Marx in general include, in addition to Cornu, *op. cit.*: R. Garaudy, *Humanisme marxiste* (Paris, 1957); *Recherches internationales à la lumière du marxisme*, 14 (1960), *Sur le jeune Marx* (contains several articles); G. Mende, *Karl Marx' Entwicklung vom revolutionären Demokraten zum Kommunismus* (Berlin, 3d ed., 1960); T. I. Oizerman, *Deutsche*

Zeitschrift für Philosophie, 10 (1962), pp. 1147-1161. See also Pappenheim, *op. cit.,* and what probably is the first book in English which considers the *Manuscripts* in some detail: H. P. Adams, *Karl Marx in His Earlier Writings* (London, 1940).

9. Karl Marx, *Der historische Materialismus, Die Frühschriften,* herausg. *von* S. Landshut *und* J. P. Mayer (Stuttgart, 1932, 2 vols.), vol. I, *Nationalökonomie und Philosophie;* new edition by S. Landshut: *Karl Marx, Die Frühschriften* (Stuttgart, 1953). The first edition appeared in the same year (1932) as the MEGA edition, but is incomplete and the transcription of the text is open to criticism.

10. *Op. cit.,* p. XXXVII.

11. H. Popitz, *Der entfremdete Mensch* (Basel, 1953).

12. E. Fromm, *Marx's Concept of Man,* with a translation from Marx's *Economie and Philosophic Manuscripts* by T. B. Bottomore (New York, 1961); *see* also the reviews by A. J. Gregor, *Studies on the Left,* 3, No. 1 (1962), pp. 85-92, and F. Bartlett and J. Shodell, *Science and Society,* 27, No. 3 (1963), pp. 321-26.

13. Tucker, *op. cit.; see* also the review by A. J. Gregor, *Studies on the Left,* 2, No. 3 (1962), pp. 95-102.

14. P. Bigo, *Marxisme et humanisme* (Paris, 1953), p. 34.

15. *See* G. Lukacs, *Existentialisme ou marxisme?* (Paris, 1948); A. Schaff, "Marxism and Existentialism," *Monthly Review,* 14 (1962), pp. 12-18, 100-111.

16. In the *Communist Manifesto* the "true socialists" are attacked for the nonsensical use they made of such terms as "exteriorization of human essence." But Marx continued to use the words occasionally in a materialist sense. In the manuscripts of 1857-58, published in Moscow (1939-41) under the title *Grundrisse der Kritik der politischen Ökonomie,* we find in a study of surplus value: "The stress is laid not on the objectivization of the power that labor has placed opposite to itself, but on the effect of alienation on it. . . ." (Berlin edition, 1953, p. 715.) In *Capital,* III, Part I, Ch. 5, Sec. 1 we find the words reminiscent of the *Manuscripts:* "The relations of capital conceals indeed the inner connection [of the facts] in the complete indifference, exteriorization and alienation in which it places the worker in relation to the conditions of the realization of his own labor." (Zurich edition, 1933, p. 108.) On Marx's life-long concern with alienation, *see* also F. Pappenheim, *op. cit.,* p. 83.

TRANSLATOR'S AND EDITOR'S NOTE ON TERMINOLOGY

1. *The Logic of Hegel,* tr. Wallace, 2nd ed., p. 180.

2. *Ibid.,* p. 209f.

3. "Theses on Feuerbach, VI," in *Reader in Marxist Philosophy,* p. 317.

THE ECONOMIC AND PHILOSOPHIC MANUSCRIPTS OF 1844

PREFACE

1. At this point Marx crossed out the following paragraph in the manuscript:

Whereas the uninformed reviewer who tries to hide his complete ignorance and intellectual poverty by hurling the "utopian phrase" at the positive critic's head, or again such phrases as "pure, resolute, utterly critical criticism," the "not merely legal but social—utterly social—society," the "compact, massy mass," the "oratorical orators of the massy mass," this reviewer has yet to furnish the first proof that besides his theological family affairs he has anything to contribute to a discussion of worldly matters.

Marx refers here to Bruno Bauer who had published in *Allgemeine Literatur-Zeitung* two long reviews dealing with books, articles and pamphlets on the Jewish question. Most of the quoted phrases are taken from these reviews in *Allgemeine Literatur-Zeitung* (Heft 1, December 1843; Heft 4, March 1844). The expressions "utopian phrase" and "compact mass" can be found in B. Bauer's article *"Was ist jetzt der Gegenstand der Kritik?"* published in *Allgemeine Literatur-Zeitung*, Heft 8, July 1844.

Allgemeine Literatur-Zeitung (General Literary Gazette), a German monthly, was published by B. Bauer in Charlottenburg from December 1843 to October 1844.

Marx and Engels gave a detailed critical appraisal of this monthly in their book, *The Holy Family*.

2. *See* Note 6, Section 2 of Introduction.

3. At this point Marx crossed out the following paragraph:

Besides being indebted to these authors who have given critical attention to political economy, positive criticism as a whole—and therefore also German positive criticism of political economy—owes its true foundation to the discoveries of Feuerbach, against whose Philosophie der Zukunft *and* Thesen zur Reform der Philosophie *in the* Anekdota, *despite the tacit use that is made of them, the petty envy of some and the veritable wrath of others seem to have instigated a regular conspiracy of silence.*

Meant are the following writings of Feuerbach:

Ludwig Feuerbach, *Grundsätze der Philosophie der Zukunft (Principles of the Philosophy of the Future)*, Zürich und Winterthur, 1843; and *Vorläufige Thesen zur Reformation der Philosophie (Preliminary*

Theses on the Reformation of Philosophy) published in *Anekdota,* Bd. II.

Anekdota is Marx's abbreviation for *Anekdota zur neuesten deutschen Philosophie und Publicistik (Unpublished Materials Related to Modern German Philosophy and Writing),* a two-volume collection published by A. Ruge in Switzerland. It included Marx's *Notes on the Latest Prussian Instruction to Censors* and *Luther—the Arbiter between Strauss and Feuerbach,* and articles by Bruno Bauer, Ludwig Feuerbach, Friedrich Köppen, Arnold Ruge, etc.

4. Marx has in mind B. Bauer and his followers, who were associated with the *Allgemeine Literatur-Zeitung.*

5. At this point Marx crossed out the following paragraph:

In this connection the critical theologian is either for ever repeating assurances about the purity of his own critique, or tries to make it seem as though all that was left for criticism to deal with now was some other immature form of criticism outside itself—say eighteenth-century criticism—and the backwardness of the masses, in order to divert the observer's attention as well as his own from the necessary task of settling accounts between criticism and its point of origin—Hegelian dialectic and German philosophy as a whole—from this necessary raising of modern criticism above its own limitation and crudity. Eventually, however, whenever discoveries (such as Feuerbach's) are made about the nature of his own philosophic presuppositions, the critical theologian partly makes it appear as if he were the one who had accomplished this, producing that appearance by taking the results of these discoveries and, without being able to develop them, hurling them in the form of catch-phrases at writers still caught in the confines of philosophy. He partly even manages to acquire a sense of his own superiority to such discoveries by covertly asserting in a veiled, malicious and sceptical fashion elements of the Hegelian dialectic which he still finds lacking in the critique of that dialectic (which have not yet been critically served up to him for his use) against such criticism—not having tried to bring such elements into their proper relation or having been capable of doing so, asserting, say, the category of mediating proof against the category of positive, self-originating truth, etc., in a way peculiar to Hegelian dialectic. For to the theo-logical critic it seems quite natural that everything has to be done by philosophy, so that he can chatter away about purity, resoluteness, and utterly critical criticism; and he fancies himself the true conqueror of philosophy whenever he happens to feel some "moment" in Hegel to be lacking in Feuerbach—for however much he practices the spiritual idolatry of "self-consciousness" and "mind" the theological critic does not get beyond feeling to consciousness.

Here "moment" is a technical term in Hegelian philosophy meaning a vital element of thought. The term is used to stress that thought is a process, and thus that elements in a system of thought are also phases in a movement. The term "feeling" *(Empfindung)* denotes a relatively low form of mental life in which the subjective and the objective are still confused together. "Consciousness" *(Bewusstsein)*— the name given by Hegel to the first major section of his *Phenomenology of Mind*—denotes those forms of mental activity where a subject first seeks to comprehend an object. "Self-consciousness" and "mind" denote subsequent, higher phases in the evolution of "absolute knowledge" or "the absolute."

When Marx speaks of the categories of mediating proof *(vermittelnder Beweis)* and positive, self-originating truth, he may have thought of these sections of Hegel's *Logic,* in which he compares immediate knowledge with mediating knowledge *(see* W. Wallace, *Logic of Hegel,* pp. 132*ff)* ; they lead him to a critique of the different proofs of the existence of God.

6. Marx may here refer to the *Life of Jesus* by D. F. Strauss (1835) and Feuerbach's *Essence of Christianity* (1841).

7. At this point Marx crossed out the following paragraph:

How far, on the other hand, Feuerbach's discoveries about the nature of philosophy required still, for their proof at least, a critical settling of accounts with philosophical dialectic will be seen from my exposition itself.

As to the promise Marx makes, he fulfilled it within a short time in *The Holy Family,* written in collaboration with Engels.

WAGES OF LABOR

1. Compare what Marx says here about the determination of wages, combination amongst workers, etc., with *The Wealth of Nations,* by Adam Smith (Everyman Library edition), Vol. I, pp. 58-60. In the first three sections of this manuscript, Marx, as he himself points out later, is constantly drawing upon the words of the classical political economists, and particularly of Smith. This is often the case, as here, even where Marx does not explicitly indicate that he is quoting or paraphrasing. The text of *The Wealth of Nations* used by Marx was Garnier's French translation of 1802 *(Recherche sur la Nature et les Causes de la richesse des Nations; par Adam Smith. Traduction nouvelle, avec les notes et observations*; par Germain Garnier, Tomes I-V, Paris, 1802). Adam Smith (1723-1790), Scotch economist, published his *Wealth of Nations* in 1776.

2. A. Smith, *Wealth of Nations,* (Everyman edition), Vol. I, pp. 60-61.

3. *Ibid.*, pp. 71-72, and pp. 50-51.

4. *Ibid.*, p. 77.

5. *Ibid.*, Vol. I, p. 230; also pp. 61-65, where Smith illustrates these three possible conditions of society by referring to contemporary conditions in Bengal, China, and North America.

6. *Ibid.*, p. 230; in Marx's manuscript the last clause of this sentence is in French, being taken direct from Garnier's translation, Vol. II, p. 162.

7. *Ibid.*, Vol. I, p. 84 (Garnier, Vol. I, p. 193). This is a condensed version of some sentences of Smith.

8. *Ibid.*, Vol. I, p. 70.

9. In this sentence the phrase "economic system" has been used to render the German term *Nationalökonomie*—the term used by Marx in these manuscripts for "Political Economy." Here, and occasionally elsewhere, Marx seems to use *Nationalökonomie* to stand not simply for Political Economy as a body of theory, but for the economic system, the developing industrial capitalist system, portrayed and championed by the classical political economists.

10. *Ibid.*, Vol. I, p. 57.

11. Pierre Joseph Proudhon (1809-1865), French socialist and political theorist. Against his *Philosophie de la Misère* (1846) Marx wrote his *Misère de la philosophie* (1847).

12. *Die Bewegung der Produktion, eine geschichtlich-statistische Abhandlung*, von Wilhelm Schulz (Zürich und Winterthur, 1843). Schulz (later called Schulz-Bodmer, 1797-1860), was a radical democrat, later docent in Zürich. In *Capital* Marx cites this book, "in many respects to be recommended."

13. The god of Greek mythology identified with Time.

14. *Théorie nouvelle d'économie sociale et politique, ou Etude sur l'organisation des Sociétés*, par C. Pecqueur (Paris, 1842). This and all succeeding quotations from Pecqueur, Buret and Loudon in this section are in French in Marx's manuscript. Constantin Pecqueur (1801-1887) was a French economic writer and socialist.

15. *Solution du problème de la population et de la subsistance, soumise à un médicin dans une série de lettres*, par Charles Loudon (Paris, 1842), p. 229. This work was a translation into French, slightly abridged, of an English manuscript which seems never to have been published. In 1836, however, Loudon did issue at Leamington a short pamphlet in English, *The Equilibrium of Population and Sustenance Demonstrated*; but the French work referred to is a substantial book of 336 pages.

16. *De la misère des classes laborieuses en Angleterre et en France*, par Eugène Buret, I-II (Paris, 1840). Eugène Buret (1811-42) was a French economist and writer. This book was a kind of predecessor of

Engels' book on the situation of the laboring classes in England (1845),
but Buret, though eloquent in his description of the misery of the
workers, preached only social reforms.

PROFIT OF CAPITAL

1. *Traité d'économie politique,* par Jean-Baptiste Say (*Treatise on
Political Economy*), 3ème édition, tomes I-II (Paris, 1817), first published in 1803.
2. This is a summary, not a direct quotation. Several of the following
quotations are similar.
3. Smith has "good, moderate, reasonable profit."
4. Smith distinguishes between three parts in the annual produce,
the rent of land, the wages of labor, and the profits of stock. The interests of the first two groups he considers as being strictly connected
with the interest of society as a whole.
5. Smith claims that in raising the price of commodities the rise of
wages operates as simple interest in the accumulation of debt, the
rise of profit as compound interest.
6. Marx uses the French terms *capital fixe* and *capital circulant.*
7. The whole paragraph (including the quotation from Ricardo's
book on the *Principles of Political Economy and Taxation* and from
Sismondi's *Nouveaux principes d'économie politique*) is an excerpt
from E. Buret's book *De la misère des classes laborieuses en Angleterre
et en France,* T. 1 (Paris, 1840), pp. 6-7. Marx quotes the French
translation in French.
8. i.e., the lower the standard of living, the higher the house rent.
9. Marx alludes to the following passage: "In a perfectly fair lottery,
those who draw the prizes ought to gain all that is lost by those who
draw the blanks. In a profession where twenty fail for one that succeeds, that one ought to gain all that should have been gained by the
unsuccessful twenty." (Smith, *loc. cit.*, Vol. 1, Bk. I, p. 94.) Smith's
point is that, especially in the salaried professions, the chances of annual gain are often far from those in a fair lottery.

RENT OF LAND

1. This sentence is not clear.

ESTRANGED LABOR

1. Estranged Labor—*Die Entfremdete Arbeit*: as to the term "estranged," see *Entfremdung* in "Note on Terminology," and the Introduction.
2. Objectification, *Vergegenständlichung*: the process of becoming
an object.

3. Loss of realization, *Entwirklichung*. A better translation might be "devaluation." Marx, in true Hegel fashion, opposes *Verwirklichung*, here translated as *realization*, to *Entwirklichung*, the taking away of reality. Here *realization* is meant as accomplishment, performance, making something real. Marx states that the accomplishment of labor turns into its opposite.

4. Alienation, *Entäusserung*. See *Entäusserung* in "Note on Terminology" and the Introduction.

5. Sensuous, *sinnlich*: what can be observed by means of the senses.

6. Species being, *Gattungswesen*, a term used by Feuerbach, who takes as the *Gattung* mankind as a whole, hence the human species.

Species nature (just like species being), *Gattungswesen*: man's essential nature, *menschliches Wesen*; see *Wesen* in "Note on Terminology."

The following passages from Feuerbach's *Essence of Christianity* may help readers to understand the ideological background to this part of Marx's thought, and, incidentally, to see how Marx accepted but infused with new content concepts made current by Feuerbach as well as by Hegel and the political economists:

"What is this essential difference between man and the brute? . . . Consciousness—but consciousness in the strict sense; for the consciousness implied in the feeling of self as an individual, in discrimination by the senses, in the perception and even judgment of outward things according to definite sensible signs, cannot be denied to the brutes. Consciousness in the strictest sense is present only in a being to whom his species, his essential nature, is an object of thought. The brute is indeed conscious of himself as an individual—and he has accordingly the feeling of self as the common center of successive sensations—but not as a species. . . . In practical life we have to do with individuals; in science, with species. . . . But only a being to whom his own species, his own nature, is an object of thought, can make the essential nature of other things or beings an object of thought. . . . The brute has only a simple, man a twofold life; in the brute, the inner life is one with the outer. Man has both an inner and an outer life. The inner life of man is the life which has relation to his species—to his general, as distinguished from his individual nature. . . . The brute can exercise no function which has relation to its species without another individual external to itself; but man can perform the functions of thought and speech, which strictly imply such a relation, apart from another individual. . . . Man is in fact at once I and Thou; he can put himself in the place of another, for this reason, that to him his species, his essential nature, and not merely his individuality, is an object of thought. . . . An object to which a subject essentially, necessarily relates, is nothing else than this subject's own, but objective nature. . . .

"The relation of the sun to the earth is, therefore, at the same time a relation of the earth to itself, or to its own nature, for the measure of the size and of the intensity of light which the sun possesses as the object of the earth, is the measure of the distance, which determines the peculiar nature of the earth. . . . In the object which he contemplates, therefore, man becomes acquainted with himself. . . . The power of the object over him is therefore the power of his own nature."

(*The Essence of Christianity*, by Ludwig Feuerbach, translated from the second German edition by Marian Evans, London, 1854, pp. 1-5.)

7. Marx' term *gegenständlich* can be translated by "objective," but what is meant is an adjective belonging to *Gegenstand,* object. We believe that *gegenständliche Welt* may be rendered best by "world of objects."

8. *Gegenständlich, wirklich,* in Marx, see previous note. Just as *gegenständlich* belongs to *Gegenstand,* so does *wirklich* belong to *Wirken,* to work. A better translation might be: "man's relation to himself only becomes for him a relation of objects and of work."

9. This obscure sentence becomes somewhat more intelligible, if we remember that in Hegelian terminology "identity" often stands for "unity." There is, Marx seems to say, a unity of opposites between wages and private property, since wages result in private property, and private property is the result of the wage system. Labor, in this process, plays only a mediating role: wages and property are the real poles.

10. Marx calls estrangement *die wahre Einbürgerung.* This means "truly becoming a part of society." The sentence seems to mean that alienation is the key to society.

ANTITHESIS OF CAPITAL AND LABOR

1. Page XL of Marx's second manuscript opens with these words. The beginning of the sentence is unknown, because the first 39 pages of the manuscript are missing.

2. Ricardo, Mill, etc.

3. Being-of-self, *Sein für sich selbst,* another Hegelian expression. Here it stands for "a fully self-contained being."

4. *Révolutions de France et de Brabant, par* Camille Desmoulins, *second Trimestre, contenant Mars, Avril et Mai.* Paris, *l'an premier No. 16,* p. 139f.; No. 23, p. 425f.; No. 26, p. 580f. Desmoulins was the famous journalist among the Dantonists of the French Revolution; the year is 1793.

5. All German conservative writers of the early 19th century.

6. Jean-Charles Simonde de Sismondi (1773-1842), already mentioned before, French historian with socialist tendencies.

7. Justus Möser (1720-94), a lawyer in Osnabrück, wrote the *Patriotische Phantasien* (1774-76), in their day quite influential. The conservative professor in Halle, Heinrich Leo (1799-1878), wrote a history of the Middle Ages (1830).

8. French and English economists of the early decades of the 19th century.

PRIVATE PROPERTY AND LABOR

1. This refers to p. XXXVI of a lost manuscript of Marx.

2. "For itself," *fuer sich:* a Hegelian term used in antithesis with "In itself," *an sich.* "In itself" means roughly "implicit" or even "unconscious"; "For itself," similarly, can be read as "present to itself," "conscious (ly) ," "explicitly."

3. Substance, *Wesen.* Elsewhere on this page *Wesen* is rendered as "essence." See "Note on Terminology."

4. It is here that Marx introduces the term "fetishism," which later played such an important role in *Capital.* He had read C. Debrosses, *Du culte des dieux fétiches* (1760), in a German translation of 1785.

5. See F. Engels, *Outlines of a Critique of Political Economy,* published in the present volume.

6. Superseded, *aufhob* (rendered below "done away with"). See under "Note on Terminology."

7. Man's externalization in the thing, *reale Entäusserung des Menschen*: the process of alienating, *Veräusserung*: See under *Entäusserung* in "Note on Terminology."

8. Marx writes that the economists *"zugleich den Menschen zum Wesen und zugleich den Menschen als ein Unwesen zum Wesen machen,"* opposing *Wesen,* essence or being, to *Unwesen,* literally, non-essence or non-being, but also meaning something, or somebody, having lost touch with humanity.

9. François Quesnay (1694-1774), prominent French physician, who wrote *Tableau économique* (1758), expounding the physiocratic doctrine.

PRIVATE PROPERTY AND COMMUNISM

1. As in the previous section, this refers to a page of a lost manuscript.

2. Transcended, annulled, done away with; see *Aufheben* in "Note on Terminology."

3. Marx probably attacks as "crude communism" various opinions that he may have heard in Babouvist circles, perhaps also expressed in long forgotten pamphlets. Neither Babeuf nor Buonarotti stood for the destruction of talents or the "community of women." There was a Babouvist poet Sylvain Maréchal, who in 1796 proposed a *Manifeste*

des Egaux with exclamations such as this: "Let, if necessary, all arts perish, if only real equality be reached!" The Babouvist leadership rejected it. Community of women, as far as we know, was never preached by any socialist or communist; the closest to it may have been Plato, whose aristocratic Guards had no marriage ties, but men and women were considered equals in the selection of partners. Dézamy's *Code de la nature* (1842) suggested something similar for his whole utopian community. Communist sects have occasionally preached polygamy, e.g., some Anabaptists of the 16th century. We may remember how Marx and Engels in the *Communist Manifesto* ridiculed the idea that communists are in favor of the community of women; on the contrary, they wrote, this is an established bourgeois custom, if not in theory, the more in practice.

4. Marx here deals with the communist schools of Cabet (see Note 6 below) and others.

5. In German: *Dieser Kommunismus ist also vollendeter Naturalismus-Humanismus.* Naturalism and humanism are terms taken from Feuerbach.

6. Etienne Cabet (1780-1856), creator of utopian "Icaria." After 1848, he tried to build Icaria in the U.S.A., first in Texas. The Icarian community near Corning, Iowa, lasted until 1895.

François Villegardelle (1810-1856), French publicist, follower of Fourier.

7. Robert Owen (1771-1858), British utopian Socialist, started as a successful Scotch textile manufacturer. From 1825-28 an Owenist colony existed in New Harmony on the Wabash (now Indiana).

8. Assertion of life, *Lebensäuszerung.*
Alienation of life, *Lebensentäuszerung.*
Realization, *Verwirklichung.*
Loss of reality, *Entwirklichung.*

9. *Einundzwanzig Bogen aus der Schweiz, Erster Teil* (Zürich und Winterthur, 1843), p. 329. The author Moses Hess (1812-1875) was the German socialist who influenced Marx and Engels in their formative years; he later became a Zionist.

10. Essential powers, *Wesenskräfte*: i.e., powers belonging to me as part of my essential nature, my very being. See *Wesen* in "Note on Terminology." Another translation might be "faculties."

11. We have translated Marx's *Sinn* by "meaning" and "sense." Marx writes: *"nur Sinn für einen ihm entsprechenden Sinn hat."*

12. In places like this, where Marx talks about need (*Bedürfniss*), we may compare what he says with the thesis of Feuerbach: "Only the being in want (*nothleidend*) is the necessary (*nothwendig*) being. Existence without need is superfluous existence. . . . A being without want is a being without cause (*Grund*). Only the being rich in pain

is a divine being. A being without pain is a being without essence. . . ." (*Vorläufige Thesen, Werke,* II, p. 234.) We see Marx attempting to endow this abstract statement with a social meaning.

13. *Generatio aequivoca,* spontaneous generation. The *Principles of Geology* by the English scientist Charles Lyell, which presented the evolutionary point of view in the study of the earth's formation, appeared in 1830-33. Marx must have known of this book, which was widely discussed in those days. The term "geogeny" is not often used; it stands for the theories accounting for the formation of the earth, it could be called historical geology. MEGA, I, 3, P. 124 has "Geognosie," a term introduced by the German mineralogist Abraham Werner (1749-1817) for the study of the formation of rocks (by aquatic action). The term "geogeny" used by the latest editors seems more appropriate in our text. However, Alexander von Humboldt, in his widely read works (from 1807 on) used the word "geognosy" quite frequently. *Spontaneous generation*—of living creatures such as infusoria from mud. *Aequivoca,* equivocal, ambiguous, indicates uncertainty as to the origin of such creatures.

14. Since the manuscript ends here, we can only guess what the meaning of this last sentence is. Milligan believes that by "communism as such" is meant crude, egalitarian, communism, such as that propounded by Babeuf and his followers. However, since Marx speaks of communism as the necessary shape of the next future, as the "negation of negation," he may well have thought of human emancipation beyond the abolition of private property, to a "synthesis" in an even richer stage of human emancipation, after alienation has been conquered. He returns to this point in the next section, but here again the text has been mutilated.

THE MEANING OF HUMAN REQUIREMENTS

1. Forces of human nature, *menschliche Wesenskraft;* human nature, *menschliches Wesen.*

2. *Conditio sine qua non,* the condition that must necessarily be fulfilled.

3. *Prometheus:* . . . No craft they [i.e. men] knew
   With woven brick or jointed beam to pile
   The sunward porch; but in the dark earth burrowed
   And housed, like tiny ants in sunless caves.
   No signs they knew to mark the wintry year.
   The flower-strewn Spring, and the fruit-laden Summer,
   Uncalendared, unregistered, returned—
   Till I the difficult art of the stars revealed,
   Their risings and their settings—
                         —Aeschylus, *Prometheus Bound,* transl. J. S. Blackie.

It was Prometheus who gave fire to men: "and flame-faced fire is now enjoyed by mortals."

4. James Maitland, Baron Lauderdale (1759-1839), Scottish politician and author, wrote *An Inquiry into the Nature and Origin of Public Wealth*, (1809, 1819).

Thomas Robert Malthus (1766-1834), curate of Albury (Surrey), author of the much quoted *Essay on the Principle of Population* (first ed., 1798). Later he became a professor of history and political economy in the East India Company college at Haileybury, near Hertford.

5. When Marx wrote, Abd-al-Kadir was fighting the French in Morocco and Algeria. Slavery of Christians in Morocco was only abolished in the early 19th century. As to the trade in conscripts, we remember the Hessian soldiers in British service during the war of the Revolution.

6. Michel Chevalier (1806-79), French author and politician, was in the 1830's editor of the paper of the disciples of Saint-Simon. In 1840-42 he published an extensive study of U. S. railroads.

7. James Mill (1773-1836), English economist, expositor of the utilitarian philosophy of Bentham, developed Ricardo's ideas in *Elements of Political Economy* (1821-22).

8. Marx seems to refer to Fichte's philosophy of the *Ich*, "Ego," myself.

9. In the manuscript the lower left corner of the page is torn off. Just the right-hand endings of the last six lines remain, making restoration of the text impossible. It is possible to surmise, however, that Marx here criticizes Hegel's idealistic "transcending" of estrangement; found among the words that have survived are the following: —"in the old German way—in the way of Hegel's Phenomenology."

10. The bottom of the page is torn. Three or four lines are missing.

11. See "Rent of Land" above.

12. Marx's and Hegel's *bürgerliche Gesellschaft* is translated by "civil society," not by "bourgeois society." Marx himself defines "civil society" in the same sentence. Hegel's definition, in his *Philosophy of Right*, Sect. 157, is "an association of members as self-subsistent individuals in a universality which, because of their self-subsistence, is only abstract." In Hegel's system "civil society," in the development of the Idea of Ethical Life, takes a place between the family and the state.

13. *"Der Lebensäuszerung als Lebensentäuszerung,"* here translated as "the living of life as the estrangement of life."

14. *Wealth of Nations*, Book 1, chs. II and III (but quoted with omissions, transpositions, etc.). See the section of the present *Manuscripts* on the "Wages of Labor."

15. Adam Smith, Vol. 1, p. 20.

16. Destutt de Tracy, *Eléments d'Idéologie. Traité de la Volonté et de ses Effets (Elements of Ideology. Treatise on the Will and its Effects)*, Paris, 1826, pp. 68, 78.

17. Say, *op. cit.*, p. 300 and p. 76*f.*

18. F. Skarbek, *Théorie des Richesses sociales, suivi d'une Biographie de l'Economie Politique (Theory of Social Wealth, Followed by an Account of the Development of Political Economy)*, t. I-II, Paris, 1829, t. I, p. 25*f.* Fryderyk, Graf Skarbek (1792-1866), Polish-French historian and economist.

19. James Mill, *Elements of Political Economy*, (London, 1821), pp. 5-9.

20. That part of the third manuscript which serves as a supplement to p. XXXIX of the second manuscript breaks off at this point on the left side of p. XXXVIII. The right-hand side of p. XXXVIII is empty. Then follows the "Introduction" (pp. XXXIX-XL), already printed at the beginning of this collection. Then comes a passage on money (pp. XLI-XLIII), which we present hereafter.

THE POWER OF MONEY IN BOURGEOIS SOCIETY

1. This word is illegible.

2. Ontology is the doctrine of being, of essence, often taken in the sense of "metaphysics." Kant rejected it, since he claimed that we can never know the essence of things. Hegel uses the term, and in his *Encyclopaedia* writes: "Ontology terminates in self-knowledge, and self-knowledge is ontologically significant" (sect. 171). Marx's ideas of the very essence of human feelings are summed up in the five points that follow.

3. Goethe, *Faust*, Part 1—Faust's Study, III. Goethe's *Faust*, Part 1, translated by Philip Wayne (Penguin 1949, page 91). The last line reads in German: "as if I had twenty-four feet."

4. Act 4, Sc. 3 (Marx quotes the German translation by Dorothea Tieck; he quotes it again in *Capital*).

5. An end of the page is torn out in the manuscript.

CRITIQUE OF THE HEGELIAN DIALECTIC

1. Reference is made to the concluding portion of the part which directly precedes these words and which (because the chapter about Hegel, which Marx qualified in the "Preface" as the "final chapter," has been put at the end of the volume) is given above under the editor's heading "Private Property and Communism."

2. Bruno Bauer, *Kritik der evangelischen Geschichte der Synoptiker (Critique of the Synoptic Gospels)*, Band 1-2, Leipzig, 1841; Band 3,

Braunschweig, 1842. In religious literature the authors of the first three Gospels are known as the Synoptics.

3. *Das Entdeckte Christentum. Eine Erinnerung des Achtzehnten Jahrhundert und ein Beitrag zur Krisis des Neunzehnten. (Christianity Discovered: A Memorial of the Eighteenth Century and a Contribution to the Crisis of the Nineteenth)*, von Bruno Bauer (Zürich und Winterthur, 1843).

4. *Die Gute Sache der Freiheit und meine Eigene Angelegenheit (The Good of Freedom and My Own Affair)*, von Bruno Bauer (Zürich und Winterthur, 1842).

5. Otto Friedrich Gruppe (1804-1876), anti-Hegelian author.

6. See notes to the Preface.

7. Certificate of poverty.

8. References are made to the *Allgemeine Literatur-Zeitung* of the Bauer brothers, against which Marx and Engels were going to write their *Holy Family*.

9. Feuerbach views negation of negation, the definite concept as thinking surpassing itself in thinking and as thinking wanting to be directly awareness, nature, reality. (Reference is here made by Marx to Feuerbach's critical observations about Hegel in §§29-30 of his *Grundsätze der Philosophie der Zukunft*.)

10. What follows here are the main chapter and section-headings of Hegel's *Phenomenology of Mind*. Here and in later quotations from the *Phenomenology*, the translator has followed Baillie's translation very closely, departing from it only on the few occasions where this was necessary to keep the terminology in line with that used throughout the present volume.

11. *Enzyklopädie der Philosophischen Wissenschaften*, von G. W. F. Hegel (Heidelberg, 1st edition, 1817, 3rd edition, 1830). Hegel's *Encyclopaedia of the Philosophical Sciences* is a single volume falling into three main parts: the subject of the first is Logic. (*The Logic of Hegel*, translated by William Wallace 2nd edition, Oxford, 1892); the subject of the second part is the philosophy of nature (of which no English translation has been published), and that of the third the Philosophy of Mind (Hegel's *Philosophy of Mind*, translated by William Wallace, Oxford, 1894).

12. See Note 2, "Private Property and Labor."

13. "The unhappy consciousness," etc.—Forms of mind, and phases and factors in human history distinguished and analyzed in particular sections of Hegel's *Phenomenology*. See our Introduction.

14. Hegel mentions political economy in Sect. 189 of his *Philosophy of Right*: "Its development affords the interesting spectacle (as in Smith, Say and Ricardo) of thought working upon the endless mass of details . . . and extracting therefrom the simple principles of the thing and directing it." Hegel quotes Adam Smith in his Jena lectures

of 1803-04, where he points out how modern industry through refined division of labor and the introduction of machines creates "in a great people an immense system of community and mutual dependence, a life of the dead moving in itself, a life dead in its motion . . . that like a savage animal needs constant strict control and taming." (*Jenenser Realphilosophie*, ed. J. Hoffmeister, I, p. 239).

15. In the *Deutsche Zeitschrift für Philosophie*, 4 (1956), 6 (1958), the question is discussed whether Hegel did not, on occasion, see the negative side of labor. Reference is made to the *Philosophy of Right* Sects. 243-246, where Hegel mentions the existence of poverty and is pessimistic about the means to alleviate it, concluding that expansion of markets to backward lands may help through "the inner dialectic of society." On this subject he certainly had little to offer. However, this does not seem to be the point that Marx makes. Marx criticizes Hegel because he did not see that labor's essence was in alienation.

16. The terms *selbstisch, Selbstigkeit* are translated by "egotistic" and "selfhood." The meaning is rather that of "referring to the ego"— no moral quality is involved.

17. Phenomenology, doctrine of the appearances (phenomena). Kant had used the term for the doctrine of the appearances of the motion of bodies. Hegel took the term over for his doctrine of the modes of development of the mind, from the simple knowledge of the immediate to the knowledge of the absolute. See the Introduction.

18. The paragraph which follows is a transcript of the second and third paragraphs of the last chapter of Hegel's *Phenomenology* (Baillie's translation, 2nd edition, p. 789).

19. Thinghood, *Dingheit*. This term was introduced by Hegel in the *Phenomenology* at the beginning where he introduces the "observation," which leads to the "thing." *Dingheit* is the abstract general medium in which all specific determinations of the thing are seen in their generality. *Dingheit* is also called *das reine Wesen*, pure essence. Marx, a little further in the chapter, gives his own definition, introducing the concept of alienation. See the Introduction.

20. Externalization, *Entäusserung*. See "Note on Terminology."

21. Substance, *Wesen*.

22. Being, *Wesen*; nature, *Natur*; system, *Wesen*; be-ing, *Sein*. See *Wesen* in "Note on Terminology."

23. Nonsensical, *unsinnlich*, in the literal sense of "outside the senses."

24. To be sensuous is to suffer—*Sinnlich sein ist leidend sein*. Here "to suffer" should probably be understood in the sense of "to undergo" —to be the object of another's action. Note the transition in the next sentence from *Leiden* (suffering) to *leidenschaftlich* (passionate).

25. Here Marx has taken the impersonal pronoun *es* (it) to represent *Bewusstsein* (consciousness); but it seems that Baillie is more correct

in reading this as standing for *Selbstbewusstsein* (self-consciousness).
In the first quotation of this passage (p. 179) Marx simply uses *es*
without specifying what it represents, and the translation has followed
Baillie in interpreting it as "self-consciousness." In the present repetition of the passage, Marx's specification of the "it" as "consciousness,"
has been followed in the translation.

26. Marx refers to §30 of Feuerbach's *Grundsätze der Philosophie der
Zukunft,* which says: "Hegel is a thinker who transcends himself in
thinking."

27. This sequence gives the major "categories" or "thought-forms"
of Hegel's *Encyclopaedia* in the order in which they occur and are
superseded. Similarly, the sequence above, from "private right" to
"world history," gives the major categories of Hegel's *Philosophy of
Right,* in the order in which they there appear.

28. The conventional conception of theology, jurisprudence, political
science, natural science, etc.

29. In German text *Selbstentfremdung, Wesensäuszerung, Entgegen-
ständlichung* and *Entwirklichung* of man are contrasted with his
Selbstgewinnung, Wesensänderung, Vergegenständlichung and *Verwirklichung.* These sharp verbal contrasts are somewhat lost in the English
translation.

30. *The Logic of Hegel,* tr. by Wallace, ¶ 244. "Intuiting" is here
used to render *Anschauen.* In popular usage *Anschauen* means "to
contemplate," but Hegel is here using the word, like Kant, as a
technical term in philosophy meaning, roughly, "to be aware through
the senses." "Intuiting," likewise, should be understood here not in
its popular sense but as the philosophical term which is the recognized
English equivalent of *Anschauen.*

31. Time, Motion, Matter, Light, etc., are forms distinguished within
Hegel's *Philosophy of Nature.* Becoming, etc., are of course categories
of the *Logic.* Marx gives only a summary of Hegel's actual definitions.
For instance, Sect. 200 of the first edition of the *Encyclopaedia,*
teaches: "Time as the negative unity of being-outside-of-oneself is
also a mere abstract, ideal being, which since it is, is not, and since
it is not, is."

32. This last quotation is the opening paragraph of the chapter on
the philosophy of nature in the *Encyclopaedia.*

33. Hegel's *Philosophy of Mind,* tr. by Wallace, ¶ 381. But in rendering these passages from the *Encyclopaedia,* the present translator has
not followed Wallace closely.

APPENDIX

1. *Outlines of a Critique of Political Economy* is the first economic
work of Frederick Engels in which he examines the bourgeois economic system and the basic categories of bourgeois political economy

from the standpoint of socialism. It appeared in the same *Deutsch-Französische Jahrbücher* of 1844, in which Marx published his critique of Hegel's *Philosophy of Right* and his essay on the Jewish question. Engels' work made a deep impression on Marx and as late as 1859 in the Introduction to his *Critique of Political Economy* he called it "a brilliant outline of a critique of economic categories." Certain weaknesses in the exposition by the 23-year-old observer of English economic life are apparent to students of the mature work of Marx and Engels. They do not impair the originality and the keenness of Engels' analysis, unique for his day. See the Introduction.

2. Friedrich List (1789-1846), a well-known German economist, advocated the abolition of customs barriers within Germany but at the same time the protection by tariffs, etc., of German industry from foreign competition.

3. Marx expanded on this definition of Smith as the Luther of political economy in the section on "Private Property and Labor." Buret (see Note 16, "Wages of Labor") called Smith "the Bacon of political economy."

4. "Exchangeable value," English term quoted by Engels.

5. Thomas Perronet Thompson (1783-1869), an officer in the anti-Napoleonic wars, wrote *Corn Law Catechism* (1827), influential in the struggle which led, in 1846, to the abolition of the corn laws.

6. John Wade (1788-1875), English publicist and historian.

7. Dec. 16, 1835.

8. A. Alison, *The Principles of Population, and Their Connection with Human Happiness,* Vols. I, II (London, 1840). Archibald Alison (1792-1867), Scottish lawyer and historian, opposed the theory of Malthus.

9. Thomas Robert Malthus (1766-1834), see Note 4, "The Meaning of Human Requirements."

10. The old name for Australia.

11. Three pamphlets appeared under the pseudonym of "Marcus," namely: *On the Possibility of Limiting Populousness,* by Marcus, printed by John Hill, Black Horse Court, Fleet Street, 1838, 46 p.; *The Book of Murder! A Vade Mecum for the Commissioners and Guardians of the New Poor Law . . . Being an Exact Reprint of the Infamous Essay on the Possibility of Limiting Populousness, by Marcus, one of the three . . . now Reprinted for the Instruction of the Labourer,* by William Dugdale, 37, Holywell Street, Strand.; *The Theory of Painless Extinction,* by Marcus. Cf. N.M.W.: *Advertisements* 29. VIII. 1840.

An anonymous pamphlet, *An Essay on Populousness, printed for private circulation; printed for the author.* 1838. 27 pp.—contains the basic ideas of the "Marcus" pamphlets. *See* also Thomas Carlyle, *Chartism* (London, 1840), p. 110*ff.*

12. The Poor Law of 1834 meant to outlaw relief payments to the

able-bodied. Repeal of this law was one of the demands of the Chartists.

13. Humphry Davy (1778-1829) taught at the Royal Institute in London; wrote *Elements of Agricultural Chemistry.*

Justus Liebig (1803-73), established at Giessen a famous chemical laboratory; wrote *Organic Chemistry in its Application to Agriculture* (original German ed., 1840).

14. A. Alison, *op. cit.*, p. 548.

15. Andrew Ure (1778-1857), Scottish chemist. His *Philosophy of Manufactures* (2d ed., London, 1835) was widely read, Marx quotes it repeatedly in *Capital.*

16. Engels refers to a work on England's social history which he intended to write and for which he was collecting material during his stay in that country (November 1842-August 1844). In this work Engels meant to devote a special chapter to the condition of the English workers. Later he changed his mind and decided to write a special book about the English proletariat. He did so on returning to Germany. The book, *Condition of the Working Class in England,* was published in Leipzig in 1845, in German. The first English translation was prepared by the American, Florence Kelley Wischnewetzky, and appeared in New York in 1887. It has been republished in *Karl Marx and Frederick Engels on Britain* (Moscow, 1953).

NAME INDEX